C000258802

# BEACON FOR CHANGE

# BEACON FOR CHANGE

How the 1951
# FESTIVAL OF BRITAIN
Helped to Shape a New Age

Barry Turner

First published 2011 by
Aurum Press Limited
7 Greenland Street
London NW1 0ND
www.aurumpress.co.uk

Copyright © 2011 Barry Turner

The moral right of Barry Turner to be identified as the author
of this work has been asserted by him in accordance with the
Copyright, Designs and Patents Act 1988.

All rights reserved. No part of this book may be reproduced or utilized in any
form or by any means, electronic or mechanical, including photocopying,
recording or by any information storage and retrieval system, without
permission in writing from Aurum Press Ltd.

A catalogue record for this book is available from the British Library.

ISBN 978 1 84513 524 9

1 3 5 7 9 10 8 6 4 2
2011 2013 2015 2016 2014 2012

Typeset by SX Composing DTP, Rayleigh, Essex

Printed and bound in Great Britain by the MPG Books Group

# CONTENTS

'1951 should be a year of fun, fantasy and colour, a year in which we can, while soberly surveying our great past and our promising future, for once let ourselves go . . .'

*Gerald Barry*

'I want to see the people happy.'

*Herbert Morrison*

'To me the Festival of Britain represented the spirit of optimism, which was then among the British people, who had fought so hard, and endured so much. A better future was within our grasp and we were ready to accept the challenge of building a new Britain.'

*Barbara J. Walsh, festival visitor*

# INTRODUCTION

The 1951 Festival of Britain was a commercial and cultural showcase for the promotion of trade and the edification of the people. A century earlier, Britain had basked in the reflected glory of the Great Exhibition, the high point of Victorian world patronage, when over six million visitors had traipsed through Joseph Paxton's Crystal Palace to gawk at the mechanical wonders of the age. None since had matched the splendour and excitement of that event and in 1951, with Britain in its post-war doldrums, it took a high degree of courage, even audacity, to throw the spotlight on a bedraggled phoenix arising from austerity and disenchantment. Yet the miracle happened. On a soggy, derelict site on the south side of the Thames, Britain was recreated as an image of the future, a proud country which had much to offer to the store of human happiness.

Inevitably, prediction was tarnished by experience. The Festival style, owing much to Scandinavian and, to a lesser extent, Italian design, was light and spacious and, above all, sensitive to social and environmental needs. What came after was distorted by a national culture that favoured picturesque cosiness over the more practical and, some thought, sterile design of the northern Europeans. To take one of many small examples, the flat-fronted gas and electric fires displayed at the Festival as heat efficient and a saving on space were admired for their ingenuity but largely rejected by consumers wedded to the bulbous imitation log fires which were better at suggesting warmth than actually delivering it.

Likewise, Festival architecture, though evident in schools (2,500 were built between 1944 and 1955), hospitals and new towns called forth by the welfare state, was long resisted by the lobby for old-fashioned values, which favoured Tudor-style beams and mock Georgian portals. After the Festival, the conservation movement was strengthened by the horrors of what really was modern, such as the outcrop of city tower blocks, to annul the fear of rural Britain disappearing under low-rise urban mass. The love of concrete, so flexible, so durable, so easy and cheap to produce, inspired creative architects, but most were frustrated by planners and developers who thought good taste was to do with shrimp cocktails. Alongside the concrete monoliths, the love affair with the car gave right of way to vehicles over the right of ordinary citizens to live in communal harmony.

All this was anathema to those who inspired the Festival, though ironically they are often blamed for the errors of judgement perpetrated by their successors. To look back now at what the Festival stood for and what it had to offer is to discover a spirit of imagination and adventure that only in recent years has begun to realise its full potential. Memories of the Festival are a potent reminder of what we might have achieved much earlier had we had the wit to recognise the challenge.

Ah, memories. My Festival of Britain was a day trip to London. For a thirteen-year-old from what was then deepest rural Suffolk, this was a big adventure. It started with a disappointment. Not quite sure of what I was in for, I was certain of only two things; the Festival promised not only a fun fair the likes of which had never graced our local playing fields, but, best of all, illuminations, this at a time when a few coloured lights in a shop window were cause enough to stand and stare. Neither of these was I destined to enjoy. The excursion train from Bury St Edmunds to Liverpool Street was scheduled to return in the early evening when it was still light, allowing us too little time to visit the Battersea Pleasure Gardens, some way up river from the main exhibition site on the South Bank near Waterloo.

It was thus a sulky schoolboy who embarked on a rare visit to the capital, the journey brightened by my making short work of the sandwiches that were supposed to have been held over for lunch. Unloaded in the steam and sooty smells of Liverpool Street, I and my gaggle of school friends, all in uniform caps, dark blue blazers and grey flannel trousers, were shepherded on to the Underground (a first for many of us) to emerge in Wonderland.

My strongest Festival memory is of the broad-brush impression of newness, a contrast to all else that could be seen from the Thames embankment and, indeed, of anything we were used to at home. The Festival colours were startling, a happy departure from the shades of black and white that branded the post-war years. Everybody remembers the Dome of Discovery. But do they, really? The aerial pictures of the South Bank utilised to illustrate countless brochures and articles show the Dome as the pre-eminent spectacle, but close to ground level it merged easily into the surrounding network of shining lightweight buildings and broad walkways with a surprise round every corner.

For me, and I think for many youngsters, the Festival was the first indication that learning was discovery and that discovery could be fun. No doubt we picked up something of the essential message of the Festival, that Britain was emerging from hard times to lead a revolution in domestic design and technology that promised a better life for all. But it was the individual exhibits, though tame by modern standards of animated display, that caught the eye and the imagination. Wandering the Festival you could see how things might work if modern science were to be engaged as the servant of progress.

At the time I had no idea why the Festival had been mounted or who had organised it. Later, when I became convinced that the Festival was one of those pivotal cultural events too easily ignored or quickly passed over by historians transfixed by political minutiae, I came across the name of Gerald Barry, newspaper editor turned exhibition impresario, who inspired the Festival as a popular demonstration of national renewal and who managed the enterprise with flair and imagination while operating within a tight budget. Barry's unpublished Festival diary, letters and notes, to which his family has generously allowed me access, provide an invaluable record of attainment against formidable odds. Would that Barry or someone of his calibre had been in charge of the Millennium celebrations. How much less talk there would have been of overspend and underachievement.

My day in London in 1951 was not my only connection with the Festival. Like many other towns and cities across the country, my home town of Bury St Edmunds marked the year with its own programme of events. The emphasis was on amateur performance, starting with an afternoon of song and dance by local schools. For this unalluring occasion my second year at the boys' grammar was dragooned into swelling an audience that consisted chiefly of proud parents. We were in the front row; bored witless until the finale when a girl of generous appurtenances demonstrated her handstands and cartwheels. Above a bare midriff she had on a frilly top secured by a ribbon round her waist and another ribbon tied behind her neck. In mid-act the ribbon at her neck snapped. This gave no concern while she was upright, since she was able to use one hand to hold everything in place, but when she went into her cartwheeling act her modesty, delectable beyond the wildest dreams of hormonally challenged teenagers, was revealed to all. Encouraged by our wild applause this true artist gave an encore. I never did find out how the adults reacted. They had all left the hall while we in the choice seats were taking our time rearranging our clothing.

A performance of a more refined nature was mounted by the town's Operatic and Dramatic Society with their open-air production of *Twelfth Night*. Fancying myself as a critic and having firm views on Shakespeare's comedies (not exactly a laugh a minute), I entered an essay competition with the prize to be awarded for the best ideas on making the Bard intelligible to modern audiences. I came second in the under-15 category. Years later, when I was sorting out my father's attic, I came across a news cutting from the *Bury Free Press* with a picture of me receiving a book voucher and shaking hands with John (soon to be Sir John) Gielgud. I had no recollection of this and can only assume that I had not then heard of the great actor. Also featured was the winner, whose name I recognised as that of a boy from a nearby public school who subsequently became a leading political commentator. This puzzled me since I knew that he was my senior by at least three years and thus, by rights, disqualified from my age group. Renewing acquaintance-ship forty years after the event I invited him to explain. 'Simple,' he said. 'I lied about my age.'

I learned much from my Festival year, but it took longer to realise that in dealing with politicos, a touch of cynicism is no bad thing.

# CHAPTER ONE

The Festival of Britain was foremost a family outing. Some came for the spectacle of futuristic designs and bright colours, others to see modern technology in action, still others to experience a cultural reawakening after years of drab uniformity. But on one point everyone who paid their five shillings admission (four shillings from mid-afternoon) was agreed; they were there to enjoy themselves. Herbert Morrison, speaking for the government, wanted 'to hear the people sing' while Gerald Barry, the Festival impresario, said that what he was offering was a 'tonic to the nation'.

The notion of having fun was distinctly novel in post-war Britain. Leftward-leaning historians who spend too long in the archives get hooked on the thrills of a social revolution, the creation of a welfare state by the first Labour government to command an absolute majority at Westminster. The Beveridge Report with its promise to combat the five great evils – want, disease, ignorance, squalor and idleness – caught the spirit of the time. But for the typical family, it was jam tomorrow, or maybe some day far off. Meanwhile, the daily routine was making do on very little, a routine that had a long tailback, with the war giving a further twist to the spiral of material decline that had started with the depression and mass unemployment of the 1930s.

Everything that mattered was in short supply. Butter, meat, tea and coal were all rationed and when, in 1949, restrictions were lifted on the sale of sweets and chocolates, the rush on the shops was so great the concession had to be withdrawn. Twenty million Britons lived in homes without baths and hot water while nearly a fifth of London's homes were officially classed as slums. In the borough of Fulham alone, not otherwise designated as deprived, single-room accommodation was the lot of 7,000 families. Then to cap it all, came the winter of 1946–7, the harshest on record – the longest period without sun, the fiercest snowstorms, the lowest temperatures. Snowdrifts up to ten feet or more were whipped up by gale force winds. Cars, trucks and even trains disappeared under a white shroud, sometimes for days on end.

While the government could not be blamed for the weather, it did come under attack for failing to meet the demand for coal, then the main source of domestic heating and industrial energy. The assumption that the miners would rescue the country from its meteorological crisis was based on the optimism engendered by nationalisation. Taking the mines into public ownership (along with the railways, waterways, gas, electricity, the airways, the Bank of England and iron and steel) was supposed to usher in a new age of labour relations with management and workers in happy harmony. The reality was no change. Union leaders wanted better pay and conditions for their members, and they wanted it now while their bargaining position was strong. When the government refused to give way (many other special cases were in line waiting to see how the miners would fare), there was no alternative to cutting energy supplies.

The package of restrictions introduced was draconian. Even the most pessimistic commentators had not anticipated the complete suspension of household electricity supplies for three hours in the morning and two hours in the afternoon. Television was closed down and the Third Programme, the cultural channel of BBC Radio, went off the air. All broadcasting had to cease at 11 p.m. The plug was pulled on greyhound racing, one of the few sports it was possible to hold in freezing weather, and there was to be no afternoon cinema. Newspapers were reduced to wartime size and some weekly journals like the *Spectator*, the *New Statesman* and *The Economist* were told to stop publication altogether.

As one factory after another locked its gates, the number of jobless rose from a few thousand to over a million. Before the winter was over, unemployment was to hit two million with another half million workers on short time, in total over 15 per cent of the nation's workforce. One of the most painful images, long recalled from the winter of 1947, was of sullen householders with old prams and handcarts queuing outside gas works and coal merchants. It was like the 1930s all over again. There was one piece of good news in the offing. In February 1949, clothes came off rationing.

The challenge for the government was in persuading the country that there was a future worth working for. It was an uphill task. Cynicism was matched by a social malaise. Remembering the late forties, a boringly repetitive refrain comes to mind: 'It can't be done, Guv'. A Gallup poll revealed that 42 per cent of Britain's population – and 58 per cent of those below the age of thirty – would emigrate 'if free to do so'.[1] A young ex-serviceman spoke for many when he told an interviewer, 'I wish I were anywhere but this goddamned country. There is nothing but queues and restrictions and forms and cold and no food.'

He might have added that with Britain's worldwide commitments – British troops were stationed in West Germany, Austria, Italy, Libya, Malta, Cyprus, throughout the Middle East and in an extensive patchwork of colonial outposts – there was a serious risk for anyone who had recently served in the military of being recalled to the colours. In July 1947, the National Service Act introduced conscription for eighteen months, a period soon extended to two years, for all men aged eighteen to twenty-six. In 1950 Britain spent 6.6 per cent of its gross domestic product on defence, more than any country except the Soviet Union.

The euphoria of victory in Europe had long since given way to an overriding sense of grievance and bitterness. The Festival was intended to change all that. A national pick-me-up, the party of a century had a serious underlying purpose, to demonstrate that Britain had within itself the talent, imagination and energy to create a new society. Gerald Barry spoke of encouraging higher standards, 'to bring into being new works of art, new social amenities for the people . . . to give the younger architects, artists and designers a chance to prove their talent . . . and to leave behind some permanent contributions to the future'.[2] A framework for the Festival planners was thus established. An inviting image had to be created melding pleasure, education and inspiration.

The idea had as its starting point a proposal put to the government in 1943 by the Royal Society of Arts. Founded in 1754 to foster inventiveness and creativity, the RSA was — as it remains — a place where designers, artists and industrialists could find common ground. It was here in John Adam Street, just off London's Strand, that the fashion for exhibitions evolved, initially for painters to display their canvases, but after the creation of the Royal Academy, chiefly for manufacturers to promote their latest products. Ever more ambitious projects led to the Great Exhibition of 1851, the proudest moment in the RSA's history, though chief credit for the success of that enterprise must go to its royal sponsor, Prince Albert, who made of it a ringing proclamation of British leadership.

The Great Exhibition set a standard, adopted by all the successor trade exhibitions in Britain, France and the United States, of spectacular displays (the Crystal Palace, built with a single glass and iron framework and covering 19 acres, was alone worth the price of admission) which sought to 'improve the taste of the middle classes, to inform manufacturers about mechanical improvements and to morally educate the working class'.[3]

Nothing quite so patronising entered the official records of 1951, but the broad principle of exposing fresh ideas to an unsophisticated audience in a language they could understand guided much of mid-twentieth century thinking. The response was positive, even enthusiastic. Learning was in vogue, as proved by the wartime popularity of the Army Bureau of Current Affairs, BBC programmes such as *The Brains Trust* and the oversubscription of a multitude of adult education classes and lectures. Equality meant equality of opportunity and while this assumed decent living standards for all, it also imposed on the intellectually advantaged a duty to inform and instruct. The sovereignty of the lowest common denominator was to come later.

The RSA's proposal for a festival, to be held in 1951, was given a sympathetic hearing by the coalition government, confident by 1943 of ultimate victory over Germany. The political talk was of reconstruction and rejuvenation. A festival could be an important part of that. Further encouragement came in the form of an open letter in the *News Chronicle* to Sir Stafford Cripps, the then President of the Board of Trade. The writer, Gerald Barry, who also happened to be the paper's editor, favoured an international fair in the grand tradition. He was pushing at an open door.

Cripps, an austere politician, was also a visionary dedicated to modernising Britain's economic base. Barry's proposal appealed to him as a much-needed stimulant to British exports, particularly to the States and other dollar economies. Already in hand were plans for a Britain Can Make It exhibition, organised by the Council of Industrial Design for the post-war reopening of the Victoria and Albert Museum in South Kensington. Put together by Basil Spence, a young Scottish architect, Britain Can Make It promoted clean, modern design, displaying more than 6,000 products from 1,300 firms newly switched over from war work. A centenary celebration of 1851 would do yet more to prove that Britain was ready to move on from the mass production of the cheap and tawdry for uncomplaining markets in the sterling area. It might even shake up those tired heirs to the Industrial Revolution, owners and managers who, when times were bad, complained that they could not afford to invest and when times were good assumed that they didn't have to.

Prompted by Barry, Cripps set up a committee 'to consider the desirability of organising an exhibition in London in 1951'. Chaired by Lord Ramsden, it started deliberations in September 1945 and reported six months later. Allowing that Ramsden, a former Tory MP, was an enthusiast for building trade links, particularly with the Commonwealth and colonies, it was predictable that his committee should wholeheartedly endorse the guiding principles of the Great Exhibition by prescribing a 'first category international exhibition to be held in London . . . to demonstrate to the world the recovery of the United Kingdom from the effects of the war in the moral, cultural, spiritual and material fields'.

Having stated his committee's position, Ramsden set out the options for the site. The choice was narrowed by what were, in Ramsden's view, two essential requirements. First, the exhibition should surpass the New York World's Fair of 1939 'in scale and technical achievement' and the Paris Exhibition of 1937 'in aesthetic excellence and personal appeal'. Both these events had spread themselves liberally, Paris over 250 acres, New York over 1,216 acres. Ramsden compromised on a minimum of 300 acres. To find such a space was challenge enough but Ramsden made it tougher still by his second requirement, that the site should be in central London.

Hyde Park was top choice, not least because it was the original home of the Crystal Palace, but thought was also given to the area close to Waterloo Station on the Thames' south bank, much of it laid waste by the Luftwaffe. The unsavoury reputation of the district with its narrow streets and back-to-back slums stretching to the Elephant and Castle may have given pause, though limits on the available

area, short of wholesale demolition, were another deter-
rent. A throwaway comment was later picked up as
significant. The success of the 1937 Paris Exhibition, said
Ramsden, was partly because 'full use had been made of the
banks of the Seine'. There were those who wondered, could
not the Thames serve the same purpose?

The delivery of Ramsden's report in March 1946 had as
its immediate effect the concentration of political minds.
Filling in the details produced a raft of objections, starting
with the likely cost. It was all very well for Ramsden to assert
that 'no money or effort should be spared' but there were
too many other claims on public finances to permit any
great budgetary freedom. Then again, Hyde Park was judged
a non-starter as an exhibition site. At a time when many of
London's parks were still under wartime cultivation or in
use as military installations, Hyde Park was that rare thing,
a large open space for general recreation, not to mention
lunchtime strolls by civil servants from the neighbouring
government buildings.

For a second round of deliberation a committee of
government insiders representing relevant departments
was brought into play. At this stage, the brief was still to find
a site that could accommodate an international exhibition
to rival the pre-war extravaganzas in New York and Paris.
This assumed up to fifty million visitors over six months
with an exhibition staff of at least 10,000. Given that
London, unlike Paris and New York, was short on broad
boulevards and that traffic congestion, even with petrol
rationing, was already a planner's nightmare, the consensus inevitably favoured a site close to but not in central
London, preferably one that could provide a permanent
home for an annual British Industry Fair.

The search for the ideal venue spread far and wide. Woolwich Arsenal and adjoining marshes offered 650 acres but they were eight and a half miles from the West End. Even further away from the city's heartland were Trent Park in Cockfosters (950 acres) and Hampton Court Park (450 acres). Closer in, Battersea Park, covering 215 acres including 15 acres of lake, found favour, as did Sydenham, where the Crystal Palace had been reincarnated until it burned down in 1936, and Alexandra Palace, a grandiloquent Victorian edifice in north London, designed for 'recreation, education and entertainment'.

Among the more original proposals was to clear 15 acres of accommodation at Wormwood Scrubs, a Victorian prison overdue for replacement, which taken in conjunction with neighbouring ground would serve as a permanent exhibition centre. The idea fell foul of Home Office economies. Wormwood Scrubs, with all its inadequacies, still holds prisoners.

There was another look at the South Bank in the light of proposals by the London County Council (LCC) to transform the bombed area into a cultural and recreational centre. But no sooner was this considered than all the familiar qualms resurfaced. The site was too small, it was divided by a railway ('unless a connection could be driven through under the road and rail bridgeheads') and there was no embankment to hold back the Thames.[4] Eventually the consensus settled on Osterley Park in West London, one-time home of the Earls of Jersey, where a neoclassical stately home was set in 300 acres of landscaped parkland.

While the civil servants were huddled together, the RSA came back into the act by staging a Festival Conference for interested individuals and organisations. To say that it was an eclectic gathering is to put it mildly. Wartime regulations had spawned a profusion of trade and professional bodies, most of which were keen to contribute their expertise. Together they set the parameters for subsequent debates on whether to hold a festival and if held, on its scope and size.

The cheerleaders were headed by Alfred Bossom, an architect who had owned a successful American practice before being elected Conservative MP for Maidstone. With his acquired transatlantic energy, Bossom was impatient with convoluted discussions. 'Let's get on with it' was his entreaty. Site size was an irrelevance since the Festival could be split between a nucleus in London and numerous specialised exhibitions further out. As to the cost and labour involved, believing it could not be done was all part of a British malaise. 'We are held down by the feeling "We can't do it". We've got to throw off this lethargy.'[5]

First on his feet to make strenuous objection to Bossom's crack about national lethargy was a Mr Jacobs from the London Trades Council, speaking on behalf of the trades unions. There was no lethargy among his members, he declared, before launching a long diatribe which suggested lethargy and defeatism at every turn. London couldn't cope with thousands of visitors, the transport system was sure to break down and criminal elements would thrive in the chaos. Anyway, skilled labour would be far better occupied on less frivolous projects.[6]

It took the wonderfully named Dowager Lady Swaythling, representing the Electrical Association of Women, to reintroduce a note of buoyancy with a call for 'vision and progress'.[7] Taking up the theme, several speakers agreed the case for rejuvenating the South Bank, 'until recently the heart of London', proclaimed Miss J. Tyrwhitt of the Association of Planning and Regional Construction, adding that not far from Waterloo was 'the London of Shakespeare, the London of Dickens'. The conference ended on a positive note with a promise from the chairman, Viscount Samuel, to make their conclusions known in Whitehall.

At which point the government had second thoughts. The official explanation for abandoning an international exhibition in favour of one focusing exclusively on Britain was that to do otherwise was to risk overloading the exhibition circuit while at the same time contravening a 92-nation convention designed to bring some order to what had threatened to become a festival free-for-all. Signed in 1928, the convention limited international exhibitions to one every three years. Since Belgium and France had already pencilled in 1950 and 1953, the earliest date Britain could claim was 1956 or 1959. In theory.

In practice, it would have been easy for Britain to argue its case and it is significant that neither Belgium nor France took up their options. But the government no longer had any wish to push its diplomatic advantage. The fear of runaway costs was paramount. When the decision was taken to narrow the scope of the Festival, Britain was heading towards a financial crisis brought on by the terms of an American loan. The deal had been for the pound to become freely convertible one year after the start of the loan, in July 1947. This meant that countries holding sterling could convert their pounds into dollars, which they promptly did. Within six weeks, the British Treasury had run out of dollars and convertibility was suspended. By then, Britain had spent $3.3 billion of a loan expected to last until 1951. In September 1949 the pound was devalued from $4.03 to

$2.80. As the government endeavoured, with increasing desperation, to meet the cost of better housing, health and education, there was nothing left over for what some ministers, let alone their opponents, regarded as marginal expenditure.

To the pain of financial stringency was added the embarrassing reminder that Britain had not done too well from recent international exhibitions. At the 1937 Paris Exposition Universelle, the British pavilion had been dwarfed by the aggressively assertive profile presented by Germany, Italy and the Soviet Union. There were unfond memories of the German-built 54-metre tower, topped by an eagle embraced by a swastika. The equally grandiose Soviet display featured a stainless steel statue of an excessively muscular worker bearing a hammer and sickle to the height of a six-storey building. This demonstration of raw power was to be repeated at the 1939 New York World's Fair, only this time 'Big Joe', as it was christened by New Yorkers, held in its outstretched hand a five-pointed red star, ten feet in diameter. At night the star was lit by a 5,000 watt lamp. If the war had seen off Nazi propaganda, the Soviet Union remained an aggressive performer on the world stage. In any international festival, it would feel compelled to upstage the host country, a provocation to the US to play the same game. Britain would be outclassed and the government knew it.

The thumbs-down to an international exhibition entered the official record with a parliamentary question to the President of the Board of Trade on 28 March 1947. Cripps conceded that 'large scale demands on labour and materials' would 'impede the progress of urgent tasks of reconstruction' and were therefore unacceptable. However, he promised 'some national display' in 1951. With this, Cripps lost interest in an enterprise that could not, in his view, do anything to help promote British exports. So the buck was passed to Herbert Morrison who, as Deputy Prime Minister and Leader of the House of Commons, had chief responsibility for keeping up morale on the home front.

Morrison was an old-fashioned, progressive socialist, having been converted at an early stage in his career to an 'evolutionary conception of society on the biological analogy'.[8] Unlike his colleagues on the far left, he had no wish to smash the social system. Acknowledging the good things in life, he simply wanted to make them more readily accessible. He had faith in the power of education to raise the general level of aspiration and achievement. The idea of a Festival to celebrate Britain's recovery from the war and to point the way to a better future had a strong appeal for him. Here was an opportunity to combine learning and entertainment, a powerful combination thought Morrison, while at the same time giving commerce and the arts a chance to show what they could do.

In a meeting with the RSA on 16 July 1947, H.A. Marquand, Paymaster General, outlined Morrison's initial thoughts, which had 'not yet been considered by the government and were still highly confidential'.[9] Responsibility for the Festival was to be devolved to various quangos such as the Arts Council, the Council of Industrial Design, the British Film Institute and the National Book League.

There was still no decision on a Festival site. At this stage the likelihood was that separate exhibitions would be held where premises happened to be available. But it was soon clear that this could only serve to diminish the impact of the undertaking. The concept of a combined exhibition began to take shape with science, design and architecture under one umbrella. Morrison worked away at his ministerial colleagues, indulging, according to Max Nicholson, his permanent secretary, in 'a little gentle arm twisting' by virtue of his responsibility for drawing up Cabinet agendas.

To be truly national the Festival had to be as far as possible above party politics. Since the Conservative opposition, led by Winston Churchill, 'the greatest living Englishman', was bound to oppose anything that might do the Labour government some good, Morrison set out to appoint a group of planners who could boast impeccable non-partisan credentials. His first choice of front man was Lord Ismay, Churchill's chief of staff throughout the war. 'Pug' Ismay was a gifted soldier-administrator, schooled in infinite patience by the vagaries of his former chief. In semi-retirement, he was numbered among the great and the good on hand for missions too sensitive for the usual political or diplomatic channels. Administrative ability apart, Ismay had the great advantage of being liked and trusted by Churchill, whose antipathy to all things Labour might in this instance be muted if his old friend was in charge.

When Ismay was summoned to Downing Street he had just returned from two 'wholly frustrating' weeks at UN headquarters in New York, where he had been trying to persuade India and Pakistan to come to an accommodation over the disputed territory of Kashmir. The invitation to meet Prime Minister Clement Attlee and his deputy suggested another unwelcome overseas appointment. He went, as he said, 'in fear and trembling'. In the event, to be asked to chair the Festival Council came as a huge relief, even though, 'It seemed a very unsuitable assignment for one who was a complete ignoramus about science and somewhat of a philistine about the arts.' But since anything was better than going abroad again on a hopeless assignment, he accepted immediately.[10]

The Council was a roll call of the British establishment, including such august figures as Sir Kenneth Clark, John Gielgud (not yet dubbed), Sir Malcolm Sargent, Sir Alan Herbert and, for the Conservatives, R.A. Butler and Walter Elliot, ready to dispense their wisdom on behalf of the Festival. In prime position for the job of planner in chief was Gerald Barry. His early advocacy of an international exhibition put him in the spotlight but it helped that he was a friend of Max Nicholson. Before the war, Barry had given a platform to Nicholson by publishing his 'National Plan for Great Britain' in what Barry himself, the publication's editor, described as an 'obscure' journal called *Weekend Review*.[11] This had led to the creation of the think tank Political and Economic Planning (PEP), the progenitor of the National Health Service.

The son of a clergyman and a product of Marlborough (which he hated) and Cambridge, Barry had served in the Royal Flying Corps in the First World War before launching into journalism. Perennially young looking, he was said to be 'anxious, sensitive and conscientious'.[12] He was also 'friendly with an enthusiastic manner and a sharp uplifted nose that seemed to truffle for ideas and jokes'.[13] Everyone agreed he was, without question, an enthusiast who 'did not recognise the words "No" or "I can't". He was a perfectionist who would not rest, or let others do so, until the smallest details were exactly right.'[14]

Editor of the *News Chronicle* from 1936, Barry's pursuit

of radical causes including the reform of the sex and censorship laws set him against the paper's chairman, Laurence Cadbury, 'one of the most conservative of those who claimed to be liberals'.[15] Judging from the bundle of memos filed by Barry, the owner meddled in editorial matters almost on a daily basis, with the cartoonist Vicky (a Barry discovery) heading the list of staff who offended Cadbury's sensibilities.

Pushed out of the editor's chair at the *News Chronicle* in November 1947, Barry was keen to land the Festival job but he was not an easy catch. He departed with a handsome payoff – £15,000 in cash and £10,000 in first preference shares in Daily News Ltd, the equivalent today of around half a million pounds. He could afford to wait. Moreover, there were others ready to engage his services, and at a salary higher than that on offer from the government. Writing to Morrison he argued, most tactfully, that £3,000 a year, £500 more than the official rate, would be just about acceptable 'in the light of my commitments to my family and dependants and to my own market value in the future'.[16]

There was also the matter of expenses, 'which in an appointment of this kind are likely to be not inconsiderable'. Barry wanted an allowance agreed at the outset. The Treasury was not keen on this idea. From the dusty enclaves of Whitehall came a stern missive to Max Nicholson confining the prospective Director General to 'ordinary government arrangements' for senior staff. These included 'first class travel and subsistence at Class A rate'. As for entertainment, the routine was to notify in advance 'such lunches and dinners as he finds it desirable to give'. He could expect to be recompensed at the rate of fifteen shillings a head on the proviso that he exercised 'reasonable discretion and austerity'. Barry had some thinking to do, but after assurances that the Treasury 'will try not to stand in the way of meeting my reasonable needs' and a promise to respect his holiday plans, he wrote a gracious letter of acceptance.

Morrison's patience was justified. He knew that in Barry he had a capable administrator whose journalistic record as an independent radical gave him friends on both sides of the political divide. The *News Chronicle* was a liberal newspaper at a time when the Liberal Party, with just twelve MPs (falling to nine in the 1950 election), was a busted flush and thus no threat to anyone. Moreover, the Liberal philosophy of providing a social structure in which individual talents could thrive, was ideally suited to the spirit of the Festival. Broadly accepted by all parties and accounting in large measure for the decline of the Liberals as an electoral force, the freedom for all to make the most of their lives was embodied in a man who had devoted his career to promoting equality and personal fulfilment.

This is not to say that Gerald Barry was an abstract idealist. He was a firm believer in putting the modernist architect at the centre of post-war reconstruction and such was his faith in economic and social planning that he was on record as advocating the nationalisation of land.[17] As he saw it, the challenge of twentieth-century civilisation was 'to combine order with individuality, controls with essential freedom'. The job of the architect was 'to bring grace and vanity into the deadening uniformity of modern living'. It was not enough to replan the structure, 'we must also reanimate the spirit'.[18] But while he described himself as a rebel, his radicalism was tempered by his respect for tradition and for symbolic institutions. It was not by chance that the Church and the monarchy were to take leading roles in the Festival. Whatever his radical credentials, Barry offered a safe pair of hands.

As Director General of the Festival, Barry was given the broadest possible brief. Morrison wanted 'a national display illustrating the British contribution to civilisation, past, present and future in the arts, in science and technology and in industrial design'. Barry and his team of specialist advisers (officially the Festival Executive Committee) were at a loss to know where to start.

We had to create a Festival of *Britain*, the whole of Britain. It was a completely new idea: nothing like it had ever been attempted in any country before, and if it were to be accomplished with results worthy of the intention, the planning of it seemed likely to involve us in an alarmingly wide range of national and local activities. It was not simply a matter of organising one exhibition, or several exhibitions; nor of matching these with a number of arts festivals in suitable places. The moment we began to look at this programme, formidable enough in itself, we saw clearly enough that its social and economic application would entail preparation in many categories of the national life that could be no direct concern of our own organisation but the timely and energetic tackling of which would have a decisive effect on the success or otherwise of the whole undertaking.[19]

There were just five members of the Executive Committee. Along with Barry, Bernard Sendall was Controller of Home Services and Cecil Cooke Director of Exhibitions, both at the Central Office of Information;

Mary Glasgow was Secretary General of the Arts Council; and Leonard Crainford, formerly administrator of the Royal Shakespeare Company, was Secretary to the Festival. Sendall was critical to the smooth running of the operation. 'An Englishman to the roots of the blue-black beard that lay beneath his swarthy cheeks, a loyalist to his masters and to their cause whatever it or they might be and, in general, dedicated to sustaining the traditional values of old England',[20] having worked in Churchill's private office:

> He was adept at drafting and could make a U-turn in policy appear to be an absolutely logical consequence of unchanged circumstances. He could imply a threat in a way that appeared innocent and open. He could hint at a deal in a matter so ambivalent that a subsequent withdrawal could be carried off in a perfectly gentlemanly manner. He was in fact a past master at the craft of government by paper, a latter-day Francis Bacon, and despite the depth of his guile and his deeply discreet nature a very nice chap and a devotee of English county cricket.[21]

After the Festival, Sendall was made Deputy Director General of the Independent Television Authority.

Said Barry, 'We sat before our blotting pads industriously doodling, in the hope perhaps that a coherent pattern might eventually emerge, on the same principle that if you set down twelve apes before twelve typewriters they will (or so it is said) in the course of infinity type out the complete works of Shakespeare.'[22] Playing for time, Barry started researching 1851.

While waiting for a pattern to emerge from the doodles it seemed sensible at least to start collecting information about our illustrious predecessor. Even surface scratching at once brought to light fascinating material, catalogues, guide books, souvenirs of all kinds and an astonishing variety of plain and coloured prints. In a shop in Kensington Church Street I found something like a complete set of the Nash water colour engravings, the pick of which we had mounted in maple frames as appropriate decoration for the Festival offices. I recall that even this mild degree of enquiry started to raise the prices of 1851 relics. Dealers and public quickly became 'Crystal Palace conscious'.[23]

Other, more hostile influences were already at work. As Barry formulated a broad plan, the opposition was marshalling its forces. Leading the way were the Beaverbrook newspapers, the *Daily Express* and the *Evening Standard*, both dead set against what they chose to call 'Morrison's Folly'.

Barry soldiered on. He had two years, eleven months and two days before, as he put it, 'the curtain was due to rise'.

## CHAPTER TWO

There were two essential qualifications for joining the Festival creative team. One was to know the cheapest route between a bright idea and its realisation. The other was to know the right people. Barry ticked off his list of appointments by working his way through his address book. As Director of Architecture, in effect his chief of staff, Barry's choice fell on 39-year-old Hugh Casson, 'a little, slender man with sharp features and untidy hair'[1] whose thriving architectural practice was modernist without being so modern as to upset the cultural establishment.

Noted for a self-deprecating humour (he claimed that at school, Eastbourne College, his 'highest attainment was a "second" in bird watching') and a talent for charming his way out of trouble, Casson was a frequent contributor to the *News Chronicle*, where he was known to Barry as a fellow enthusiast for the role of architecture as an instrument of social engineering.

The offer was made over coffee. 'The job was full time and the salary was £1,000 pa. If possible, I was to start at once.' Barry warned him, 'There's not likely to be any building to do — it's just keeping an architectural eye on things. But it looks like being fun.' Casson accepted on the spot.[2]

Also of like mind and background to Barry was Ralph Tubbs, who was to give the Festival its icon, the Dome of Discovery. Tubbs was a friend of Casson, but again it was the columns of the *News Chronicle* that had first brought him to Barry's attention. He was also well known as the author of *Living in Cities*, a spinoff of a futuristic exhibition he had put together in 1940, and of its sequel, *The Englishman Builds*, published at the end of the war. In these two short books, Tubbs gave vent to his anger at the way unbridled modernisation had wrecked the lives of those it was supposed to serve: 'The centre of the city is a jungle of commercial blocks, neo-classic or pseudo-modern, through which the congested traffic creeps in a dense haze of petrol fumes; in the 'underdeveloped' quarters the slums linger on, while around the town spreads unending suburbia.'[3]

Like Barry, Tubbs was strong on family life as 'the basis of a happy existence'. But the machine age had undermined the family, replacing it with 'vicarious pleasures as the sole reason for living'. The result was 'social disintegration'.[4] The remedy according to Tubbs was for urban planning to consider the wants of the ordinary family. Though much in favour of new building materials such as reinforced concrete and plywood, for inspiration he looked to a romantically idealised past when 'taste had lain with the informed aristocrats and with hand craftsmen'.[5] John Ruskin and William Morris were Tubbs' standard bearers. Like them, he and Barry shared an almost pathological aversion to the Victorian 'middle class industrialists and slave-driven machine operatives ... unequipped in mind to evolve new standards of beauty for the new conditions'.

Instead, 'mass production was devoted to the multiplication of shams and cheap finery'.[6]

Others of the Festival inner circle had cut their teeth in the wartime Ministry of Information (MoI) or had participated in the Britain Can Make It exhibition of 1948. Among them was Russian-born Misha Black, founder of the Design Research Unit, a major influence on design education, and according to Casson 'one of the most experienced exhibition designers in Europe'. Throughout the war, Black had been principal exhibition architect at the MoI. He was a great one for winging off memos to colleagues with his latest thoughts, however oblique or half-formed. Casson reported to Barry that, such was the correspondence created by Black, his secretary lumped it all together in a file labelled 'Mishallaneous'.[7]

Other veterans of the MoI were Ian Cox, the Festival's director of science and technology, and Executive member Cecil Cooke, in charge of exhibitions. Then there was James Gardner, one-time coordinating designer of Britain Can Make It, 'an imperturbable pipe-sucking and decisive figure, rather like an officer in an R.C. Sherriff play, with a sharp sense of theatre and a genius for improvisation and lightning draughtsmanship'.[8] Gardner was on Casson's three-man Design Group, but with his quirky sense of humour he was soon set loose on the Pleasure Gardens at Battersea where he was his own master, at least while the budget held up. The third member of Casson's triumvirate was James Holland, who had also cut his teeth on Britain Can Make It, 'a relaxed replica of James Stewart with a gently sardonic manner and a weary experience of mounting wartime exhibitions in unlikely places and difficult circumstances'.[9]

The Festival was later criticised by those who thought there should have been more competition for the top jobs. But given the pool of designer talent, it is unlikely that a markedly different employment profile would have resulted from open selection. Most architects were hardly more qualified or gifted than jobbing builders, and in the 1940s there were no design schools dedicated to giving consumerism a facelift. Moreover, a tight schedule argued against the longueurs associated with interviewing panels. But if Barry never felt the need to apologise for trawling the old pals network, this had little to do with practicalities. He had a mission brief to put on show the 'British contribution to civilization, past, present and future' and he wanted lieutenants around him who shared his broad vision of what this really meant.

Michael Frayn, writing twelve years after the Festival had closed, called them the Herbivores — 'the do-gooders . . . or gentle ruminants, who look out from the lush pastures which are their natural station in life with eyes full of sorrow for less fortunate creatures, guiltily conscious of their advantages, though not usually ceasing to eat the grass'.[10] Certainly, paternalism was the driving force of the Festival, as it was throughout government, with ministers implying, if not stating openly, that they did not need telling what was best for the people. But Frayn's implication of complacency was unjustified. A certain intellectual arrogance was mitigated by a genuine desire for popular approval. To this extent the Festival was a propaganda exercise, a concerted attempt by mostly young designers to show that their alternative to conventional taste would make for happier lives.

But what precisely were they reacting against? Tubbs and

others wrote of the horrors of jerry-built houses and overcrowded streets, but it was claustrophobic design in all its forms that was the enemy — over-furnished rooms with fussy embellishments, clichéd decorations and the superfluous twists and twiddles of the typical Victorian façade. Barry shuddered when a young architect professed to find virtues in Manchester Town Hall.[11] John Betjeman and the Victorian Society had still to find a voice. There was a reaction too against slavish devotion to the past, to middle-class homes with their tacked-on neo-Georgian accessories and to what critic and humorist Osbert Lancaster dubbed the 'stockbroker Tudor' villas of the *nouveaux riches*.

What the new boys were for was bold, clean lines, light and space, a satisfying amalgam of practicality and beauty. If Victorian monstrosities had to be cleared away to make room for enlightened creativity, so be it. The attentions of the Luftwaffe, followed by two Town and Country Planning Acts that gave local authorities the power to compulsorily purchase blitzed and derelict sites at 1939 prices, created the opportunity for young planners to realise their dreams. Their inspiration was part American but mostly European, with Scandinavia and Germany as predominant influences. Italy too; art historians point to the Milan design fairs as a major influence. But in the end, it was northern Europe that held sway, because it was there in the Nordic democracies that modern design was combined with a social message that had strong appeal to those who looked to a more egalitarian society.

Hugh Casson gave his festival 'Oscar' to the 1930 Stockholm Exhibition. He was not alone. The impact made by the exhibition in Europe and beyond was the result of a happy conjunction of time and place. Sweden was in transition as it evolved from farm and forestry to become a modern industrial state. Social democracy was still young (the party did not govern alone until 1932), but ideas of an advanced welfare system financed by rapid economic growth were already taking hold. In this heady ambience a new generation of architects and designers found their voice. Taking their cue from Walter Gropius of Bauhaus fame they embraced functionalism, a philosophy that required designers to relate more closely to the purpose a building or object was intended to serve, to make design an instrument of efficiency as well as beauty. The Stockholm Exhibition was their showcase.

What was a provocation to cultural backwoodsmen came as a delightful revelation to those who had caught the spirit of modernism. Djurgården, the waterside site for the exhibition where the National Maritime Museum now stands, was a medley of colour and light. There were three main sections, illustrating the home, including good quality apartments at modest cost; furniture and household goods – clean, smooth lines in furniture, colourful and easily manageable kitchenware, unfussy ornaments; and the urban framework – transport, garden equipment and street furniture. The link was the functionalist concept of producing 'more beautiful things for everyday use'.

The Stockholm Exhibition had a lengthy pedigree. The association of family health and contentment with room to move and good fresh air could be traced back over half a century of architectural innovation across mainland Europe. In Sweden, functionalism had its first display at the Home Exhibition organised by the Swedish Society for Industrial Design as early as 1917. The Bauhaus school of functionalist design, founded in 1919, prompted influential exhibitions such as Die Wohnung in Stuttgart and Weissenhof in Frankfurt, both in 1927.

'Our object', wrote Walter Gropius, 'was to liberate the creative artist from his other-worldliness and reintegrate him into the workaday world of realities; and at the same time to broaden and humanize the rigid, almost exclusively material mind of the businessman.' Gropius, Le Corbusier and the Finnish architect Alvar Aalto founded CIAM (International Congresses of Modern Architecture), which came up with 'Charte d'Athène', a statement of their convictions hammered out at their 1933 conference held on a ship moored off Athens.

But it was the Stockholm Exhibition that made the greatest impression on the public imagination. Visitors, of whom there were four million in a country of just six million, were attracted as much by the festive mood generated by the exhibition's chief architect, Gunnar Asplund, as by the official presentations. As the organiser of a more modest functionalist exhibition in Turku, Alvar Aalto was bowled over by the sheer sense of fun at Djurgården: 'Over the whole rests a festive spirit, almost childlike and uninhibited. Asplund's . . . aim has been a grand party . . . a composition in houses, flags, floodlights, flowers, fireworks, happy people and clean tablecloths.'[12]

British visitors, including a party of nearly a hundred members of the Architectural Association, were particularly impressed, doubtless experiencing a release of the frustration of working in a cultural environment that was, for the most part, locked in the past.

In the August number of *Architectural Review*, Morton Shand heaped praise on Asplund and his colleagues, who had shown 'a real grasp of functionalism and the aesthetics of the machine and its products'. Asplund had demonstrated that steel and glass could give a building lightness, airiness and charm. Shand thought the three-storey Paradise Restaurant, in glass and steel, with a cubistic group of sculptures suspended from the ceiling, the best building of its kind to date and the 74-metre Advertising Mast with its Press Gallery a masterpiece.[13] Even *The Times'*, not noted for its modernist tastes, praised the exhibition for its intelligence, charm and daring. There were of course hostile critics, not a few of them in Sweden, but the overall impression was distinctly favourable.

British popular opinion remained largely immune to continental influences, though it was not only young designers who found it hard to understand why the huge majority of the citizens of one of the world's richest countries should be content to spend the best part of their lives in miserable little houses in mean streets breathing industrial stench. As for the rest, for the rising middle class the home of one's own was semi-detached, two up three down, in a suburban sprawl that put narrow respectability before style or even comfort. Behind the lace curtains, linoleum flooring ('guaranteed to minimise dust'), flock carpets, knobbly-legged chairs, kidney-shaped dressing tables with chintz surround and padded bed-heads told of a style confined by complacency and low expectations.

But if functionalism had an uphill battle to win approval, lessons were learned. In 1933, a group of architects led by W. Wells Coates, an architect dedicated to building in new materials and who was to design the Telecinema for the Festival of Britain, Maxwell Fry, who argued in *Design in Modern Life* that a town should be planned to grow like an ordered, well-controlled forest rather than a jungle, and David Pleydell-Bouverie set up Modern Architectural Research (MARS) as an adjunct to CIAM. Showing work at the MARS exhibition of 1938 were several designers, including Ralph Tubbs, who were soon to be marked out by Barry and Casson for Festival engagements.

Meanwhile, Wells Coates made his name with the Lawn Road Flats, still Hampstead's architectural gem, a classic of 1930s design emphasising simplicity and efficiency to a degree that was 'nearer to the *machine à habiter* than anything Le Corbusier ever designed'.[14] His clients were Jack and Molly Pritchard, who were in the vanguard of promoting an art expression that looked to the present and future for its inspiration. Jack Pritchard had done more than most to win acceptance for the elegant, lightweight furnishings favoured by Aalto and the Danish architect Arne Jacobsen. He was also instrumental in lifting Gropius out of Nazi clutches.

A pattern was beginning to emerge that put modernist designers at the core of social change in post-war Britain. Their first real opportunity to show collectively what they could do came with Britain Can Make It. In just fourteen weeks, nearly one and a half million people made their way to the Victoria and Albert Museum to discover what precisely Britain could make and what the new style had to offer. The product selection took in Furnished Rooms, Women's Dress, Furniture, Furnishing and Fabrics, and Future Design. The first attracted the strongest interest, along with the Shopwindow Street which was 'continually blocked by crowds'.

But there was criticism that nothing exhibited could be bought since it was all marked down for export. A wit suggested that the exhibition should be renamed 'Britain Can't Have It'. Perhaps for this reason, only 29 per cent of visitors believed that their tastes had been altered by what they had seen.[15] What was the point of getting excited about things that were not immediately within reach? On the other hand, there was undoubtedly a resistance to change, evidenced by the tendency of a ration-weary public to romanticise the pre-war 'good old days'.

One good reason why the government encouraged modern design was that it attracted the sort of business that was paid for in dollars. In 1945, Hugh Dalton, the President of the Board of Trade, had drawn attention to the design revolution in the USA which 'made many of our exports old fashioned and less acceptable'. And it was not just the government who argued thus. Geoffrey Holme, editor of *The Studio*, was one of many visitors to the USA who stated what should have been obvious: 'There is a great need and a demand here for the specially made thing of good design, fine craftsmanship and superb quality of material . . . For a long time I have believed this to be our chance. To compete in methods of pure mass production is the height of folly. One has only to see to believe this.'[16]

The same message came from the government's business task-force in America. Its leader, Neville Blond, himself a successful businessman, was driven to distraction by the blatant disregard for market realities: 'Everything we sold was in black, dark blue or brown . . . On the West Coast, where bright colours prevailed, a Lancashire suit or a Midlands' motor car were too depressing for words.'[17]

But it got worse: 'How was it that after winning an order for a fleet of London taxis, the manufacturer could respond with a flat refusal to put in left hand drive. Apparently, the adaptation of the production line was too much trouble for a single order. But why did it have to be a single order?'[18]

The fact was that British exporters had become complacent, cushioned as they were by tariff-protected Commonwealth and colonial markets and latterly by the easy predictability of wartime production. But the war was over and imperial markets were no longer secure from competitors, invariably American, who benefited from new plant, new technology, superior sales and service organisations and, above all, original and attractive design.

Britain needed to catch up, and fast. Early attempts, including the Britain Can Make It exhibition, fell short of expectations. The Festival of Britain was to be a much grander affair, an undertaking no less than to galvanise an entire nation.

# CHAPTER THREE

Two months after his appointment as the Festival's
Director General, Gerald Barry made his first report to his
governing council.[1] At this stage without administrative
backup, he was camping out on the upper floor of the RSA:

One could not have had surroundings more delightful
to work in . . . The Secretary, Mr Luckhurst, went out
of his way to be kind and accommodating to his
tiresome intruders, and the porter in his pleasant
green livery was most solicitous for our comfort, being
early at hand with the inevitable cups of tea. I had a
pleasant room, and was amused to find myself sitting
opposite a contemporary painting – a self portrait –
of the architect Charles Barry. For company I had
some typing paper, pencils and a blotting pad; also
one colleague, Leonard Crainford.[2]

A few ground rules were soon established. Work was to
be devolved to six agencies, four of them already in place –
the Arts Council, the Council of Industrial Design, the
Central Office of Information and the British Film Institute
– and two set up specifically with the Festival in mind – a

Council for Science and Technology and a Council for Architecture, Town Planning and Building Research. Each of these had a representative on Barry's executive. There was a Committee for Scotland and another for Wales.

First thoughts were of three separate exhibitions – one for science, one for architecture and town planning and a third for the applied arts – 'a kind of Britain Can Make It on a much larger scale'. But it was soon realised that there was so much overlap as to make the three-way division artificial. So it was that the consensus favoured a combined exhibition offering 'not only a truer and more comprehensive picture but also a more interesting and dynamic show than was likely to be achieved by the original plan'. This would be supplemented by a series of smaller specialist exhibitions, together with locally organised festivals throughout the country.

Aspirations were high. The aim was 'to leave some mark on our history . . . in encouraging more of the right sort of recruits into the arts and sciences; in permanently raising the status of artists and scientists; in setting permanently higher standards, and so eventually in establishing British supremacy in culture and the humanities'.[3]

There was another objective – largely unspoken but none the less real. The British people were in need of reassurance that, having won the war, they were not about to lose the peace. It wasn't simply that living conditions were harsh. There was resentment at all the highly visible indications of a country in decline. The Empire was breaking up, Western Europe was heading for recovery with, incredibly, the Germans leading the way, while the Americans were as pushy as ever but, so it appeared, more against their supposedly closest ally than their former enemies. A once confident Britain, secure in its status as a great power, was having to get used to demotion. It was a painful adjustment.

Barry certainly recognised the problem and the challenge. It was not enough for his Festival to project a future bright with technological and scientific promise. That could apply to any developed country. If the Festival was to succeed it had to offer something more, a demonstration of how the British, though battered by adversity, were still a people apart, deserving respect for their achievements and attention for what they had to offer. In Barry's imagination, the Festival was to be a lesson in national identity, a reason to be proud. Prompted by Hugh Casson, the idea began to take shape of telling the story of Britain in exhibition form, so that by learning about the past, those who came to the Festival would gain courage for the future. Or, in Morrison's words, they would see for themselves a 'new Britain springing from the battered fabric of the old'.[4]

But this is to step ahead in the plot. For concepts to take practical shape, dedicated workers had to be recruited. Once Casson and his team of designers were up to strength, the search began for enthusiasts to fill other critical jobs. One of the happiest appointments was that of Paul Wright, who was to take on the task of marketing the Festival.

As a temporary civil servant, 34-year-old Paul Wright had recently suffered a severe reality check. He had resigned from the Coal Board, disillusioned by myopic management and, probably, though he was reluctant to admit this, an intransigent workforce. At a loose end and worried about his overdraft, Wright found himself discussing the future with Gerald Barry, who lived in a neighbouring village.

Neither could believe their luck. Wright was looking for a job and a purpose, a role that would satisfy his need to put something into the community. Barry also had a need, equally pressing, to find someone with flair and enthusiasm to take on the promotion of the Festival at home and overseas. And here, on his doorstep, was the ideal candidate. With his vision of a humane and more generous society, Wright breathed the very spirit that Barry was trying to engender for the Festival. Together they strode over the West Sussex downs, exchanging ideas on how the Festival could be made 'a springboard for the nation's young creative talent'.[5]

As the team began to take shape, brainstorming weekends were spent at Barry's Sussex home near Petworth. Forge Cottage, a happy melange of old and new, was the perfect stimulant to evolving a Festival philosophy. Although its façade was conventionally rustic, the rear of the house, known as the Elephant Room, was high and spacious, fronted with curving glass, 'conjuring a series of grand and intimate spaces'[6] including a mezzanine and roof terrace. The architect was F.R.S. Yorke, whose bestselling *The Modern House* established the standard of excellence for Festival architecture. The setting of Forge Cottage also helped:

> In the daytime we sat round a table on the terrace with our sleeves rolled up, or paced the lawn in eloquent pairs, like walrus and carpenter, trying to grasp the immensity of our task and marshal the shoes and ships and sealing-wax into some sort of order and coherence. Below us the early summer landscape rolled away in succeeding folds of green and gold to

the distant wave-crest of Chanctonbury, and the long, low horizon of the downs. In the middle distance stood the oaks of Bignor Park, dressed in the lime-green of their first foliage. Their beauty we inherit from an age of men that had such faith in the future of their country and so robust a sense of responsibility to their successors that they planted, not for themselves, but for their great-grandchildren. Here was our incentive.[7]

One of the more ebullient contributors to this country-house think tank was Huw Wheldon, who spoke for the Arts Council and was marked out for greatness as the future presenter and editor of *Monitor*, the BBC flagship arts programme, and subsequently as managing director of BBC Television, where he presided over a golden age of comedy, drama and documentary. Wheldon was one of the few who came from outside the Festival magic circle, though he had connections that stood him in good stead: his father, Sir Wynn Wheldon, was chairman of the Welsh Festival Committee, while his own job before he moved to London was to run the Welsh offshoot of the Arts Council. A need to soothe nationalist sensitivities (in those days far stronger in Wales than in Scotland) gave the young arts administrator a head start with his interviewing panel. A week after his grilling, at the end of January 1949, the job was his.

Wheldon had the great virtue of not taking the arts too seriously. In the front rank of the Arts Council were too many sombre-minded people who spoke and acted as if exposure to music, theatre, literature or paintings was an experience to be endured for the good of the soul. He

recognised the potential for raising the level of appreciation of the arts but knew very well that the only way to do
this was to show how culture could be fun. He made the
point famously by declaring that if it came to a choice, he
'preferred fireworks to ballet', though his ideal, figuratively
speaking, was a combination of the two. In this he was at
one with Barry.

Having settled on a narrative exhibition – 'Britain's
contribution to civilisation – past, present and future' – a
further critical decision was to resist all commercial
blandishments. 'There was to be no space to let,' ruled
Barry. 'No one would be able to have his goods on exhibit
by paying to do so; they would get there by merit or not at all.
There would be no Hall of Woollens or Pavilion of
Sweetmeats or Garden of Horticulture; there would be no
mammoth mounds of apples or effigies of Royalty in edible
fats.'[8]

This last grotesque was not entirely fanciful. For the 1924
British Empire Exhibition, held at Wembley, the Canadian
pavilion had unveiled a life-size statue of the Prince of
Wales carved out of butter. The subject complained that it
made his legs look too fat.[9] Another horror, fortunately
beyond living memory but none the less a powerful
disincentive, was the 1851 French tribute to Queen Victoria
– a statue eighteen feet high in zinc, a material not subsequently favoured for large sculptures. Barry shuddered
at the thought.

Given the severe limits on public funding (the Festival
budget was £12 million, later reduced to £11 million), it was
a bold decision to reject company sponsorship. Advertising
could quite easily have doubled the resources available to
architects and designers, though shortages of raw materials

might well have kept the lid on extravagant building. But whatever the financial considerations, control was what really mattered, and Barry had no intention of sharing it with a bunch of hard-nosed money makers who, in his view, wouldn't recognise good design if it got up and hit them in the mouth.

This is not to say that Barry was oblivious to commercial imperatives. Excluding any reference to the Commonwealth and Empire may have been motivated partly by the desire to focus on British achievements (though would not this have included the imperial tradition?), partly by a natural reluctance to grab hold of a political hot potato. With India gaining independence in 1947, Britain's retreat from Empire was well under way. The strategy produced Churchillian eruptions that might have threatened the existence of the Festival if it had tried to portray the past, the present and, most dangerously, the future of the colonies. But, crucially, the Festival was promoted as a dollar earner, and that meant attracting American visitors whose warm feelings towards Britain, such as they were, rarely if ever extended to British command over large parts of the world map. So, for the sake of the balance of payments, Commonwealth and Empire were not just sidelined but dismissed from the field.

With the broad picture in place, the pressing issue was accommodation both for the Festival itself and for the people who were to run it. A headquarters was found, courtesy of the Ministry of Works, off the Strand, close by the Savoy Hotel. No. 2 Savoy Court, a home to the Free French throughout the war, had been lately occupied by the Electricity Commission, a body made redundant by the industry's nationalisation. It was, recalled Barry, 'a solid

Edwardian affair with massive mahogany doors and panels, belonging to the days when a room was still a room and not a centrally heated box'.[10] He was surprised to find 'in this temple of electricity . . . large open fireplaces and a profusion of exposed wires and switches trailing over walls and skirtings as though electricity had been introduced by sceptical Commissioners as a temporary experiment'.[11]

There was some distress at the RSA when Barry and his core staff announced they were moving out. Though the move was to take them only a short way along the Strand, the loss of influence for the RSA implied by the departure of the Festival staff was privately acknowledged by Barry, who valued his independence. Once installed in their new quarters, there was space for Hugh Casson and his Design Group, who had been camping out in an unheated office in Cadogan Gardens. Paul Wright, who was already showing a flair for public relations, scored a coup by securing 1951 as the Festival telephone number. Around this time, the Festival was recognised as a separate government department, free from the COI but now caught in the bright beam of the Public Accounts Committee. Links with the government were via Bernard Sendall, designated deputy chairman, and, at the Treasury, George Campbell, 'who had the essential probing nose and projecting eyebrows, and seemed to delight in finding ways round his own regulations'.[12]

But the most urgent question was still unanswered. Where was this Festival to be held? Having at one time pulled ahead as the favourite location, Osterley fell out of the running when estimates for the necessary infrastructure came in at over six times the Festival budget. Other prospective sites, already assessed, were reassessed.

Earls Court and Olympia were ruled out because they were already booked for the annual British Industrial Fair. An apparently easy option that found favour in the corridors of Whitehall was to take temporary possession of the three neighbouring museums in South Kensington – the Victoria and Albert and the Science and Natural History museums.

This produced a howl of protest from the museums' directors, who had been busy reassembling the displays dispersed and stored during the war. To have had to pack everything away again was a sacrifice too dismal to contemplate. Barry and his colleagues were of the same mind, but for different reasons. The west London museums were born of the 1851 Exhibition and were unmistakably Victorian or Edwardian in appearance. This was precisely the image the Festival rejected. It was time to look forward, not back.

A tour was made of the larger parks. The likeliest prospect was Battersea, not least because it fronted a long stretch of the Thames. It was, as Barry said, 'a little off centre' with no nearby Underground, but it had a lake and a wide circular carriageway. Moreover, the park was in need of renovation, having been recently occupied by anti-aircraft units and Dig for Victory allotments. Trouble was, local residents and politicians were resolutely opposed to anything that delayed the restoration of one of London's more attractive and popular open spaces. Confronted by a powerful lobby, Barry conceded, though as it happened, Battersea was to play a part in the Festival as the home of the fun fair, appreciated by nearly all except those who lived nearby.

Almost inexorably, attention shifted back to the South Bank of the Thames, specifically the derelict site between

County Hall and Waterloo Bridge, identified in the 1945 Greater London Plan as 'the opportunity for the greatest spectacular effect of the new London' with two new theatres, a concert hall, swimming pool, restaurants and cafés. The South Bank had a chequered history. Until the end of the seventeenth century the area was known as Lambeth Marsh. With its open fields and wide streams bordered by willows, it was largely populated by wildfowl, many of which fell to the guns of James I and his hunting companions. During the Civil War, Inigo Jones took the sensible precaution of burying his nest egg here to be recovered when public order had been restored.

From about 1690 there was music and fireworks at Cupa's (or Cupid's) Pleasure Gardens, providing a popular night out for generations of Londoners until the authorities decided that it was a magnet for thieves and pickpockets. The Folly, a huge houseboat moored on the South Bank, was famed for 'the depravity of its dancing saloon'.

After Cupa's was shut down, the area was taken over by a motley collection of industries. First to move in was lead merchant Thomas Maltby who, in 1826, built the 140-foot-high Shot Tower, one of the few buildings to be left standing by the Luftwaffe. The opening of Waterloo station in 1848 was an added attraction to industry and services including the Lion Brewery, Lambeth Water Works and the London Waste Paper Company. But none of these helped to raise the tone of the place, which remained a no-go area for the supposedly more genteel Londoners who lived on the north side of the river. Brave souls occasionally ventured to the Old Vic, then known as the Royal Coburg, 'a licensed pit of darkness, a trap of temptation, profligacy and ruin'.

The first sign of regeneration came when Emma Cons, a

devotee of temperance, reopened the Old Vic as a 'cheap and decent place of amusement'. The baton was taken up by her niece, Lilian Baylis, who staged Shakespeare for the masses. In 1922 the South Bank gained added distinction with the building of County Hall, the home of the London County Council, a short way upstream while after years of political and architectural wrangling, the new Waterloo Bridge (designed by Sir Giles Gilbert Scott) was partially opened in 1942 and completed in 1945.

But was any of this sufficient justification for staging a national festival on the South Bank? Herbert Morrison, Leader of the LCC for six years up to the start of the war and cheerleader for a wider and stronger Waterloo Bridge, was delighted by the prospect of rejuvenating what he regarded as his home territory. He had been saying as much since the mid-1930s, when he had first talked of his vision of 'an embankment promenade between Westminster and Waterloo bridges where people will be able to walk and enjoy the view on the opposite side of the river'.[13] Fifteen years later, after seven schemes had been commissioned and endlessly discussed, Morrison bemoaned the lack of progress: 'Nobody goes to the South Bank, they try not to go to the South Bank because it's nothing but mud and rotting wharves and rubble and industry and warehouses, misery and poverty and railway lines. And we must clear it up.'[14]

The Festival offered the best chance yet of putting things right. Members of the Design Panel were not so sure.

'On paper it looked marvellous,' recalled Hugh Casson. 'It was centrally placed, with good communications and within sight of Big Ben and Trafalgar Square.' But . . . 'To start with it was tiny (only 27 acres). Next it was cut in half by a public right of way and by Charing Cross railway

(Hungerford) bridge beneath which were a number of snugly housed tenants with unexpired leases and right of access. Most of the upstream half was dominated by mountains of bomb rubble.'¹⁵

There were two factors – apart from the absence of viable alternative sites – that clinched it for the South Bank. First, the Design Group was beguiled by the view, a broad, gentle bow in the river that took in a clear sight of some of London's best-loved landmarks, from the Houses of Parliament to St Paul's.

Then again, the LCC had plans for the South Bank which could happily dovetail into preparations for the Festival. Work had already started on a new 1,700-foot river wall designed to protect the site from flooding while reclaiming more than four acres and providing the essential buttress for a riverside promenade. Even more relevant to the central theme, the LCC had given the go-ahead to the new concert hall, the first major public building to be constructed in Britain for well over a decade. Scheduled to be opened in 1951, here was an essential component of the Festival blessed with its own funding (around £2 million). It was almost too good to be true.

Morrison's backing was a foregone conclusion; less predictably, R.A. Butler and Walter Elliot, Tory spokesmen on the Festival Council, were also keen. One by one, the objections of the Design Group were overcome: 'The right of way to Waterloo could be piped overhead, the arch tenants decently displaced, the contractors' working areas made more restricted, the rubble removed.'¹⁶

The real work was about to start.

# CHAPTER FOUR

The priority was to establish an action plan. This turned out to be more of a challenge than Gerald Barry had anticipated. As the editor of a national newspaper, his role had been that of a benevolent dictator. His was the grand vision, others gave it shape and substance. Doubtless he thought of the Festival in the same light. But while Barry persuaded himself that he had a clear idea of what the Festival was all about – a national restorative positioning Britain in the brave new technological world – the devil was in the detail. Barry suffered agonies of frustration as Casson and the design team wrestled with apparent irreconcilables – how to put on a show with wide popular appeal; a show, moreover, with lasting impact on the public imagination. And all this on a tight budget. As James Gardner recalled:

> In the early days, we would spend an hour or two peeling detail paper off a continuous roll, sketching over each other's layouts with coloured inks to keep our minds on the attack, then, when we had covered ten feet, we would spread it on the floor to decide which of the twenty or so variants to adopt. Walking the site later, when the buildings were up, we came

unexpectedly upon a ridiculous little brick recess. 'Don't you remember,' said Casson with a wry grin, 'that's one of those elegant breaks in line that looked so *right* on the plan.'[1]

While the South Bank waited for its facelift, at Savoy Court the debate continued on what was to be done, how it could be done and by when it could be done. As Casson explained:

> The brief demanded a narrative exhibition, a story — yet to be written, of course — to be told in proper sequence chapter by chapter, pavilion by pavilion. Tradition demanded that there had to be a central feature as memorable and dramatic if possible as the Eiffel Tower. Most important of all, the whole place, however varied in detail, had to be given a visual personality which, we hoped, would be the fruit of a common design philosophy.[2]

The excitement of being part of a trailblazing adventure soon turned to weary realisation that some of the best ideas would never lift off the paper. 'Ralph Tubbs arrived one morning with a proposal for roofing over Trafalgar Square to provide a platform main entrance, to carry from there a raised catwalk over Northumberland Avenue to join a new footbridge over the Thames.'[3] Ingenious but unattainable. The concept was reduced to a simple bailey bridge built by the Royal Engineers.

Gradually, suitably realistic ideas began to fall into place. At the centre was to be the Dome, 'the shining cranium of invention'[4] as Casson dubbed it, with the best of British invention and enterprise on display. Around the Dome would be pavilions dedicated to the land, agriculture, mining and industry, and telling the story of Britain. Downstream, on one side and to the rear of the still to be built Festival Hall, the projected themes were more people orientated – arts and crafts, education, the English at home, their character and recreation.

The river front was to be given a seaside makeover – the British on holiday – complete with a promenade, deck-chairs, ice cream stalls and, an optimistic touch, sunshades. Not surprisingly, this was the first time the Thames in central London had been visualised as anything but a commercial highway. Little would be done about the murky water and dockside smells (it would be many years before clean air became the norm), though local industries were urged to cut emissions for the duration of the Festival. Clearly, much was to be left to the imagination.

Somehow, a small site had to be so planned as to give a sense of space, allowing for easy, leisurely movement between the pavilions. This was to be achieved by a series of connecting patios, each of contrasting shapes and colours. The idea was for new points of interest to catch the eye at every turn, a device to encourage visitors to keep moving and to forget how confined they really were. The bailey bridge started within shouting distance of Trafalgar Square and Thameside piers for passenger boats, all intended to reduce crowding at the road entrances. Other aids to footsloggers included a new escalator at Waterloo Underground station.

But, given the expected popularity of the Festival, there was no getting away from the fact that a site of 27 acres was too small to accomplish all that Barry visualised. Certainly there was not enough space to show off what the planners could achieve with socially motivated architecture. The solution was to create a new town in miniature, a concept that fitted neatly into the County of London Plan and the Greater London Plan, the products of several years' toil by Sir Patrick Abercrombie, Professor of Town Planning at London University, and J.H. Forshaw, the LCC architect.

Abercrombie wanted to achieve a lower living density which allowed village-like communities to thrive within the city. Here was an opportunity to demonstrate how it would be done in practice. The selected site was in Poplar, a deprived area of the East End which had suffered heavy bomb damage. Now to be called the Lansbury Estate after erstwhile local Labour MP George Lansbury, a tireless campaigner for social justice, the new neighbourhood was to have its own schools and church, an old people's home, a pedestrian shopping centre and covered marketplace, pubs and open spaces. It was a planner's dream made real – or, to quote an observer of the work in progress, 'a modern oasis set in a vast area of overcrowded streets'.[5]

Putting the scope of the scientific revolution on display also needed more space than the South Bank could provide. With building about to start on a new wing of the Science Museum in South Kensington, the answer had to be an opening exhibition linked to the Festival. Beyond London, the Festival outreach took in an exhibition of Industrial Power in Glasgow's Kelvin Hall, the Ulster Farm and Factory Exhibition on an industrial estate outside Belfast, and two touring exhibitions: one by land, the other on the Festival ship, *Campania*, a converted aircraft carrier on loan from the Admiralty.

But more was needed to make the Festival a truly

nationwide celebration. On 8 June 1949, the Guildhall in the City of London hosted a gathering of local authority leaders from across England and Wales. They were there to hear all about the Festival and to find out what they were expected to do to make it the party of the century. The answer was anything and everything. Tidying up the park, giving the town hall a fresh coat of paint, building a new bus shelter, organising a carnival, clearing a bomb site, mending the church organ or cleaning out the village duck pond – it was all grist to the Festival mill. The provincial dignitaries went away suitably enthused.

Having had their outline plans endorsed by the Festival Council, the Design Group divided responsibilities. Misha Black and James Holland were given the upstream section with Ralph Tubbs concentrating on what was now known as the Dome of Discovery. The eastern side of Hungerford Bridge, downstream, was left to Casson and James Gardner. General management of the building programme was delegated to Freeman, Fox and Partners, a firm of structural engineers of such illustrious antiquity as to have served in the same capacity for the 1851 Exhibition, not to mention building Sydney Harbour Bridge. Rejecting the defeatism of its competitors, Freeman Fox alone was able to reassure Tubbs that his pancake-shaped Dome, 365 feet in diameter, could be built in the time available.[6]

The company's history justified its self-confidence. For the Great Exhibition, what was then Fox and Henderson had set itself the task of assembling 3,300 iron columns, 2,224 girders and 205 miles of sash bars to hold together 900,000 square feet of glass in order to make real Joseph Paxton's vision of his Crystal Palace. And all this to be accomplished in twenty-two weeks on a budget that allowed for no margin for error. By comparison, the Dome of Discovery, though throwing up its own formidable challenges, was well within the scope of Britain's leading structural engineers. The proposal was for the Dome's rib structure and smooth metal cover to be made of aluminium alloy, a material hitherto not often used for substantial buildings: 'The ribs were to thrust on to an all welded steel box ring girder, itself held aloft 40 feet above ground by a series of slender lattice steel masts leaning inwards and forming a complete triangulated support system all round the ring.'[7]

Elsewhere on the South Bank site, architects and display designers, mostly under forty and untried on any project to rank with the Festival buildings, were recruited and told to get drawing. There were over fifty of them, a number that soon rose to close on a hundred, chosen 'for their honesty of aim and sympathy of viewpoint; they all spoke the same language but each with enough variety of intonation to make it interesting'.[8] 'The talent of Britain was allowed to bloom in unison for five months,' declared Misha Black.[9] Casson might have added that they were nearly all part of his old boy network.

Among the star turns were Robert Goodden and Richard Russell, the architects for what was originally called the Communication of Ideas Pavilion. Too dull, said Casson, who doodled his way to a visual interpretation of the British character, strong of purpose but tolerant and modest, with a love of sports and a self-deprecating sense of humour. The new title was to be the Lion and the Unicorn, encompassing strength and eccentricity under one roof. Though no one liked to admit it, the Lion and Unicorn exhibition was less about real people and more about the promotion of an artificial national self-image. Possibly for that reason it turned out to be one of the most popular features of the entire Festival.

The competitive element was not entirely absent. Closely contested was the design for a Festival emblem. The profile of Britannia above a compass star with a lower border of blue and white pennants won the day against twenty other entries as the symbol that would most easily adapt to everything to do with the Festival, from promotional material, including advertisements, to letter headings and souvenirs. It could be used on any surface and in any size. The designer, Abram Games, had already made a name with his 1930s posters for Shell and BP. His inspiration for the bunting surrounding Britannia came when he was watching his wife Marianne hanging out the washing.[10]

Barry heartily approved of Games, a man in the forefront of innovative commercial art – which, as he put it, 'reaches and teaches more than any piece of fine art that is hung in an academy for a handful to admire'. Evidence of such missionary zeal was provided by his 'Your Britain, Fight for it Now' poster of 1942, a montage depicting an imagined future that featured a neat block of flats, a busy clinic and a modern school and based on Impington Village College, an all-purpose education centre in Cambridgeshire designed by Walter Gropius and Maxwell Fry. Though widely praised, the poster was rejected by Churchill, who preferred the more homely images of Frank Newbauld's Merrie England village seen at a distance by the shepherd on his way home across the South Downs, an artificial construct which, ironically, later critics accused the Festival of helping to foster.

Still missing from Barry's draft plan was the magic touch,

the Eiffel Tower effect, to give the Festival a distinctive image that would be memorable after other national events had been long forgotten. An open competition attracted, among other fantastical visions, a blob with a hole in it, three triangles having an argument in space and a needle poised on nothing.[11] The last, and the winning entry, was Britain's first example of high-tech architecture – an outsized exclamation mark! Rising 300 feet, this slender steel and aluminium structure, seemingly free-standing, was held in place by high-tension cables slung between three steel beams. Lit from the inside, at night it was a pointer that could be seen all over London. Like the Eiffel Tower, it served no practical purpose except to make people stop and stare and wonder.

This startling, futuristic icon was created by architects Hidalgo Moya and Philip Powell, along with engineer Felix Samuel, who commanded half the budget for his foundations. As Philip Powell recalled, 'Jacko [Moya] and I did separate entries. I did a pyramid, a slightly tapering thing, with a zigzag bracing and coloured pattern but Jacko's first sketch felt so right that there was no point going further and we collaborated after that. But it was Jacko who evolved the design.'[12] However, they had no name for it, so another competition was held. It was won by Mrs Sheppard Fidler, wife of the chief architect of the Crawley Development Corporation, who combined the words 'skyhook' and 'nylon' to come up with Skylon. She told reporters that writing poetry had heightened her imaginative powers.

Clearing the South Bank raised the question of what to do with the few buildings already there, of which the Shot Tower was the most conspicuous. Abandoned by its owners,

Associated Lead, who had moved to Chester, the tower was a throwback to the days when lead shot was made by feeding molten metal through a colander, then dropping it from a great height (there were 322 steps to the top) into a large copper bath. First thoughts were of giving the tower a hefty whack with a wrecking ball. But sentimental Londoners were averse to losing a favourite landmark. The solution was provided by Ian Cox, who suggested adapting it to the twentieth century by fixing it up with a radio telescope. Visitors would be able to watch on screen as signals were sent to the moon and reflected back in two and a half seconds. For added interest, a lighthouse beam would shine out from the pinnacle. The firm of Chance Brothers, who had made the panes of glass for the Crystal Palace, was invited to supply the equipment.

Then there was the old Lion Brewery, in place for over a century, which also claimed its share of sentimental regard. This was due not so much to the quality of the beer as to its symbol, a seven-ton sculpture that adorned the classical frontage. The decision was to let the building go – it had no place in a modern festival – but to save the lion, said to be unique because it was made of Coade's artificial stone, though what this was precisely no one could say, since Mrs Eleanor Coade had taken her recipe to the grave. Only recently has Coade stone been reinvented. Rifling through the order books of the south Devon quarry where Mrs Coade obtained her materials, Stephen Pettifer, a Wiltshire sculptor, calculated the exact proportion of clay relative to other materials used to produce the toughest artificial stone before Portland cement.[13]

The lion, now painted red, was to be relocated to a new home next to a ticket office opposite Waterloo Station Gate.

(It now adorns the south side of Westminster Bridge.) It nearly didn't make it. The first attempts to lower the beast from its perch were abandoned when the cable of its wooden cradle snapped. Returning for a second try, the workmen were again sent scuttling when the entire façade threatened to collapse. Mission accomplished, the demolition men moved in.

While the South Bank was being cleared of rubble and work started on the river walk, the Festival message of 'a new fashioned variation on the old fashioned theme of patriotism'[14] began to take firmer shape. But not without contention. The Festival was supposed to be all about Britishness, but a consensus had yet to be reached as to what the word really meant.

Since vocal minorities in Scotland and Wales were unlikely to submit to any definition of nationality that equated Britain with England, there was much talk of strength through diversity, a concept that defied logic but allowed the superficial impression to be given of a united country. In Wales, where 26 per cent of the population spoke their native language, the interpretation of diversity was to focus exclusively on things Welsh, with the National Eisteddfod at Llanrwst and festivals at Llangollen, Swansea and St Davids. A government-sponsored rehabilitation of some hillside farms, showing how they could be made more productive and profitable, was thought to be worthy but only what the government should have been doing anyway. Scotland had its exhibition of Industrial Power, but as its organiser, Alistair Borthwick, pointed out, 'Festivals imply festivities and it is beyond dispute that there are few objects which inspire joie de vivre to a less extent than boilers and turbines.'[15] More fun was to be had from an audacious and highly newsworthy claim to independence when, in December 1950, a raiding party of four students stole the Stone of Scone, the symbol of Scottish sovereignty, from Westminster Abbey.

Nationalist demonstrations were studiously ignored by the Festival team, who struggled to reconcile diversity with a convincing description of British identity. Readers of the official guide were told that there was no one characteristic peculiar to the British people but that the various characteristics 'when taken together, could not be mistaken for any other nation in the world'. Writing on the twenty-fifth anniversary of the Festival, Ian Cox put more of a gloss on the diversity theme:

> What is it that gives the British character and British achievement such diversity? What is the link between the past and the present that gives us such faith in the future? What provides the spark for British initiative? The answer to all seemed to lie in the great variety and diverse natural resources of the island of Britain, a mixed race of people and an innate curiosity within these people which urged them to explore and discover in every sphere. Interactions between these factors, which are permanent, provide the continuity between past, present and future.[16]

What Cox described as the intellectual plan, 'as distinct from the architectural one', was met by showing how British life had evolved over the centuries. In theory, this provided essential guidance for the choice of the contents of the various exhibitions, but it also meant that the conveners had to look back to the country's imagined past while giving a foretaste of the future, a recipe for muddle and confused messages.

For one thing, depicting the national identity in terms of a people of mixed origins evolving into a homogenous society came up against the demographic facts. Though immigration was still at modest levels, it was a little surprising that no note was taken of the 1948 British Nationality Act, which allowed for unrestricted entry to Commonwealth citizens. That same year the first post-war immigrants from Jamaica arrived in Britain on board the *Empire Windrush*. In July, Home Secretary James Chuter-Ede told the House of Commons,

> Some people feel it would be a bad thing to give the coloured races of the Empire the idea that, in some way or the other, they are the equals of people in this country. The government do not subscribe to that view. We believe wholeheartedly that the common citizenship of the United Kingdom and Colonies is an essential part of the development of the relationship between this Mother Country and the Colonies.[17]

The West Indian newcomers joined the half million Irish, 140,000 black and Asians and 160,000 wartime refugees among those living and working in Britain who had been born overseas. Add those who were first-generation British and there could be no doubt that the country was already multi-racial and multi-cultural.

Moreover, differences in class and gender, though largely ignored by the Festival, spoke against national unity. The sin of omission that showed up most obviously was the treatment of the place of women in society. While their contribution to the war effort, in the services and factories or single-handedly running households, had enhanced their self-respect and self-confidence, it was true that after 1945 most employed women were happy to return to domesticity. Equally, sex equality had few friends in the governing classes: everywhere there was encouragement for women to throw off the guise of masculine capability in deference to the traditional concept of feminine beauty (for the young) and maternal warmth (for the not so young).

To that extent, Barry and his colleagues cannot be entirely blamed for overlooking the early signs of post-war feminism. But with so much emphasis on labour-saving devices in the home (visitors were told that electric cookers, washing machines, central heating and refrigerators would soon be within reach of everyman – or, rather, every-woman), it was surely reasonable to expect the Festival to project likely changes in the pattern of domestic life. Yet, paradoxically for an eminent journalist with radical credentials, Barry stuck closely to social conventions. Futuristic architecture and design were to be tempered by traditional values.

Barry even favoured a pavilion devoted to the family ideal – Mum and Dad, each with their accepted roles, surrounded by loving children – until he was dissuaded by a reminder of the divorce figures, up from 10,000 in 1938 to 35,000 in 1949. That a reminder was needed at all is surprising, since Barry himself was on his second marriage and was none too happy with his exotic and unpredictable wife (the Russian-born Vera Russell, an *éminence grise* of the London art scene).

The Festival was to be resolutely middle class. This was in part aspirational and commendable, an attempt to show ordinary people who could barely make ends meet what was in prospect to make their lives easier. But it could also be insufferably patronising, as with the attempt to distinguish between middle-class and working-class homes. The demarcation was to lead to an embarrassing climbdown once the Festival had opened, when it was realised that designs for the Homes and Gardens Pavilion had matched the 'parlour' or 'best room' with fabrics and furniture that were too obviously intended for ladies of leisure. A rapid refurbishment created rooms that put real needs above purely aesthetic judgements.

The middle-class bias showed up again in the fondness for rural nostalgia, portrayed in advertisements and product displays as a necessary ingredient of the good life. The assumption was that though townspeople rarely visited the countryside they liked to know that it was there, a comfort zone of rose-bordered cottages, teashops with latticed windows, cricket on the village green and sun-baked yokels propping up the bar of the Rose and Crown. In one way or another, all these idealised scenes from country life made their appearance somewhere in the Festival, while rural poverty and the widespread lack of basic facilities, like water sanitation and electricity, failed even to get a mention.

In this the Festival took its lead from dozens of best-selling books about a mythical countryside in which the quaint and the twee were offered as vicarious pleasures to urban readers. H.V. Morton's *In Search of England*, an illustrated guide and reflection on the English countryside 'as a living thing' and as 'guarding the traditions of the race', first published in 1927, had sold more than a million copies and was in its thirtieth edition by the end of the

war.[18] Equally popular among roving sentimentalists were
J.B. Priestley (*English Journey*) and Arthur Mee (*The King's
England*).

Referring to the Ulster Farm and Factory Exhibition, the
official guide to the Festival tried to introduce a note of
authenticity. 'No longer is the countryman the old style
yokel, a rough uncultural being in corduroys, uncouth in
accent and manner.' Why, farmers even had tractors and
other machinery to do much of the hard work.

But on the South Bank, the romance of the countryside
was allowed to prevail, not least in the People of Britain
Pavilion. Here the theme convenor was archaeologist
Jacquetta Hawkes, wife of J.B. Priestley, then at the height
of his fame as an author and broadcaster. Both husband and
wife had an ambivalent attitude to modernism and both
believed that the roots of national identity were deep in the
history of the land. Why an archaeologist rather than a
historian was chosen to instruct on the People of Britain
was never adequately explained. Possibly Hawkes recommended herself by her contribution to a collection of essays
published in 1947 under the title *The Character of England*.
Barry, whose favourite historian was Arthur Bryant, no
stranger to making it up as he went along to support his
concept of Britishness, may have been attracted to Hawkes'
rendering of the bucolic idyll:

Here, close beneath the eye of the man who lies on the
downs, is the hair-fine grass, dull olive in colour and
cropped short by the sheep; among it a few dwarfish
violets and the vivid yellow coins of rock-roses whose
recumbent stems twine between the roots. The third
flower in this miniature world is wild thyme, a

spreading stain on the turf whose soft purple colour and warm aromatic smell seem to strike the senses as one. Feeding delicately upon it the Chalk-hill-blue butterfly from time to time closes its wings to show the bright rings on their undersides.[19]

This twaddle continues for several pages.

The contradiction in Barry as the modernist with reverence for tradition showed up most obviously in his eagerness to attract the endorsement of the Church of England and to involve the Church and, as an afterthought, the Council of Churches, in every aspect of the Festival. There was even a Festival Church, the blitzed and renovated St John's, where lunch hour services were held every weekday. Barry was not himself a conventional Christian. 'I am not able to believe the Christian faith as I was taught it as a child,' he wrote. (He was the son of an Anglican priest and brother to a bishop.) But he did believe in the sanctity of the individual and that life 'is something to be enjoyed to the fullest extent of which we are capable . . . to add to its happiness, its beauty or its wisdom'. Above all, he believed in the 'creative value of human love'.[20]

By working with the Church, even though he must have found the platitudinous and chauvinistic pronouncements of Archbishop Fisher hard to take, Barry hoped 'to give the British people an opportunity for renewing the expression of their faith' by appealing to 'pride in their heritage' and to what he saw as the understated contribution of the Christian experience to western civilisation. The Festival, he declared, was to be the demonstration of 'a great people collecting its spirit to face the future by remembering the past'. He continued:

Our past is a Christian past, in many more ways than the common, unthinking people are conscious of. It is so much a part of ourselves that we do not realise it . . . one of the main motive powers of our speech and our instinctive reactions in daily human contact and conduct. The Christian religion brought unity to Britain, kept culture alive through a Dark Age and gave Britain its proudest literary heritage and indeed its 'vulgar tongue': the Bible and the Book of Common Prayer. It has given us also much in music, drama and the arts: for the Churches minister to the arts as well as the arts ministering to the Churches. Perhaps the greatest instance is architecture. The Christian attitude to life, even among those who do not profess it, is interwoven into the pattern of our national life in ways which are impossible to disentangle and often difficult to delineate.[21]

And so evolved the philosophy of the Festival, a mix of 'the progressive, the paternalistic and the anachronistic'.[22] It remained to be seen if it could be fashioned for popular appeal.

# CHAPTER FIVE

In the spring of 1949, Hugh Casson, James Gardner and James Holland were in Italy for the Milan Fair. It was not a joyous experience. Their allowances were 'barely adequate' for subsistence and they were forced to travel by the 'cheapest form of public transport', which was overcrowded and inconvenient. Though their Italian hosts were more than generous, it was humiliating for Casson, as the leader of the British party, not to be able to return their hospitality.

But this was nothing compared to the hideous embarrassment of assessing the British presence at the Fair. Of all major countries, the British contribution was least inspired. A 'national disgrace', wrote Casson. On a stand little bigger than that of Haiti, a single assistant, head down in his newspaper, sat surrounded by sundry items of furniture. The only decoration was a Union Jack pinned to the back wall and two potted shrubs. The shoddy nature of the display was in contrast to the Canadian stand opposite, which 'showed an exciting and intelligent display of its national achievements'.[1]

Another British visitor was Charles Foley of the *Daily Express*, who revealed that the budget for showing the best of British was just £100 and that 'no one from the Board of

Trade has set foot in the city', though Sir Stafford Cripps was booked to lecture on Britain's recovery. This, observed Foley, should at least 'appeal to the Continental sense of fun'. The overall effect was of a country 'too proud to fight or too poor to compete'.[2]

Casson was in despair. He had just witnessed 'the worst possible advance publicity for the Festival'. Thereafter, he stayed at home, where he was able to take some comfort from reports fed back from other trade fairs – Copenhagen, Vienna, Prague and Brazil – where Britain made more of a concession to presentation and marketing as integral to commercial success. But not so much as to assume any sort of breakthrough.

Historians have puzzled over the reasons why Britain passed up so many of its post-war commercial opportunities. As the Dome of Discovery, with its pride of British invention, was soon to demonstrate, the country still had a strong manufacturing base. British technological innovation matched that of the USA in developing radar, computers, telecommunications, television and jet engines. Britain built more ships than any other country and was the leading European producer of coal, steel, cars and textiles. In the south, science-based light industries were beginning to make an impact.

Against this, and putting all at risk, was an assumption of innate superiority, a hangover from the myth of Britain's lone resistance to Hitler's Reich. Though the Battle of Britain, when the country really was on its own, must count as one of the turning points of the war, the tendency to give exaggerated significance to victory at El Alamein and other largely British exploits while downplaying American and Russian participation may have done wonders for morale but also served to engender the feeling that the rest of the world owed Britain a huge favour.

The discovery that the rest of the world did not acknowledge the debt – as when America cut off the flow of subsidies and refused to back a grossly overvalued pound sterling – was traumatic. Fear and confusion added to the problems of a Labour government elected on the promise of welfare security for all while struggling to prove the obvious, that a better life had to be worked for. Back came the public chorus, let someone else work for it.

Overlaying the mood of fatalism was an addiction to petty bureaucracy, in part a throwback to wartime regulations but equally the product of an administration dedicated to the false premise that if you looked after the pennies the pounds would look after themselves. The 1940s and 1950s were the glory days of the officious form filler and fault finder, as illustrated by two examples close to home – the policeman who stood at a halt sign ready to issue a summons to any cyclist or motorist who broached the white line even by a few inches and the minor civil servant who, called out on an emergency, delayed his departure until he had found his tie.

No wonder Barry and his Design Group were stressed to the limit in their efforts to demonstrate that it was never too late for a fresh start. Applications for the simplest requirements, made out in triplicate, were examined, re-examined and examined again for errors or ambiguities that could be used to delay sanction. The more unusual requests gave a whole new meaning to procrastination.

What would be the cost of finding, transporting, insuring and feeding husky dogs for the Polar Display, or battery hens in the Pavilion of Agriculture? What was a fair price for a full-sized statue of the White Knight or a model of a tanker's rudder? And what of the oddments? Drinking fountains and ice-cream kiosks, litter bins and signposts, trees, fireworks, toilet paper? How many or how much were needed? What would they cost? The list was endless but it had to be made and it had to be priced. There were negotiations, too, with the War Office over the Bailey Bridge, with the Admiralty over the loan of waterbus pontoons, with caterers and bus companies and floodlight experts, with the Raw Materials Commissions (building was still controlled by licence), the Royal Fine Arts Commission and the Metropolitan Water Board. Some were helpful, while others seemed 'armed invincibly', as Thomas Spratt once put it, 'against the enchantments of enthusiasm'.[3]

The plethora of agencies to be consulted each had a list of concerns that were, of course, of the highest priority. That the allocation of building materials was heavily regulated meant that demand and supply rarely harmonised. At first, steel could not be had in sufficient quantities even for ready money but wood was plentiful. Then, mysteriously, it was wood that became scarce while orders for steel were fulfilled promptly. In the first phase, it took government intervention to secure 150 tons of sheet piling demanded by British Rail to secure the foundations of the Charing Cross railway bridge. It seemed that the structure was under threat from the pumping of mud and water from the South Bank site. Before the delivery of the sheet piling could be approved, the alternative, to stop pumping, was given time-wasting consideration.[4]

The Metropolitan Police was quickly in on the act with a warning that no guarantee could be offered against London traffic grinding to a standstill when the Festival opened. There were worries too about crowd control and space, or lack of it, for parking, though in an age when there was still only one car for every sixteen citizens this did not seem to be too much of a challenge. In the event, thirteen sites were earmarked for parking.

One positive result of police pressure was the introduction of roundabouts on the south side of Waterloo and Westminster bridges. A formidable rulebook was produced by a working party 'representing all conceivable bodies concerned in London's traffic by road, rail and water'. So drastic and so effective were the traffic controls imposed by the police that a season widely prophesied as one of utter confusion ran rather more smoothly than a normal summer.[5] A Scotland Yard file on known pickpockets and confidence tricksters may have helped to keep down the South Bank crime figures.

Fearing a threat to their interests, trade lobbies such as the Waterside Manufacturers Association, the Association of Master Lightermen and Barge Owners and the London Association of Public Wharfingers queued up at the Festival Office for concessions or compensation for 'disturbance of business' and 'severe financial loss'.[6] Southern Railway train drivers feared they would be blinded by reflections from the surface of the Dome.

Relations with the London County Council were particularly delicate. A proprietorial interest in the South Bank and the proximity of County Hall, together with the

building of what was to be known as the Festival Hall (a
proposal for calling it The People's Palace was fortunately
dropped), were assumed by the council to give it the right to
consultation every step along the way. It started with the
ticklish business of having to tell the twenty or so
leaseholders of Belvedere Road that they would have to
make way for the bulldozers. This raised the ire of Mrs
Mackey of the County Café ('soup and bread 5 pence'), who
wanted to know how her business was expected to thrive if
it was cut off from her regular clientele. The same thought
now occurred to other traders about to be dispossessed, not
least George Burchett, a professional tattooist who was
currently decorating the entire body of a man who aspired
to become a Festival exhibit.[7]

Barry favoured generous compensation but siren voices
at the LCC warned against setting an expensive precedent.
An exchange of correspondence avoided the very word
'compensation', opting for the less emotive 'gift payment'.
And this was what Mrs Mackey and her neighbours
eventually settled for, though the precise sum was not
disclosed in the official papers.[8]

There must have been moments in his dealings with the
LCC when Barry reflected on the irony of trying to generate
a Festival spirit of entrepreneurial innovation in London
alongside an organisation dedicated to nitpicking and
procrastination. A simple request 'to make use of the
County Hall riverside terrace for a queue for the Chicheley
Street entrance to the South Bank' eventually elicited a
seven-point conditional response that began by seeking a
promise 'that the queue, not exceeding eight deep, be
formed against the river parapet of the terrace, proceeding
approximately two abreast down the steps and into the

northern roadway with breaks for loading and turning'. There had to be guard rails, 'adequate lavatory accommodation in an agreed position' and a pledge to clear away any litter. The Council architect wanted to be copied in on any subsequent correspondence.[9]

The descent to absurdity reached base when Paul Wright, handling Festival public relations, calculated that media interest, already intense, would justify the presence of an LCC press officer on night duty after the opening of the South Bank site. The recipient of this suggestion was the Deputy Clerk, who soon cottoned on to the likely identity of the self-sacrificing council employee, in other words the Deputy Clerk himself. He replied to Wright pleading a technical problem: 'Since I moved from Chelsea I have been trying to get the Post Office to transfer my old line to my new address but they have consistently refused saying that the local exchange is overcrowded.'

In all seriousness, he was told that he could have an extension line from Basil Street Fire Station, a measure that was likely to cause confusion when emergency calls were misdirected. The offer was declined by higher authority, much to the relief of the Deputy Clerk who confessed to Wright, 'My own instinct is all against having a telephone because of the possibility of disturbance at home.'[10] Anything but that!

In fairness, the LCC was not entirely devoid of constructive thought. It was thanks to the Council that the Festival was exempt from the laws restricting the number of shopping hours. Retailers were spared the otherwise mandatory half-day closing and the ban on evening shopping so long as no employee was expected to work more than a 48-hour week.[11] There was also an extension of licensing hours so that Festival-goers could enjoy a drink any time between 12.30 a.m. and 3 p.m. and from 6.30 p.m. to 2 a.m. on premises 'where meals, music and dancing were provided'.

If coping with an obstructive bureaucracy was trouble-some enough, the tribulations suffered by the Festival management were multiplied by a fractious and litigious labour force. The Festival decade was the heyday of the shop steward, indelibly portrayed by Peter Sellers as Fred Kite in the 1959 Boulting Brothers movie *I'm All Right Jack*. With the Communist Manifesto in one hand and the union rulebook in the other, the militant shop steward was a force for disruption, and proud of it.

Barry Evans was one of the artists commissioned to design and paint a mural of the research ship *Discovery* for the Dome:

Work inside the Dome was uncomfortable and very dark. The atmosphere was damp and cold, the lighting was minimal, one electric lamp of 100 Watts for a twenty foot or so wall was inadequate, to say the least, and a 'Valor' stove for heating the wax emulsion we were using as a medium was not enough to heat us. We were dressed in winter clothes and wearing mittens. Holding a paintbrush in cold hands doesn't make for fine painting. In addition, the noise was deafening. Right behind us was a pneumatic drill. Forklift trucks, girders crashing, workers shouting above the noise.

In order to continue painting it was necessary to move the 100 Watt lamp to the dark part of the wall. I found a chair to stand on and was about to remove the bulb when a voice behind me cried, 'Have you got a ticket?' It was Mr Torode, the union official. I looked at him in puzzlement. 'A ticket?' 'Are you an electrician,' he said. 'No,' I replied, 'I am an artist, a painter.'

'Don't you change that bulb or we are all out. You have to belong to a union, everybody has to belong to a union, what's your union?' I replied, 'I am an artist, we don't have unions.' 'You do here sonny, everybody here has to belong to a union.' I said, 'What union can we belong to?' He thought for a moment or two and said, 'You can belong to the Glassblowers' Union.' I said, 'Mr Torode, I am not a glass blower.' He replied that I couldn't work in the Dome unless I belonged to a union. So I became a paid-up member of the Glassblowers' Union and got on with my work, after he had had a word with the clerk of works and an electrician had moved our 100 Watt bulb further along the wall.[12]

It was no help that most of the Festival designers and architects were from the commissioned ranks of the wartime services, where they only had to say 'do this' and it was done. Though radical by conviction and dismissive of class distinction, they were easily thrown by challenges to their authority and generally uncomfortable in their relations with the workers.

In the early days the chief representative body was the National Association of Theatrical and Kinematograph Employees, in place by virtue of having overseen government exhibitions during and after the war. But the sheer scope of the Festival meant that no one union could dominate for very long and in short time the Transport and

General Workers Union was in competition to recruit the small army of attendants and casual workers who appeared on site.

Inevitably there were demarcation disputes, with each side accusing the other of poaching its members. For a time this was to the advantage of management, since antagonism between the unions frustrated joint action. But as the schedule grew tighter, the union monopoly over labour supply was a recipe for blackmail strikes – pay up or the work doesn't get done on time – as well as strikes to correct real or imagined grievances. Excuses for inactivity became ever more bizarre. A foreman rigger working on the Skylon caused a stoppage when, descending from dizzy heights, he tripped over a manhole cover. At once there was a cry of 'all out', and no further work took place until a promise was made to improve working conditions at ground level.

On the last day of 1949, when five men were sacked for incompetence (New Year's Eve was perhaps not the happiest timing), 250 carpenters and joiners downed tools, threatening to stay out until their brothers were reinstated. This the employers refused to do, with the result that the dispute spread until the knock-on effects closed the entire South Bank site.

Herbert Morrison did his best to get things moving by calling on Richard Coppock, his former LCC colleague and, more significantly, General Secretary of the National Federation of Building Trade Operatives, to deploy his negotiating skills. It took all of fifteen days to reach a settlement. Coppock was knighted for his efforts, though Barry doubted that he had actually made much difference. His diary quotes approvingly the comment of George Strauss, Minister of Supply and Barry's closest government contact, on hearing of Coppock's knighthood: 'A man whose personality is sufficiently remarkable to hide deficiency of character and ability.'[13]

Two weeks later the disgruntled electricians made their point by throwing the master switch. After the lights went out, Barry noted in his diary: 'A new month and the site virtually at a standstill . . . mass meeting in progress and football on the Fairway. Chalked up on a wall, "Joe [Stalin] for King" . . . a few more days of this and we've had it.'[14]

Barry hit out at both sides for their 'prep-school intransigence'. When the secretary of the Electricity Employers Association told him arrogantly, 'There's nothing I don't know about the strike business. I've been handling it for thirty years,' Barry resisted the urge to say: 'That's just your trouble.'

It was largely Barry's initiative, born of desperation, that brought the two sides back to the negotiating table. The issue was wage discrimination, with the electricians on specialised display work taking home the larger pay packet. It was settled by the payment across the board of a one-off bonus which left Barry worrying about the project's deteriorating financial outlook. Casson tried to make a joke of it: 'A good time-and-a-half was had by all.' Barry remained in sombre mood: 'There is a hole in the kitty and the swag is dwindling.'[15] This on top of an overall reduction of the Festival budget by £1 million in the wake of the 1949 devaluation crisis.

Cuts had to be made, one of the deepest being suffered by the public relations department which had been too successful for its own good. Why spend money on pro-motion when the press was giving so much free coverage? Festival stories were the fallback for every news editor with space to fill. On a single day in March 1951, the *Daily Graphic* revealed that Stanley Smith, thirty-two, would set out for America in a twenty-foot homemade boat called *Nova Espero* to boost British exports (there is no record of him reaching journey's end); the *Daily Herald* praised the International Union of Socialist Youth for organising visits from overseas for those who wanted to see democracy in action; the *Mail* announced a new five shilling piece to mark the Festival; and the *Express* complained that there were not enough Union Jacks to meet popular demand.[16]

Projects with less than an even chance of fulfilment, like the helicopter taxi service between the airports and central London and the Tours of Britain guides, were now relegated to the file of fond memories. The budgets for the Science Exhibition and the Land Traveller Exhibition were slashed in half. While the South Bank emerged relatively unscathed, most of the plans had to be revisited in order to find economies. One much-mourned casualty was the Newton-Einstein House, a device in which thrill seekers could be spun at centrifugal force, thus defying gravity. The official reason for its cancellation was the fear of 'unpleasant psychological effects', though something on the same lines, subsequently featured at the Battersea Fun Fair, would no doubt be dismissed as small beer today by visitors to modern theme parks.

And then there was the weather. Preparing the South Bank site for the builders was like working in the Great Grimpen Mire. The heavy rain of the winter of 1950–1 had raised the water table to just below the ground surface. When the London clay was turned it created small lakes which then had to be drained, hopefully before vehicles and equipment sank in the mud. It was not much consolation to know that the scene offered unrivalled entertainment for the onlookers lined up on Hungerford footbridge. Promoted by the popular press to star of the show was 37-year-old George Brooks, who operated a mechanical bucket excavator, said to be the biggest machine of its kind in London.[17] Brooks was not entirely unfamiliar with publicity. He had a wartime record of using his excavator to drag unexploded bombs from under demolished houses. His association with the Festival was touted by reporters as another demonstration of patriotism in action.

With the excess of rain and the Thames in full flow, critics were bemused to hear of plans to build an underground reservoir. It was, as Barry admitted, costly, and in the event it was never used, but it was judged to be an essential insurance against a summer drought, when the Metropolitan Water Board, following the rule book, would have banned the use of water for gardening. Why not take advantage of the Thames? Because salt in the tideway was a killer for trees and plants.

Not that there were any trees when the site was cleared. They had to be ordered from a nursery near Winchester. Mature trees, of which there were sixty-nine in all, were carried on roads well away from built-up areas, the trucks escorted by motorcycle outriders. As the first of these transports left the nursery on its slow two-day journey, the driver had to climb a telegraph pole to disentangle branches from overhead wires. Villagers en route came out to applaud the contemporary version of Great Birnam Wood on its way to Dunsinane.

'Having trees,' Barry decided, 'we must also have birds.' Ornithologists were called in to advise on attracting plumage a little more exotic than that of the London pigeon.

The answer was bird boxes, but bird boxes having an entrance hole of a certain size. A hole the size of a florin would attract the birds we sought: a half-crown hole would attract too weighty a visitor. . . . Moreover, the bird boxes must be placed in the trees in the autumn. We must not wait until the spring when the birds start nesting. If the bird boxes were obviously new the birds would be suspicious. They must be given time for the London winter to make them dirty and rainsoaked. Evidently birds prefer the picturesque and dilapidated antique to the modern council house.[18]

Few of the bird boxes were ever occupied. The deep eaves on some of the Festival pavilions proved to be a more inviting nesting place. There was, perhaps, a lesson here for architects with their best-laid plans for human habitation.

A collective sigh of relief greeted the news that construction could start more or less on schedule. The euphoria did not last long. After the summer respite Britain was heading towards one of the wettest winters on record and the wettest spring since 1815. 'It almost seemed as if Fate was against us, so persistent were our troubles,' wrote Barry.[19] Towards the end of the year and into the early weeks of 1951, 'RAIN', heavily underlined, is a word that appears in Barry's diary with monotonous regularity. In an effort to plan more effectively, he made direct contact with the senior people at the Meteorological Office, only to be told that it was impossible to forecast accurately more than two days ahead.

On New Year's Day 1951, Barry was beside himself with

frustration. 'Blizzard followed by thaws. Then rain. We shall be hard driven indeed to open on time.'[20] It was eventually reckoned that over five months, 20 per cent of the potential working time had been lost to the weather.

The weather and a recalcitrant workforce were not the only causes of distress. The bailey bridge fell into the river (more entertainment for the bystanders), a water main burst, the gun mounting for the radar equipment fell from the top of the Shot Tower – 'causing the tower to jump off its foundations', wrote Casson with only slight exaggeration – and rats ate through the electric cables. In mid-1950, in an attempt to tighten up the administration, a Controllerate of Architecture was set up, though as Reyner Banham, a modernist cheerleader among Festival consultants, observed dryly, the duties of the Controller, Howard Lobb, 'were not very clearly defined'. In the event Lobb 'attended all progress meetings and reported to us with great regularity any defects he spotted in the contractors' workmanship'.

It was not just those responsible for the Festival structures who had their problems. Deciding what to put in the various exhibition halls caused headaches. Responsibility for selecting items, cataloguing and storing them and, eventually, placing them in position fell to the Council of Industrial Design, a role that elevated the profile of the Council, hitherto an institution to promote good design as a subject in itself, as the arbiter of standards across industry.

Over 10,000 products ranging 'in size from locomotives to lipsticks and in value from many thousands of pounds to a few pennies'[21] were judged worthy of display. Other examples of British enterprise that were not quite up to scratch were put on a stock list that, on publication, comprised 20,000 items from 5,000 manufacturers. By today's standards there are few surprises in the Festival selection. But it is easy to underestimate the impact of products that are now commonplace. In 1951, washing machines, water heaters, fridges, vacuum cleaners and electric irons were beyond the experience of well over half the population.

Even to modern eyes the South Bank was not without its oddities, rather too many of them in the estimation of those who saw the Festival as an opportunity to educate and enlighten an otherwise untutored public. There were memories of the 1937 Paris exhibition when the British regard for cosy tradition had made the country look ridiculous in the eyes of more assertive nations – something never, it was hoped, to be repeated. Kingsley Martin, editor of the *New Statesman*, was among those who had commented on the ridiculous peculiarity of the British section:

> When you went in, the first thing you saw was a cardboard Chamberlain fishing in rubber waders and, beyond, an elegant pattern of golf-balls, a frieze of tennis racquets, polo sets, riding equipment, natty dinner jackets and, by pleasant transition, agreeable pottery and textiles, books finely printed and photographs of the English countryside. I stared in bewilderment. Could this be England?[22]

Well, it was England of a sort, the favoured image of the upper class. No one imagined the Festival would be like that. At the same time, as Barry was quick to recognise, if the Festival was to become exclusively educative, the public, sensing that it was being patronised, would stay away in droves. The solution was to give the devotees of eccentricity their own space where they could indulge the British delight in laughing at themselves.

The Lion and the Unicorn Pavilion was designed by R.D. Russell and Robert Goodden, who rose to the challenge of creating a 'spacious, airy and serene' setting (or, as *The Times* called it, 'a large shed') for the 'exposition of the British character with overtones of national traditions and achievements'.[23] They were held up for want of an adequate brief on what would be shown. Barry was uncharacteristically vague:

> There were certain ideas which were not only a part of British character and behaviour but which so to speak, exported, had had an influence outwards in the world – Freedom was an obvious example. These ideas were expressed through the language, literature, the visual arts, education, radio, films. Could these somehow be gathered up into an intelligible and coherent exhibit? . . . Eventually certain basic subjects were chosen as typical: the language itself as the chief means of communicating the ideas of these strange islanders, the language now spoken by two-hundred-million people, its various modes of expression from the sublimity of the Bible and the poets to modern clichés and slang. Then the Freedoms: the three basic and binding Freedoms of justice, worship and political liberty, and the story of the struggle through the centuries by which they had been won; love of nature and the

country life; skill in workmanship; and finally a glance at the eccentrics.[24]

The glance turned out to be a long look, but if Barry was disturbed by the inconsequential nature of many of the exhibits, he never showed it. A scriptwriter was hired, accomplished nothing and retired exhausted. There was more luck with the second choice. Appointing himself 'resident jester' was 35-year-old Laurie Lee, poet, novelist, journalist and maverick, who was still eight years off his classic *Cider with Rosie*. In November 1950, Lee launched an appeal in *The Times* for 'models made of unlikely materials' and 'machines built for unpredictable purposes' to illustrate the eccentric side of the British character. The response was overwhelming:

With our occupation of Savoy Court began a traffic in mysterious objects of every improbable shape, colour and use. They stood about on directors' desks or window sills or in the corners of passages, continually passing in and out, always being changed, turning the appearance of the building into something between a Fulham Road junk-shop and an eastern bazaar. Sometimes they were large and had to be coaxed into the lift, the commissionaires handling them with an aloof Cockney tolerance, like a man being asked to hold someone else's baby in a bus. No doubt they tapped their foreheads on the quiet. Models of every description, plans, maps, paintings, odd chunks of sculpture, lengths of luscious material, toy fountains — such assorted bric-a-brac became the accepted furniture and adornments of the place, spreading an irresistible mood of sharrawaggy and slightly unhinged romance. And when one day I opened the door of the little room where the gentleman in charge was collecting *objets trouvés* for the Lion and the Unicorn Pavilion, it was neither out of idleness nor perversity on his part, but of sheer devotion to duty, that he was found standing in tranced contemplation of a stuffed performing rabbit.[25]

Some would-be contributors were held off at the pass. The offer of Dr McClure's experimental chamber organ, 'to demonstrate the practical means whereby 19 sounds can be made to the octave instead of the usual 12 but with the use of the standard keyboard', was politely declined. Musical experts advised that 'though [the organ] was possibly an attraction to the specialist, it would not be of sufficient general interest for central exhibition on the South Bank'.[26]

Also rejected was 'a very beautiful table made from Trinidad wood' from a correspondent who wanted a stand at the Festival to promote his Trinidad Mango Rum Liqueur. Hardly an eccentricity but well within the category of inappropriate exhibits was the 'modest display of artificial limbs' submitted by the Ministry of Pensions. More eccentric but far less appropriate was the model of the South Bank made out of toilet rolls.

But Laurie Lee did get an egg roundabout and a smoke-grinding machine, though what practical use, if any, either of them might have had was never explained. A surprising but popular late entry was a 'suitcase attachment with wheels to eliminate the drudgery of carrying'; surprising because this was the sort of invention that might have occurred to the Victorians — except, probably, that in their day travellers who were wealthy enough to have heavy baggage could call on porters to carry it.

Among the items regretfully turned down were a 'brilliantly engineered machine, twenty feet square, with the sole object of blowing out matches, a deflatable rubber bus for going under low bridges',[27] a violin and mandolin made from used matchsticks (both eminently playable) and the archives of the British Snail Watching Society. Utilitarian offerings such as that from the Metropolitan Drinking Fountain and Cattle Trough Association were found places outside the Lion and the Unicorn Pavilion. Inside, exhibits were captioned in heavily larded prose. 'Britain's crust like a cloth has been dipped in the ocean, soaked, rinsed and hung up in folds to dry.'[28]

It was all hugely popular, though whether visitors, caught up in the fun of the thing, saw in the Lion and the Unicorn what Barry hoped they would see ('the two opposing facets of the British character, the stolid, unimaginative Lion and the highly individualised, eccentric, unpredictable Unicorn') must remain in doubt.

# CHAPTER SIX

The Battersea Fun Fair was the Festival's poor relation. Though from the very beginning an amusement park was assumed to be an integral part of the Festival, it did not take a surveyor to show that there was not enough space on the South Bank to build it, or an accountant to figure out that there was nothing in the budget to pay for it. Clearly, more money had to be raised, but not at the taxpayer's expense. The self-appointed guardians of the public purse, mostly working for the Beaverbrook and Rothermere newspapers, were sure to rise in self-righteous anger at state expenditure on such frivolity. But suppose the fun fair and its attachments could be promoted as a self-financing, indeed profitable enterprise, a worthy government investment with a substantial return to the taxpayer?

With Battersea Park in mind, just three miles up river from the South Bank, this was the scheme that Barry, with support from the London County Council, put to Herbert Morrison: a government-sponsored company with access to Treasury funding. With the politician's native instinct for protecting his back, Morrison gave qualified approval, subject to an inquiry led by civil servants and local authority representatives. Their report landed on his desk in April

1949. With the usual standards and control provisos, the working party was mildly supportive as long as the Pleasure Gardens could maximise revenue by staying open for five years.

The case was not strong enough for Morrison, who also took note of the implacable opposition of elements on Battersea Borough Council. Having seen off the Festival itself, the wealthy, influential Chelsea residents on the north side of the river were not about to welcome 'undesirable visitors' to their elegant doorstep. Yet Battersea Park was the only possible Thameside site within practical reach of the South Bank. Impasse.

Barry was not prepared to let the matter drop. Indeed, as the Festival began to take shape and he realised that he was unable to rein back the dedicated enthusiasm of such as Ian Cox and his scientific team, he was even more determined to offer visitors light relief to balance the weight of the serious information they would be expected to absorb. He needed more than the eccentrics' corner of the Lion and the Unicorn Pavilion to create a mood of innocent frivolity. The concept Barry had in mind was a throwback to the eighteenth-century pleasure gardens – fantasy, fireworks and bright lights – but without the debauchery that eventually led to their closure:

Here, in part of this park, we shall lay out gardens and lakes where there will be many opportunities for various kinds of entertainment, from bands and dancing to the more rollicking attractions of the traditional fun-fair. There will be restaurants and cafés here, too, and illuminations at night. What we have in mind is not just a fun-fair – though there will,

as I say, be that, in one corner of the gardens – but
something more spacious and leisurely – something
new for London – or, perhaps, I should rather say
something old, something going back to the spirit of
Vauxhall Gardens.[1]

'Elegant fun' was a phrase that cropped up frequently in
Barry's speeches and articles. In this he echoed Dr
Johnson, who had spoken admiringly of the Vauxhall
Gardens as 'that excellent place of public entertainment . . .
peculiarly adapted to the taste of the English nation, there
being a mixture of curious show and gay exhibition, music,
vocal and instrumental, not too refined for the general ear
. . . and good eating and drinking for those who choose to
purchase that regale.'

The Vauxhall Gardens, which thrived from 1661 to 1859,
when the railway cut it off from the river, was a model for
Europe with its tree-lined avenues, music pavilions,
theatre, shops, taverns and eating houses. At darkness, 'the
bell rings and summons us to the best and by far the most
beautiful entertainment of the evening – the fireworks'.
Taking his cue from Vauxhall, Barry studiously avoided
talking about a fairground, with its implications of raucous
behaviour. Traditional breathtaking thrills such as a
rollercoaster and a water-splash would be matched by
gentler activities to be enjoyed by all ages.

Barry has been criticised for ignoring the wishes of the
average family in favour of 'the fantasies of escape, pleasure
and extravagance' of middle-class planners.[2] This is unfair.
While it is true that 'vulgarity' is never a word to be
associated with Barry, his presentation for the Festival
Pleasure Gardens had as much to do with practical politics

as with his own tastes in entertainment. Opponents of the scheme were more likely to be mollified by contemplating the quieter pleasures.

But more importantly, Barry had in mind a contemporary spinoff from Vauxhall, the highly successful Tivoli gardens in central Copenhagen. Tivoli was and remains one of the best loved of Danish institutions. In close proximity and competing for attention are theatres, concert and dance halls, restaurants and cafés, exhibitions, a boating lake and a fun fair. In the summer a daily programme of attractions helps to draw the crowds. A Danish family in pursuit of a day's outing in the city does not have to think long before making its choice.

In Barry's view the Tivoli experience was far superior to the more ebullient entertainments on offer in America. But when visited by Billy Rose, a doyen of New York showmen, who had made his name as the producer of Aquacade, the only paying proposition of the 1939 World's Fair, Barry felt bound to listen. He was pleasantly surprised:

Everyone, it seemed, had advised Mr Rose to charge a fairly steep price to see the Aquacade. Mr Rose having invited their advice decided to ignore it. 'Cut down the price and put up the numbers, Mr Barry.' On the subject of cleanliness he was more specific. 'Everyone told me what I needed at the Aquacade, Mr Barry, was plenty of smart showgirls, plenty of legs ... I didn't want a show for old men and adolescents. What I wanted was a good healthy family show, a show for a man to bring his wife and kids to and feel comfortable ... What did I do? I decided to keep it clean. And what happened? Within ten days I said to my wife…it's o.k. – we're home.' 'What do you mean we're home', she said…'we've only been running ten days. How can you be sure?' 'I will tell you how I was sure, Mr Barry. That morning two nunneries had block-booked a couple of hundred seats apiece.'

Billy Rose was clearly a man after Barry's heart. They were in accord too on the need to flavour education and enlightenment with a potent measure of innocent fun:

Some time ago the City of Houston, Texas, decided to run an exhibition. This put Fort Worth on its mettle and the City Fathers decided to call in Billy Rose. Fort Worth and Houston are only 40 miles or so apart which in the United States is hardly the difference between Putney and Mortlake…The citizens of Houston had put up 4 million dollars to promote their exhibition. 'How much can you give me?', asked Mr Rose of Fort Worth. 'A million dollars is a lot of money, Mr Barry, but it isn't as much as 4 million. What did I do? I got out a poster, I got out stickers, I plastered the whole State of Texas with announcements saying: "Houston for education – Fort Worth for entertainment". Mr Barry at the end of the season I had played to 2 million dollars, and Houston was in the red.'

Mr Rose was, of course, perfectly right. That is why we were determined if we could to have the Pleasure Gardens as well as the South Bank and only regretted that shortage of space forbad us to put the two on one site. That is why we had dancing at the Fairway at the

South Bank, and the Guards beating Retreat and Tattoo of an evening.[3]

As the Festival designer with iconoclastic tendencies who did not take life too ponderously, James Gardner (a risky choice) was given the task of reproducing Tivoli in Battersea Park. While he set off on a Scandinavian tour, 'at my own expense', he noted caustically, Barry drew up a modified blueprint to meet political and residential objections. Apart from the concept itself, now with heavier emphasis on cultural enlightenment and innocent delights, the main concession was to commit to one year only and to budget accordingly. The result was the setting up of Festival Gardens Ltd, backed by public funds to the tune of just over £1 million. With revenue estimated at just under £1 million, it was a gigantic miscalculation on both counts. However, a budget that was less than two-thirds of the original attracted nods of approval.

The formalities took time, not least because an Act of Parliament was needed to exclude the public from 38 acres of Battersea Park while building was in progress. It was not until late November 1949 that Gardner was finally given the go-ahead. Freed from South Bank responsibilities, his reporting line was no longer to Hugh Casson but to Festival Secretary Leonard Crainford, who was appointed secretary, in effect, managing director of the new company. Crainford's chairman was Sir Henry French, a retired civil servant said to have wide interests in the film industry. The governing board was led by Barry and three other members of the Festival executive including the director of finance, the vigilant George Campbell. They were backed by representatives of the entertainment industry and local government ranging from impresario Sir Charles Cochran to Sir Charles Loder, a member of the Council of the Royal Horticultural Society.

A longstanding friend of the Director General, Crainford was an early recruit to the Festival executive where he was valued for his experience in arts administration – a rare qualification in those days. But however successful he had been in managing the RSC, the Battersea Pleasure Gardens were way beyond his experience. Even if he had come with all the managerial virtues, he would have had his work cut out reining back a free spirit like Gardner. That said, the partnership started promisingly. Having decided that most of the budget would go on infrastructure – 'pumps, piers, paving and planting'4 – and the like, Gardner argued for sponsorship for the major exhibits. This was anathema to Barry and strictly prohibited on the South Bank, but needs must . . .

Gardner set off on a round of his commercial contacts, attracting an enthusiastic response from Guinness for a clock that went mad each quarter-hour, with unlikely characters such as a highly animated ostrich popping out of their dens, from the Lochhead Hydraulic Brake Company (a mermaid in bronze), Nestlé (a crèche), Sharp's Toffee (a Punch and Judy show) and Schweppes (a grotto celebrating wind, fire and water), and from the Worshipful Company of Brewers for three beer gardens.

The designer-in-chief was getting into his stride. Justifiably so, since after a year wasted in talk there was only fifteen months left to put together a show worthy of a royal opening. But the sudden acceleration of activity must have caused concern for Barry, Crainford or French, or possibly all three. In any event, Gardner suddenly found himself under threat from the theatre designer Olivier Messel, very much an establishment figure, who had been asked to produce a rival layout for the consideration of the Festival Committee.

Gardner was convinced that Barry was behind the attempted coup. Maybe, but Gardner, with a hefty chip on his shoulder, was probably too quick to assume that Barry was instinctively suspicious of mercurial brilliance. A likelier explanation is that money worries had begun to surface (Gardner subsequently conceded that the only way he could balance the budget was to claim sponsors where none existed), with the result that someone with sufficient pull had demanded a second, and possibly cheaper, opinion. As it happened, Messel did not come up to expectations. Having given the project his divided attention he had the raw cheek to turn up at Gardner's office with a face-saving proposition.

He smiled at me appealingly with those big brown eyes, like a pet dog begging for a titbit. 'G, darling,' he hesitantly stuttered, 'you are so clever at *visualizing*. Could you be a *dear* and prepare a perspective of my ideas for the presentation?' He opened a folio full of pretty sketches, rococo pastiche wedding cake but beautifully done, and just Barry's cup of tea. My fingers itched to make an aerial perspective of it all — so I did. Though I felt I was being used, I had to carry on with my own scheme, knowing full well I would probably be left with the odd marginal bits like entrances and public conveniences.

Came the day of reckoning:

Messel and I wait in uncomfortable silence in an outer office as bleak as a police station interview-room, even down to the brown lino. A long-faced gentleman peeps round the door and beckons Messel (I begin to wonder if I am there). He goes off with the rendering I have prepared for him — white grotesque pavilions peeping through a tapestry of trees, elegant Canaletto-style figures grouped in sun-dappled glades, even a gondola on a pretty lake. A romantic pastoral stage set? It was a bloody good rendering.

For forty minutes I watch the hand creep past the Roman numerals on the flyblown clock, then a buoyant Messel bustles back. 'G, darling, *your* turn now. They will simply adore your scheme. I'll be so *thrilled* if you get it and I am *sure* you will.' So in I go and address myself to Sir Henry French at the head of the table. I decide that the way to win is to look practical. I describe the features introduced to give pleasure, but then go on to discuss the key practical considerations, car-parking, circulation, cost and timing — the last item being critical as here we are, after starting eighteen months late, discussing a revision of the layout. With that I win the day, I suspect much to the chagrin of Gerald Barry who is sitting next to French.[5]

The follow-up was a solicitor's letter threatening action if Messel's sketches were shown to have influenced the final plan. Now the ideas really began to flow.

Monday mornings find our mini committee of four sitting round a dining table in a hired room off Sloane

Street, discussing how to give the thousands of tired mums, arthritic ancients, young lovers and exuberant teenagers more than a good time — something memorable — without their very presence destroying the little world of delight they have come all this way to see. The world's problem in microcosm. I aim to avoid pastiche — nostalgic plaster as I remembered seeing it at the great White City Exhibition when aged four, my father with pomaded moustache and straw boater, ma with hair up in a bun and a lacy flat hat, all too Edwardian. On the other hand I must keep clear of abstract art which the mass of visitors will not even pretend to understand (feeling that the intellectuals are putting one over them).

I table ideas. An avenue of revolving flower beds? No. (Hell, a lovely coloured drawing thrown away.) A toadstool maze? No. A Punch and Judy theatre? Yes. A ping-pong ball fountain? Yes. Alas, it only worked on the drawing board, too much wind. . . . Giant tortoises creeping around with exotic plants on their backs? No. An underground grotto, the Four Winds, with smells of seaweed and spices? Yes. An aviary filled with budgerigars, three hundred or more — they're social birds? Yes, if you can get the budgerigars.

A mouse village? Agreed. Every item agreed at these meetings would bring some unforeseen side effect with it. In this case the mice began to eat their village, so I added a little timber yard where they could sharpen their incisors when not running in and out of the houses.[6]

One of the most memorable flights of imagination was inspired by alcohol at a dinner for sundry artists and journalists at the Café Royal. George Him, known for his children's books illustrated in hand litho, was heard to extol the joys of climbing trees:

> I thought about it. We could not have people actually climbing, but we could have a spiral stairway leading to a series of slender walkways bridging through the branches from tree to tree – and have some fun up there; an owl with its revolving head, a great grinning cat on a swing, a toy town mounted along a bough with an underground railway hanging under it and a Chinese dragon illuminated at night. The fun fair people said no one would pay to climb a spiral stair, but the committee said 'yes' so it was on.[7]

And then there was the Emett railway. Rowland Emett was famed for his wispy drawings of ludicrous contraptions that appeared regularly in *Punch*, the weekly satirical magazine favoured by middle-class readers eager for something, anything, to laugh at in austerity Britain. His Far Twittering and Oyster Creek Railway, with its long-funnelled locomotives modelled on Stephenson's *Rocket* and its befuddled employees (association with British Railways were inevitable), was the best loved of his creations.

Oblivious to the political implications, which incredibly failed to surface, Gardner invited Emett to make fantasy real. The railway turned out to be a showstopper, recovering its entire cost within three weeks. The only hiccough came when the well-known radio performer Gillie Potter, otherwise known as the Sage of Hogsnorton, claimed copyright over the invented village of Far Twittering. Emett had to settle for Far Tottering.

Other recreational indulgences jostled for attention. On the principle that for a day out eating is the first priority, fun seekers were promised six restaurants, three of them self-service, a tea shop, two snack bars, three pubs, a wine garden, children's tuck shops and several refreshment kiosks catering for 'all tastes, all ages and all pockets'. At the end of a scaffolding pier, which the experts said was unsafe but which was still in place fifteen years later, Gardner built a Mississippi Showboat complete with a whirling paddle wheel, smoke belching from tall funnels and the music of Old Kentucky on a barrel organ. Inside was Oscar the Octopus, a rubber construction so realistic that complaints were made to the RSPCA about the tight confinement of such a large creature.

Recalling the popularity of the dance pavilion in the Gothenburg pleasure gardens, another simulation of Vauxhall, Gardner decided to go one better with a vast circular tent held in place by steel cables. It was the largest single pole tent ever erected. The fabric alone weighed fifteen tons. In the Riverside Theatre, a pastiche of Regency, Victorian and Modern styles designed by Guy Sheppard, who had made his name with the Ballet Rambert, Leonard Sachs, soon to achieve television renown with his Palace of Varieties, presided over old-time music hall. Night after night, performers Hattie Jacques, Bill Owen and Bernard Miles set out to demonstrate that the old routines were the best.

Positioned on the eastern side of the gardens, as far away as possible from the sensitivities of the Chelsea burghers, the fun fair offered a Big Dipper (there were those who thought it a timid affair, but it was thrilling enough for young people starved of excitement), Skywheel, Bubble-Bounce, Flyo Plane and Water Splash — American imports for the most part, purchased by a delegation of fairground operators on a government-sponsored trip to the States. The party had been led by Major Leslie Joseph, a board member of the Festival Gardens, owner of a pleasure beach at Porthcawl and chairman of the farcically named National Amusement Council, who was to play a much bigger role in the Battersea saga. Predictably, when the press caught on to this dollar profligacy in the Festival accounts, there were handwringing editorials bemoaning government extravagance and probing questions in the House of Commons seeking an explanation for the latest example of state lunacy.

Battersea's pride and joy was the Grand Vista, 'a lacy screen like the Crystal Palace with a great bank of trees behind it, then a lake with fountains . . . and shallow steps leading down in the Venetian manner, flanked by two high colonnades'.[8] John Piper designed the colonnades while one of his close friends, Osbert Lancaster, whose pocket cartoon in the *Daily Express* made him a household name, brought his lively imagination to bear on the rest of the display. The Grand Vista was the setting for the twice-weekly fireworks. Acrobats and high-wire performers occupied the lakeside stage. On carnival nights visitors wearing fancy dress were admitted free.

Battersea was a triumph over such adverse circumstances that it was a miracle it happened at all. For a start, the project was beset by mismanagement, for which Gardner must take part of the blame. Roaring ahead with the handing out of contracts, he left it late in the day before warning Crainford that Festival Gardens Ltd was seriously over-committed with little prospect of covering the deficit. When he did come clean Crainford, who should have been keeping a closer watch on the figures, remained calm, even agreeing to take over from Gardner the responsibility for signing the monthly accounts. It is hard to believe that Gardner did not know what he was doing. Crainford was now directly in the firing line. It was not long before he heard the sound of safety catches being released.

If money had been the only problem it is possible that he might have survived. But there was more bad news as it became crystal clear that there was no chance of the Pleasure Gardens opening on time. In this context the chief culprit was the weather. The wet and even wetter early weeks of the year had taken their toll on the South Bank, but the meteorological impact on Battersea was far greater.

Belatedly, it was realised that the original park had been laid out on reclaimed river bed. This meant that in the exceptionally wet winter, the site became, as Gardner put it, 'a sponge which was full to overflowing'. Turning up one day to inspect what he hoped would be progress, he found instead bulldozers and other equipment half submerged in London clay. Worse still, the tidal water of the Thames was rising at a terrifying rate. Gardner could hardly believe his eyes.

The river is higher than the footpath, only held back by a fragile footing designed to support the railings. A cluster of barges is floating serenely by almost at eye-level. My mind freezes as I see the neatly angled waves in their wake chasing each other along the wall towards me, here and there toppling over it to wet the pavement.[9]

On 31 December, Barry took his young son Stephen on an inspection tour of Battersea. He gained no comfort from what he saw. 'Crainford still claims it will be ready in time,' he noted in his diary, 'but today it looked as though this will require a major miracle.'[10] He added disapprovingly that the labour force 'managed to look listless and leisurely'. On the first day of 1951 there was a blizzard, followed by a thaw, followed by rain. On 2 January, Barry was back on site prior to a meeting of the Pleasure Gardens Presentation Committee. He was not best pleased.

> Spent the morning going over Battersea site in detail. Blizzard stopped just before we began, but the whole area is under mud and snow and not a hands-turn of work is being done. The men are happy enough playing crap in their shelters, but, when work becomes feasible again, instead of their jumping to it to recover lost time, the first half-day is spent in finding lost tools. A different psychological climate from the South Bank.[11]

Attempts to economise merely served to antagonise otherwise loyal staff. One overstreched employee wrote:

> I gather the firm are trying very hard to cheat us out of our holidays, on the grounds of expense. Pip and I are preparing with others to make a genuine fight for it, if necessary going to the Minister of Works himself. I think they want to give us ONE day a month instead of

the 2 or 2½ we were promised – which is ludicrous when half the staff have worked 7 days a week for months![12]

A week later, Barry found 'Plenty of work going on but in what conditions. A morass, a pudding.'[13]

Jokers talked of 'Batter on the Sea'. Meanwhile, an attempt was made to mitigate the worst effects of the weather by pumping the surface mud into tanker trucks and ditching it down river. Gardner came up with a new schedule that set the opening date back three weeks, soon stretched to five weeks.

In early March, the Deputy Prime Minister told a hostile Commons that the likely cost of Battersea, at £2,400,000, was over twice the original estimate with expected revenue unchanged at around £1 million. He made it known to Barry that this confession of failure was 'the worst thing that had happened to him in his whole political career'.[14]

Barry made haste to persuade Sir Henry French 'to dictate a letter to Morrison saying he would recommend to the emergency board on Thursday that "a person or firm" of indisputable standing be immediately appointed to take over control of the Company's finances'. He went on, 'Nothing now can save the holocaust but at least this might help to restore public and institutional confidence – and much better we should take the initiative ourselves than have an outsider imposed upon us.'[15]

Barry was chiefly concerned with saving his friend Leonard Crainford, but he was also watching his own back. He blamed the entire fiasco on the 'puritanically impelled' Stafford Cripps, who had only agreed to the Battersea project on condition that no public money was lost. Now, 'the Festival itself will get the blame for blunders for which it is not responsible and over which it has virtually no control'.[16] Meanwhile, Morrison had reluctantly succeeded the terminally ill Ernest Bevin at the Foreign Office, leaving Festival matters to Richard Stokes, the newly appointed Lord Privy Seal and Minister of Works. Like all recently promoted politicians, Stokes was keen to make his mark. He did so by firing Leonard Crainford.

The first Gardner heard of it was when he picked up a copy of the *Daily Express* where the story, headlined 'Festival No. 2 Man Out', was on the front page. The shock was all the greater since it was his own photograph, not Crainford's, that accompanied the report, an indication of the managing director's low profile. Gardner was suitably distressed ('It was like being hit with a rubber bullet'[17]) but soon recovered. Not so Barry, who felt that Stokes had acted precipitously and that his friend had been treated unfairly:

So all my efforts to save him have been bypassed (I had Pug [Ismay] and French sworn to fight for him, but they were not given an opportunity). The same morning I have news that the new baby has died! How the fates do cram it on. Poor Leonard. How well he has taken the double blow – my own feelings are too bitter to describe – by an additional coincidence the whole thing occurs on the very anniversary (third) of our starting work together and alone on Festival of Britain in the RSA building. He spent that afternoon and evening with us at Chester Place and I drove him to his lodgings.[18]

Along with Crainford, the chairman of Festival Gardens,

Sir Henry French, was also eased out. During his appearance before the Commons Public Accounts Committee it emerged that he had been unaware of a rewritten deal with contractors which gave them the freedom to revise their original estimates to their own advantage. He was also hazy on the thumping bonuses paid to keep men on the job. Warnings from George Campbell that the finance was out of control had been ignored.

French was succeeded by Sir Charles King, formerly engineer-in-chief at the War Office, who was credited with wide experience of difficult construction work. He was to combine the roles of chairman and finance director. In place of Crainford there was fun-fair expert Major Leslie Joseph, soon to be Sir Leslie. The appointment came as an unpleasant surprise to James Gardner, who though himself sensitive to social slight, could be savage in his assessment of those who failed to measure up to his creative energy. He quickly decided that Joseph, a 'self-satisfied Welshman' who 'might well have been the proprietor of a provincial drapery emporium',[19] was nothing but a curse on originality. And on good taste, he might have added when, after a few days away, he returned to Battersea to find that 'some primeval monster had staggered round the site vomiting tarmac'.

Three wide shallow steps, planned for the head of the main vista, had become an undulating slope of glistening tarmac like treacle poured over a pudding. There was an all-pervading smell of tar. It was clear that Joseph . . . had determined that he must have the Pleasure Gardens ready for the Royal opening as planned. In my absence he had instructed the contractor to lay tarmac wherever a walkway was indicated on the plan — and to get it done before I returned.[20]

Gardner was outraged. He thought 'of all the artists, craftsmen and technical men I had enthused with the idea and got to work late hours for minimal fee'.[21] His first instinct was to appeal to Barry but he feared a rebuff from, as he put it, 'an establishment man'. So, instead, he hauled himself to the Royal Institute of British Architects where sheer persistence secured him an interview with the president. 'I explained the unauthorized tarmac blitzkrieg, he appeared to be very concerned. It was unethical for any client to modify agreed plans, and the RIBA was there to support an architect in this situation.

Within days surveyors were on site with their levels and striped poles busy marking out the paved promenades. 'My hair had gone a little whiter,' noted a weary Gardner. 'But who cared, the battle was won.'[22]

There was to be no royal opening. Fearing political entanglements, Princess Margaret crossed it out of her engagement book. The fun fair opened on 11 May, in time for the Whitsun weekend. The Pleasure Gardens in its entirety welcomed the public three weeks later. By then an additional £1 million had been pledged by the government. Judging by the enthusiastic reception of the summer visitors, it had all been worthwhile.

# CHAPTER SEVEN

Reviewing the obstacles in the path of his creative team as they stumbled their way towards the Festival deadline, Hugh Casson put the 'almost universal derision and hostility'[1] of the press high on his list. His sensitivity was understandable but overdone. Gerald Barry was more philosophical. With his long experience at the top of the newspaper industry, he recognised that setbacks accompanied by doom-laden prophesies of worse to come made good copy but did not suggest that journalists were in league to destroy the Festival. In fact, taking the press as a whole, including influential periodicals like *Country Life* and *Illustrated London News* and the provincial papers, the message was positive.

Opposition, at its most vitriolic, was limited to the *Daily* and *Sunday Express* and their sister paper for Londoners, the *Evening Standard*. There are several explanations for their antagonism. The least well known but most convincing is that the pugnacious and vengeful Lord Beaverbrook bore a grudge. In 1930 he had bought the *Saturday Review*, assuming that its editor, Gerald Barry, and his staff would stay in place to promote one of Beaverbrook's dottier projects – the creation of a United

Empire Party to bring together under one economic umbrella the disparate parts of the world map coloured in red.

That the colonies and dominions had little if anything in common beyond recognising a degree of British sovereignty, or that economic union would benefit Britain as the chief manufacturing nation as against the rest as suppliers of raw materials, did not seem to have occurred to Beaverbrook. Barry, on the other hand, recognising a dodo when he saw one, led an editorial walkout. Beaverbrook was left with an empty shell of a journal. Thereafter Barry was on his hate list.

Less personal but no less forceful was Beaverbrook's crusade against the waste of taxpayers' money. Here he was playing up to his middle-class readers, who equated the ruling Labour Party with the irresponsible distribution of largesse to socialist causes. The Festival was seen as a prime example. Notwithstanding Herbert Morrison's edict to exclude anything that was overtly political (even a reference to school meals was dropped), the promise of a better life inherent in the Festival implied, said the cynics, that it could only be achieved under Labour. Elements of the Tory Party, for whom socialism by stealth was the chief menace, encouraged Beaverbrook to pursue his conspiracy theories. No matter that he had been here before and failed.

Soon after Labour came to power, Beaverbrook had taken up cudgels against staging the first post-war Olympic Games in London. His editorial pages were filled with denunciations of such an extravaganza. Where was the money to be found? If there were spare resources, why were they not being allocated to more deserving causes? When the Games proved to be a huge success, the carping abruptly ceased. Instead, praise was lavished on sports heroes, many of whom, deprived of proper training or even an appropriate diet, beat formidable odds even to compete, let alone win.[2]

But Beaverbrook was not one to be deterred by past errors. In his jaundiced mind, the Festival was yet another populist ruse to win undeserved credit for the socialists.

Barry, with Paul Wright in attendance, made one attempt at friendly persuasion. They took the editor of the *Evening Standard* to a splendid dinner at the Garrick Club 'in the hope of correcting some of the paper's milder charges and inaccuracies'.[3] The result, seen next day, was a leader that made all the usual charges – 'Morrison's Folly' and 'Socialism through the back door' – but delivered with more than usual ferocity. The *Standard*'s follow-up was a 'rigorous inquiry' into the management of Battersea Pleasure Gardens which 'revealed' incompetence by 'ill qualified employees' and spiralling costs. That there was some justice in these strictures made it all the more vital to show spirit in putting across the counter-argument. It was time to fire the big gun.

As the great man's former chief of staff, the Chairman of the Festival Council, General Lord Ismay, was a confidant of Sir Winston Churchill. And if anyone could haul in Beaverbrook it was Churchill. Ismay was persuaded to seek an interview with his former chief. What was said behind closed doors will remain for ever secret but the outcome was not in doubt. As reported to Paul Wright, Churchill concluded the meeting with the heartening words, 'All right, Pug, you old fool, you can have your damned festival.' Sweet reason, doubtless heavily laced with flattery, had done the trick.

Well, perhaps not quite. While by early 1951 there was a notable softening in the Beaverbrook campaign, this might be traced as much to evidence that readers were persuaded that the Festival was not such a bad idea. A Gallup poll found 58 per cent support as against 28 per cent who, in the light of world events (the American-Chinese confrontation in Korea raised the spectre of a third world war), favoured postponement or cancellation. It was significant that the results of a 'for or against' survey conducted by the *Express* were never published.[4] Instead, a leading article suggested that since the Festival budget had already been spent, the public might as well make the best of it.

Looking back, Barry could never get over the blatant dishonesty of the Beaverbrook vendetta, 'the continuous repetition of false statements in the editorial columns of the *Daily Express*, statements that could have very simply been checked according to the elementary routine known to the humblest journalist, by reference to Hansard or the newspaper's own cutting library or by a telephone call to the Festival Office'.[5]

Barry resisted the urge to demand retractions, fearing that it would merely encourage further excesses. But he did get in one retaliatory shot that found its mark:

A young man representing himself to be one of the Standard leader-writers [almost certainly Charles Wintour, later editor of the *Standard*] accosted me one day at some function and began to apologise for the 'stuff he had to write against the Festival'. That, he explained, was just the policy of the paper: he himself, would I please understand, was 'all for the Festival'. I told him I understood perfectly. I also told him that when he grew up he would doubtless learn not to try to have his cake and eat it. If he objected so strongly to what he was ordered to write, there lay to his hand a ready alternative. But if – and no blame to him at all for that – he preferred to go on accepting the cake, then he should have the good manners to eat it with his mouth shut.[6]

Other publications were far more supportive, with lengthy features, even special issues, devoted to the Festival. Despite the incessant rain, Barry's diary entry for 3 January 1951 strikes a jubilant note, recording that *Picture Post* 'is to give us 12 solid pages of pictures and text – admirable stuff . . . excellent'.[7] This followed over two months of discussions to get the slant of the feature just right. Barry was willing to acknowledge problems but wanted a positive message to come across. That he achieved this, apart from some 'unfortunate personal publicity', was thanks largely to an influential go-between. Lionel Birch, the assistant editor of *Picture Post*, also happened to be the chief caption editor of the Festival.

With his formidable list of contacts in the media, Barry was a publicist's dream. And whatever Paul Wright set up for him in the way of interviews and articles, the Director General was always happy to play his part. He wrote dozens of articles for dozens of magazines and newspapers, traipsed the country at the behest of Huw Wheldon and the Arts Council to beef up regional efforts to create a festival atmosphere and crossed the Atlantic to drum up American support. The free publicity he secured was worth more than the entire promotional budget several times over, a fact which Barry was forced to recognise even when the trips out of London became wearisomely repetitive.

> In the train or the back of the car, or at night when our local talks were over, we [Barry, Huw Wheldon and Paul Wright] would do much work together on other parts of the Festival. Speeches . . . were concocted pacing up and down a large empty public room in a York hotel. Nothing of particular moment to record arose from these excursions. They were pretty similar, my chief memory being of well polished mahogany tables in Mayoral Parlours or Council Rooms at which the purposes of the Festival were expounded and sharp local questions answered. One learned a great deal about the sturdy independence of the provinces and one usually came away from a place feeling it meant to do things in its own way and that by this means the events of the Festival up and down the country would achieve plenty of variety and contrast.[8]

What money Paul Wright did have to spend on advertising, he spent boldly. With an allocation of just one hundred thousand dollars for a campaign that was supposed to reach out across America and Canada, Wright decided to chance it all on one shot, a four-page, full colour advert in *Life* magazine, the first time anyone had spent that kind of money on a single ad.[9] With a readership thought to be around twenty-five million, *Life* appealed precisely to those Americans who might want to visit Britain and could afford to do so. Those in the target audience who missed out on the Festival issue of *Life* soon heard about it in news reports on what was a startlingly original initiative – the perfect marriage between advertising and public relations. To cope with the rush of enquiries, a Festival office was opened in New York.

Another publicity venture that required a relatively small amount of money to go a long way was the European bus tour. Four suitably embellished London double-deckers were enlisted to carry the Festival message to twenty-five cities in eight countries, a round trip of four thousand miles. Since, in those days of limited travel, few on the Continent had ever seen one of these towering vehicles, the novelty value alone guaranteed favourable press coverage.

Incidents along the way were given full media treatment, starting in Oslo where overhead cables along the tramways had to be lifted to let through the bus convoy. Elsewhere en route, which in addition to Norway took in Denmark, Germany, Holland, Belgium, Luxembourg and France, tyres had to be deflated to clear low-level bridges. For the four-day stopover in Paris, the buses lined up in the Place de la Concorde, a source of wonder to rival the famous Obélisque de Luxor at the centre of the Place.

A crew of eight London Transport drivers, led by the splendidly named Frank Forsdick, were English to the core, never before having ventured far from the capital let alone abroad. Unfazed by the absence of linguistic skills, they treated all foreigners with the good-natured condescension of a favoured race. Hard though it was for Barry to accept, the continental lifestyle did not win any converts.

'The food isn't up to English standards,' declared Forsdick. 'Give us a bit of old English roast beef or a plate of fish and chips.'[10] Wine was not regarded as an adequate substitute for beer. To keep everyone happy, casks of best bitter were shipped over to Paris.

Journey over, in November 1950 the buses returned to normal service. The only distinguishing marks of their adventure were commemorative plaques on the upper and lower decks of each vehicle and GB plates, a bizarre incongruity for those unfamiliar with the story.

Always good for publicity, a succession of VIPs were encouraged to inspect progress on the South Bank. Heading the list of dignitaries were the King and Queen:

A thunderstorm had been deluging down during the visit and knowing the state of the site I feared they might have to plunge through a quagmire on the South Bank. I said as much to the Queen. 'I thought it might be rather muddy,' she said, 'so I brought a pair of boots. I can change them in the motor.' From that moment I became not only her humble subject but her devoted slave. My chief memory of the tour of the site is not of the buildings, nor even of the mud, but of the Queen breaking the routine of the visit to stop and talk to the workmen. There was one who came I think it was from Bermondsey, and he mentioned the name of the street. At once the Queen remembered: she had been there during the blitz and they exchanged reminiscences. We plodded through the clay to the far end of the site to see the new view of St. Paul's under the southernmost arch of Waterloo Bridge, disclosed by demolition, a view not seen by Londoners except a few lightermen and brewers' draymen almost since the time of Canaletto.[11]

The royals were followed by stars of stage and screen. Charlie Chaplin, who was born within hailing distance of the South Bank, was unable to take up the invitation but Laurence Olivier and Vivien Leigh were happy to oblige, staying for several hours to sign autographs. Then it was the turn of the Prime Minister, accompanied by 'Lord Festival' himself, Herbert Morrison. Though it was a fine sunny morning, it had rained heavily for most of the previous week, justification enough for a change of footwear. The only trouble was that the wellingtons provided for the two guests were a size too small. What Barry described as a 'prodigious struggle' ensued; a 'ludicrous episode'. 'I was holding the PM's arm and propping him up while he stood on one leg.' The incident passed off with good humour, but 'what it will look like on the newsreels heaven knows!'[12]

When the tour finally got under way, Barry stayed close to the Prime Minister, hoping that he might be persuaded to put his signature to invitations to 'key' Americans to attend the opening ceremonies. But Attlee was notoriously short on small talk. 'His own shyness induces shyness and he did little more than utter occasional monosyllables.'

Then, stepping out of the Transport pavilion and on to the Fairway, the Prime Minister suddenly became human: 'Do you know I was looking at the weekend at Chequers at copies of the *Illustrated London News* for 1851 giving pictures of the Crystal Palace. My mother went to the opening.'[13] After this the conversation flowed, with Attlee suggesting that the VIP list should be extended to Commonwealth representatives, especially those from India and Pakistan ('a revealing touch', noted Barry).

Morrison was warmer and more forthcoming. While Attlee almost whispered a short statement to the press, Morrison held forth with a lengthy address which included a commitment to open the Festival on time. Barry smiled and remained silent. But whatever his fears, he had good reason to be satisfied. Elsewhere in the political establishment, enemy sniping was a daily hazard.

While the Conservative leadership maintained a lofty disdain, refusing even to visit the South Bank ('I haven't been to it, of course. Nothing would induce me,' a senior shadow minister told Barry), their backbench surrogates felt under no restraint. Leading the pack was the lunatic fringe of the far right. It is hard now to imagine how anyone could take seriously such MPs as Cyril Osborne, who was against the Festival because (a convoluted cause and effect) the divorce courts were choked and the prisons crowded, or Sir Waldron Smithers, who wanted Festival resources diverted to building new houses in his prosperous constituency of Orpington.

But of all the political attacks on the Festival and what it was trying to achieve, the prize for sheer meanness and petty-mindedness must go to those parliamentarians who led the opposition to Sunday opening. Having failed in their efforts to shut down the entire Festival on the one day of the week most people could get to it, the killjoys fastened on to the Battersea Pleasure Gardens as that part of the Festival most likely to succumb to pressure from sabbatarians in general and the Lord's Day Observance Society in particular. Decision time came in late November 1950, when an amendment to exclude the Pleasure Gardens from the Festival Sunday Opening Bill was debated in the House of Commons. It was the sort of occasion that gives democracy a bad name. Leading off in a long, rambling speech, Sir Herbert Williams, Tory member for Croydon East, put the case for those who believed 'that, as far as possible, we should involve people in the minimum of Sunday work'.

It was not long before the debate was bogged down in tedious detail. At the end of nearly six hours of confrontation between libertarians and the sanctimonious guardians of public morals, no one was any the wiser as to what constituted work, let alone how much of it could reasonably be permitted to disrupt Sunday family worship and the peaceful pursuits favoured by the Victorian middle class. If ever there was a case for politicians to catch up with public opinion this was it. But a Sunday newspaper poll which showed an overwhelming majority of readers in favour of opening Battersea seven days a week was dismissed derisively, while close attention was given to the risk that squeals from riders of the swings and roundabouts might interrupt Sunday School lessons – even though the nearest Sunday School was said to be more than half a mile away.

In the end, the collective wisdom of the people's representatives was for the fun to be cut from the fun fair on Sunday, leaving customers to the more sedate activities of the Pleasure Gardens.[14]

But if politics was a war game, it was at least limited to Westminster. With few pages to fill, the newspapers had little enough space to devote to the wilder lunacies of parliamentary knockabouts. As for the BBC, bound as it was by the Reithian ideal to describe and inform but never to criticise, radio chiefly and television to a lesser extent became the perfect media for spreading the Festival message. In all, the Festival featured in 2,700 current affairs and documentary programmes. 'Incomparable support,' said Barry.

There must have been times when Beaverbrook wondered if he was in the right business.

# CHAPTER EIGHT

As seen from Downing Street, the Festival was the only bright spot in a bleak year. The Attlee administration, so recently the standard bearer of a brave new world, was falling apart. In the general election of February 1950, Labour's parliamentary majority over all other parties had been cut from 146 to just five. The government was further weakened by the depletion of its front rank. Bevin's death and Cripps' last days in a Swiss sanatorium deprived the Cabinet of two of its strongest characters. A third, Aneurin Bevan, along with Harold Wilson, then the youngest minister of senior status, made off in high dudgeon when health service charges threatened their credo of free treatment for all. Attlee himself was not in good health, nor was Morrison, who much against his will followed Bevin at the Foreign Office, a job for which he was temperamentally ill equipped.

Though never happier than when glad-handing his way round familiar territory, Morrison was uncomfortable on foreign ground where the natives were liable to have an uncertain grasp of English. Moreover, everywhere he looked on the world map, there seemed to be a crisis which involved Britain. Though the Korean War was largely

American led and financed, the British contribution was a crippling burden on a weak economy and while there was national pride in the brave stand by the 'Glorious Gloucesters' at the historic battle of Imjin, there were many who wondered why British forces were there at all.

Then there was the trouble building up in the Middle East, where Britain had for generations been in pole position. The nationalists were keen to get Britain out, likewise the Americans (so much for the special relationship) as long as they could keep control of the oil. In Iran, a populist leader, Dr Mohammed Mussadiq, gained power on an anti-British ticket, pledging to take control of the Anglo-Iranian Oil Company. No sooner said than done. As preparations for the Festival neared completion, Mossadiq carried out his threat, reducing at a stroke the British share of Middle East oil production from 53 per cent to 24 per cent, while at the same time purloining the refinery at Abadan, £100 million worth of installation, Britain's single biggest overseas asset.

It was not a good time to start celebrating.

But Morrison, who continued to hold on to the Festival as if to a lifeline, never wavered from his conviction that 'we should keep the self respect and morale of the British people on a high level', which meant the Festival must go ahead come what may. Or, as he put it more idiosyncratically at an eve-of-Festival dinner at the headquarters of Political and Economic Planning, 'To have organised the Festival now may be madness, but it is the sort of madness that has put us on the map and is going to keep us there.'

A pageant like no other was planned for the opening. It was to be conducted by King George VI on the steps of St Paul's after a service of dedication led by the Archbishop of

Canterbury. Turning out in force, the establishment of
church and state was to parade in full regalia supported by
the King's Bodyguard of the Yeomen of the Guard, Yeomen
Warders of the Tower and trumpeters of the Household
Cavalry with sundry heralds and gentlemen-at-arms.

There were those who found it curious that Britain
should dedicate itself to the future with a recreation of
medieval splendour. Not so Barry, who believed passion-
ately that pride in the past was the prerequisite of a national
revival. His instinct served him well. Turning out in their
thousands, the crowds lining the royal procession were, as
*The Times* said, 'in joyous mood'. And, for once, Barry was
lucky with the weather.

> The morning of May 3 broke cool and misty, but *dry*.
> After the endless rain, London had suddenly enjoyed
> six consecutive fine days: one raised the blinds on that
> Thursday morning hardly daring to hope for a
> seventh. It was an equivocal beginning – anything
> might have been going to happen; but as the Royal
> procession drove from Buckingham Palace through
> the thronged streets to St Paul's the sun broke shyly
> through.[1]

Along with other Festival dignitaries, Barry stood at the
entrance to the Cathedral portico to await the royal party.
The procession's imminent arrival was signalled by a 41-
gun salute, fired at the Tower of London and in Hyde Park,
and by the ringing of church bells.

> Over our heads stretched a blue and white canopy.
> Below us at the foot of the wide sweep of steps were

drawn up a guard of honour of the Honourable Artillery Company, the band of the Welsh Guards, detachments of the Women's Royal Army Corps; in the centre, forming a circle round the railings of Queen Anne's statue, stood the Company of Pikemen of the HAC in their uniforms of the sixteenth century. In a vast arc facing the cathedral and all down Ludgate Hill an immense crowd surged and rippled under pressure from reinforcements behind and the restraining arms of the police in front. And here we stood at the top of the steps, a handful of men, privileged to occupy an almost empty grandstand to witness an instant of British history.

There was a lull, and some more arrivals. Up the steps came Winston Churchill, pausing above the first flight and turning with doffed silk hat and a broad smile to acknowledge the cheers of the throng. The Prime Minister, arriving immediately after, hurried shyly into the shadow of the portico almost as though alarmed by the applause: here was the contrast of two characters.[2]

A moment of light relief was provided by a stray dog set on playing games between the legs of the police horses. The spectators cheered it on as a welcome diversion before the main event, now seconds away:

The sun chose this instant to win its slow battle with the mist and sunlight glinted on helm and harness as the Household Cavalry jogged into view, escorting the Royal carriage. The King and Queen dismounted and climbed the steps, preceded by the Lord Mayor holding erect the Pearl Sword. It is a heavy sword and takes some holding. The Lord Mayor, who stands six feet four in his stockinged feet, held it as rigid as Cleopatra's Needle. So we greeted them, and they passed into the splendour within.[3]

From his vantage point on the centre aisle, Barry watched a succession of images from the age of chivalry pass before him:

Portcullis Pursuivant, Bluemantle Pursuivant, Rouge Croix Pursuivant, Richmond Herald, Chester Herald, Lancaster Herald . . . the Archbishop preceded by his Chaplain bearing the Canterbury Cross . . . the Bishop of London . . . vergers . . . the Lord Mayor . . . the King and Queen, accompanied by nine members of the Royal Family.[4]

The service before a congregation 3,000 strong was mercifully short, though the Archbishop stretched it out with a convoluted warning against a celebration without spiritual substance:

Such a Festival might be a spiritual disaster, a self-indulgence, an exhibition of pride, but neither our own character nor the harsh circumstances of our times would encourage the misuse of such an occasion. But even so the Festival might be celebrated in a kind of spiritual emptiness, devoid of aspiration or inspiration. That would be hardly less disastrous, for it would be to deny the past and frustrate the future . . .

After a hearty rendering of Blake's 'Jerusalem', a trumpeter's fanfare propelled the king, resplendent in naval uniform, on to a pigeon-proof dais mounted on the cathedral's west steps where he declared the Festival open. 'I see this Festival as a symbol of Britain's abiding courage and vitality . . . we look back with pride and forward with resolution.'

Few of those present heard a word he said. At the behest of the BBC his microphone could not be used to amplify his voice for fear of creating an echo on the nationwide broadcast. In this respect at least, British technical expertise, much vaunted at the Festival, had some way to go to catch up with American knowhow.

While the ceremonies were in full swing, there was work in progress on the South Bank. Reyner Banham, who as consulting engineer had overall responsibility for construction, gave thanks that the official opening was at St Paul's and not on site. The Festival was to be given over to the public just twenty-four hours after the Cathedral service. In that time designers were still coming up with helpful suggestions for improving their displays – nothing radical, of course, but that wall needed to come down and that walkway to be shifted six feet to the left.

The contractors adopted tight smiles and kept going. Banham waited until midnight for his final inspection. 'I was dismayed to see how much clearing up had still to be done, including the removal of a display contractor's hut still in a prominent position in the Dome.'[5] In the small hours of opening day, a man was busy killing rats that had appeared from under the floorboards as the huts were dismantled.

Exhibits were still turning up (at the last moment a

painting by Constable, lent by the National Gallery for the Lion and the Unicorn Pavilion, arrived in a taxi) and there were piles of rubbish still to be cleared. As queues began to form at the public entrances on 4 May, the last of the workmen were leaving by the back gate.

On the evening of 3 May, the top people had reconvened for an inaugural concert at the Royal Festival Hall. For Barry, Ismay, Lord Mayor of London Sir Denys Lowson and their wives, it started badly. While a selection of British music (Elgar, Vaughan Williams et al) was played by the members of five orchestras, ten choirs and the state trumpeters of the Royal Horse Guards, conducted by Sir Adrian Boult and Sir Malcolm Sargent – the VIPs were stuck in the lift.

It was said later that the load was too heavy; the engineers had not reckoned on a giant of a mayor who was not given to slimming. This error of judgement was compounded by the reluctance of the emergency staff to respond to what they assumed to be a hoax. With no response to either the bell or the telephone in the lift, 'the Lord Mayor, a burly man, took off a large shoe and hammered on the walls of the lift with sufficient violence to wake the dead'.[6]

When at last help arrived, the occupants had a two-foot climb from the floor of the lift to the corridor. Being hauled up one by one was, said Ismay, an 'undignified performance'; moreover, 'to add insult to injury, nobody had noticed that [our] box had been empty throughout the whole of the first part of the programme'.[7] They were in their seats to hear 'the most memorable event of the evening', Sargent conducting his own arrangement of 'Rule Britannia', henceforth a staple of the annual Promenade concerts at the Albert Hall.

After the morning's ceremonial extravaganza ('some-thing the British do better than any other nation in the world'[8]), Barry judged the Festival Hall opening the crowning triumph. The quality of the sound was a revelation. 'Everyone marvelled that the concert hall could be so successfully insulated from the noise, a few yards away, of the trains on Hungerford Bridge,' recalls Audrey Russell, who reported on the Festival for BBC Radio.[9]

The royals and senior politicians were on parade again the next morning for their first sight of the finished — or near finished — South Bank. Any hopes the organisers might have had of a long-term improvement in the weather were dashed by a sunrise that was wet, foggy and miserably cold, 'an unusual combination at any time, and an outrage in May'.[10] Colour and gaiety were notable by their absence. 'The bunting hung in the lifeless air as limp as wet dishcloths, the Thames was barely discernible in the mist, and a general air of damp languor hung over the scene.'[11]

To make matters worse, thanks to an error in a timetable guests had been required to assemble long in advance of the royal arrival. 'There was some disgruntlement among the great but in such conditions . . . there was a pre-disposition to complain.'[12] There was more confusion when Churchill's car was waved through, while the Prime Minister was told he had to get out at the gates and walk to the Fairway.

For a brief moment when everyone had arrived there was a semblance of order. But the best laid plans soon fell apart. Churchill started behaving like a naughty boy, insisting on riding up and down on one of the escalators. 'Perhaps he had never seen one before,' sighed Ismay.[13]

The royals, including Queen Mary in a wheelchair, were

equally disruptive. Paul Wright was assigned to Princess Elizabeth and Prince Philip. 'It was pouring with rain and we were huddled under umbrellas but it was hard to keep track of them. They would keep wandering off in different directions.'[14]

Meanwhile, the King and Queen had favoured an unprepared route into the Lion and the Unicorn Pavilion, which meant that they saw the whole thing back to front. 'Confronted with the White Knight and the Eccentrics Corner on entering, [they] must have received an unintendedly eccentric impression of the whole place.'[15]

By now 'the royal family was strung out in a straggling line over the exhibition followed by a morose, top-hatted army of VIPs. One could only hope they would all safely weather the climate and crowds and arrive where the motors were assembled for their departure'.[16] Yet, as the visit ended, impressions were not entirely unfavourable:

An hour or so later Howard Lobb, crossing over to the North bank for a late sandwich at his Club, overheard a classic scrap of conversation. An elderly Conservative M.P., sipping an after-luncheon port, was telling a younger member that he had been that morning to the opening. 'Well,' asked the youngster, 'and what was it like?' Honest even in his disillusion the veteran replied, 'Very good – I'm sorry to say.'[17]

A grand lady was also heard to give grudging approval, though she dismissed the fountain lake: 'Not a patch on Versailles.'

With no such regrets, the first paying customers who

filed through the gates in the early afternoon were equally enthusiastic. It is hard to recreate the sheer elation of experiences, new then, but now taken for granted. For the 19-year-old Arnold Wesker, the Festival was a 'new horizon . . . blasting new shapes, colours, design, creative energy, pride and confidence like a dynamic spring'.[18]

As a schoolboy, Richard Morse was struck by the 'display of street lampposts along the riverside. All types and styles were represented including those that folded down to allow the bulbs to be changed at ground level. A ten year old was fascinated.'[19] Betty Phillips, in her late twenties in 1951, took a more practical line. 'They showed you how they baked ice cream wafers, and the oven was long – terrific long oven, electric oven – it went in at one end and came out the other end all packed up as ice cream wafers, splosh one end, ice cream wafer t'other.'[20]

'The whole area was a riot of colour,' recalls Hugh Marshall, who in 1951 was an art student in Essex. 'We were engulfed in complex signage, paintings, posters and new curving and exciting shapes.'[21]

Light and space were critical to the success of the Festival. One of the big surprises for visitors was how much – possibly too much – had been accommodated in a tight urban landscape while still allowing plenty of room to move about without bumping into others. A feature everyone noticed was the imaginative use of glass, 'giving a transparency to the buildings, creating fantastic vistas of a luminous, sparkling city by the river at night'.[22] An array of cleaners was engaged to retain that sparkling effect on over half a million square feet of glass.

Fears of overcrowding proved to be wide of the mark. A widely publicised forecast of a safety limit of 20,000 on site at any one time was quickly exceeded without any fearful consequences.

Minor quibbles aside, the press reaction was enthusiastic. Old quarrels forgotten, even the *Express* and *Standard* found something positive to say. Several newspapers, including *The Times*, published celebratory issues and there was much editorial optimism that the Festival might be the turning point in Britain's post-war struggle for recovery.

In the *Illustrated London News*, Arthur Bryant, the popular historian and regular columnist, was one of many commentators to draw the comparison with 1851. 'And if the omens of 1951 are very different from those of 1851, appearances are often deceptive and the second half of the twentieth century may still prove to be what the promoters of the Exhibition so clearly and gallantly hope.'[23]

Any temptation to share Bryant's optimism was dampened by a glance at the accompanying advertisements, which suggested that Britain was still some way short of the modern age. One was for a hotel in Clacton, described as 'a must' by virtue of having interior spring mattresses in its de luxe bedrooms. What the rest of the rooms were like was left to speculation.

An attempt at a more objective assessment of the Festival appeared in *Country Life*, where Robert Lutyens, architect, interior designer, artist and only son of Sir Edwin Lutyens, Britain's premier architect, identified the essential difference from 1851. The Crystal Palace, he wrote, was authoritarian in its vision of the future while the Festival was attempting a balance between 'the enthusiasm of blond, bearded art students in duffle coats and the scepticism of so-called reactionaries'.[24] Lutyens gave the impression of preferring the authoritarian approach while refusing to acknowledge that contemporary Britain was no longer an authoritarian country.

The challenge for Barry, Casson and the rest had been to create a Festival that invigorated the imagination without attacking the foundation of all that was traditional and held sacred. Had they succeeded? The foreign press clearly thought so. From Europe and the USA came a collection of press cuttings to die for. The *New York Times* spoke of the 'demonstration of the indomitable will with which Britons can meet and survive hardships', while the *Herald Tribune* hailed 'a celebration in which all the free world can find hope'. Across Europe there was amazement and delight in the Festival image of 'an ancient and vigorous people whose creative faculties have not withered and who have much still to give of an admirably balanced political society'.[25]

There were a few dissonant voices cutting across the chorus of approval. Sir Thomas Beecham, who was miffed at not having been consulted over the Festival Hall, described that building as 'the most repellent and monstrous structure built in this grand old country for 350 years' and dismissed the entire Festival as a 'monumental imbecility', which earned a *Times* rebuke for his 'somewhat ursine' attitude. Nöel Coward was equally sniffy. The South Bank, he thought, looked 'like a dog's dinner' and as for Battersea, it was 'really the last word in squalor and completely ungay'.[26] But it was another influential critic who came closest to the consensus. 'I had expected the exhibition to provide beauty and power,' wrote Harold Nicolson. 'I had not expected it to be the very soul of wit. In place of the cemetery I had dreaded I found a maternity home, gay with pink and blue, and resonant with the cries and gurgles of the world that is to be. It is the most intelligent exhibition I have ever visited. I have never seen people so cheered up or amused in spite of a fine drizzle of rain.'[27]

The highlights were undoubtedly the Dome of Discovery, the Lion and the Unicorn Pavilion and Skylon, the latter because it seemed to defy gravity but also because, in a utilitarian age when nothing was wasted, few could bring themselves to believe that this extraordinary structure had no practical use whatsoever. Pointing towards the unknown, it was for many a symbol of hope.

The Dome – known to Festival insiders as Ralph's Tub – was impressive for its scale (it was the largest of its kind in the world and the biggest aluminium structure ever built). For youngsters there was the additional attraction of its extraterrestrial associations. Here was a flying saucer made real. It could have come straight from the adventures of Dan Dare, the futuristic space adventurer in the recently launched, all colour *Eagle* comic, or from innumerable American B-movies.

Inside there were more connections with other worlds. The display of a 74-inch telescope made for Mount Stromlo Observatory in Australia was accompanied by a caption reading, 'The explorers of outer space are the austronomers'. How long would it be before man walked on the moon? (The answer was eighteen years.) It was in the Dome that radio impulses beamed from the top of the Shot Tower were reflected back on to a giant screen. Close by, the History of the Telescope offered scale models of the instruments used by explorers of space from Galileo onwards. Adventure, in the sense of defying the odds, was a recurring theme and a powerful draw. One of the Dome's top attractions was the Polar Theatre, where a team of huskies fought their way through a realistic Arctic blizzard.

Best remembered for its oddities, the Lion and the Unicorn Pavilion irritated some by its apparently frivolous approach to life. In 'Alice through the Looking Glass', the model of Tenniel's White Knight, the flight of plaster doves from a wicker cage, the space given to eccentrics (a sort of Ealing comedy in aspic) and the random blackboard texts from Shakespeare and the Bible, Robert Lutyens sensed a pastiche in the worst possible taste. 'Take me home,' was his plea.

Others argued that the whimsy was an aid to con-templation of the more serious displays, such as the long mural by Kenneth Rowntree featuring scenes from British history, or another mural, this one by Edward Bawden, depicting country life. Borrowed treasures, including paintings by Gainsborough, Constable, Turner and Paul Nash and first editions of Shakespeare and Dr Johnson's Dictionary, were shown to good effect. There was less success in getting across in visual form abstract ideas about the law, constitution and free speech.

Sixty years on, to list in their entirety the exhibits featured in the other pavilions is an invitation to yawn. Who could possibly thrill to the sight of a working model of a power station (Power and Production), or a full-size gas turbine (Sea and Ships), or a large model of Southampton Docks with examples of passenger and freight handling (Transport), or the story of Edmondson's invention of the railway ticket, including 'displays of time-tables and other railway accessories' (Transport, again)? Not forgetting the sewage disposal plant (Health) . . .

That all this was of interest at the time, and not just to

specialists or buffs, is understandable in the context of a technological revolution in its early phase, when travel was infrequent and television had not yet entered every home. Apart from those who had been in the forces, few in 1951 had much first- or second-hand knowledge of life beyond the factory bench, the office desk or, for women, the kitchen stove. From this perspective it should not surprise us that the café in the Power and Production Pavilion, dressed up as a works canteen with modern culinary equipment, caught the imagination of those who were more used to having their lunch out of a sandwich box. It also attracted the interest of management, who were given an indication of what the trades unions would be asking for next.

Moreover, a simple catalogue of exhibits does not begin to do justice to their setting, a succession of imaginative, eye-catching displays. The landscaping for the Agricultural and Country Pavilion had to allow for a bewildering array of live creatures including prize bulls, horses, sheep and goats. The strongest memory for David Harris, one of a school party, was of 'drinking milk straight from the cows that were there as part of the farming exhibition'.[28] For the 'butterfly window' wild flowers were collected from all over the country. A daily delivery of plankton from the Lake District was judged to be essential for the well-being of exotic fish. One of the Pavilion's designers recalled the difficulties created by the innovative display techniques:

As some of the wild life exhibitions were shown in acrylic plastic – at the time a very new process – we needed five adders in mid-winter. The only way to obtain them was for the British Embassy in Paris to

prevail upon the mayor of Nice to organize an adder
hunt. In due course, an ominous box marked
'Poisonous snakes' arrived at London Airport. From
there I had to take them to the laboratory where they
had to be killed, prior to setting them in plastic. Thus
Gallic adders posed as their British cousins. But they
took their revenge. In the heat of mid-July, their
bodies swelled in such a way that they broke through
the plastic and the whole display, of which they
formed a part, was dripping with blood. People fainted
left and right, the whole area had to be roped off and,
as always when something went wrong, the designer
was called in. I put the whole gory mess in the back of
my car and tried to get rid of it through the local refuse
collection. This, however, meant hacking both
perspex and adders into small pieces to make them fit
into a dustbin. Rarely can a designer have been
required to do such a Herculean labour. No sooner
had I recovered from the shock when I was informed
that one of the large fish tanks, with all the fish and
plankton, had burst, causing a short-circuit as the
water went into the electrical controls. However, the
fish were recovered and survived until the end of the
Festival, after a new tank, this time reinforced, had
been installed.[29]

Where live exhibits were no more than wishful thinking,
three-dimensional representations were sufficiently
realistic to hold the sometimes severely tested attention of
bystanders. This was certainly true of the sea section of the
Dome, where the whaling industry was illustrated by a large
model of a blue whale 'with little men clad in sweaters and

sea boots engaged in the gory task of "flensing" the monster'.[30]

Young visitors to the Dome were held spellbound by this exhibit, as too they were by the full-scale model of the Tempest Prognosticator, the invention of the appropriately named Dr Merryweather who had observed that before the onset of a severe storm, freshwater leeches became agitated:

> The learned Doctor decided to harness the physical energy of these surprisingly hysterical aquatic bloodsuckers to operate an early warning system. On the circular base of his apparatus he installed glass jars, in each of which a leech was imprisoned and attached to a fine chain that led up to a miniature belfry – from whence the tinkling tocsin would be sounded on the approach of a tempest.[31]

The Dome also boasted a modern weather forecasting unit which claimed to predict the elements for the next twenty-four hours, though an elderly lady expressed herself most dissatisfied when the earnest young boffins were unable to tell her if it was raining outside.[32]

Inevitably the Festival had teething problems. Barry was quick to note the insufficiency of clear signposting. And many of the captions were either misleading or plain wrong. To learn that 'From the rich black coal we unlock the power of the sun' when in the real world there were frequent electricity cuts caused a few cynical guffaws, while the bold statement that 'every child has a choice between the free state education and the independent system' left parents gasping incredulously.[33] Commentaries could be insufferably patronising, as rural visitors to the Country Pavilion were quick to note. In the craft section there was rather too much emphasis on the skills of old England: wheelwrights, thatchers and basket weavers crowded out younger designers, such as furniture makers, who could see the need to adapt their crafts to domestic practicalities. Too many staff were either ill-trained or not trained at all.

The catering was a flop. The Festival's dedication to all things British was commendable so long as what was on offer could claim quality and originality. British cuisine offered neither. Nor, for that matter, did British standards of restaurant service. One of the clearest memories for Margaret Bean was lunch at the Regatta Restaurant, supposedly one of the best of the thirteen eating places on offer, on the first day of the South Bank exhibition. The surroundings were elegant, a promise of a treat in the offing. It never arrived:

> The slatternly waitress with a dirty dishcloth over her arm took our order, and an enormous helping was dumped on our plates. An order for wine caused consternation. 'Wine!' she said in horror and went away to confer with the news that nothing was available except British sherry or (I think) someone's Invalid Port. She was disappointed when we turned them down. Afterwards she wrote out the bill and stuck the pencil behind her ear, and we paid at the desk.[34]

Desmond Shawe-Taylor, music critic for the *New Statesman*, shared the disappointment:

Lured on by the novelty and freshness of colour, I drop into one of the Festival restaurants, dreaming perhaps of *cannelloni* or *quenelles de brochet*; and then, ah then, I am soon back in familiar old England. Not indeed in the fine old England of beef sirloins and saddles of mutton, but in our latter-day, take-it-or-leave-it England of lukewarm tomato soup and custard with a skin on the top.[35]

Barry tried to defend the indefensible, citing rising costs, labour shortages, untrained staff and rationing as reasons for the failure to provide value for money. He might also have mentioned sheer incompetence:

The restaurants and cafes had a testing opening day, the more so because the rainy afternoon put the open-air tea-places, with no shelter better than garden umbrellas, more or less out of action. The conse-quence was increased pressure on the restaurants under cover and some regrettable misunderstandings. One of the restaurants, which offered afternoon teas at 5s. each, had two queues waiting outside from 4 o'clock onwards and when the service of teas ended at 5.30 – leaving a gap till the service of dinners was to start at 8 – visitors had to be turned away. Had these people known earlier, there were covered cafes and restaurants elsewhere in the grounds with no time-limit on the service of teas and with scores, if not hundreds of empty chairs at 5.30.[36]

There was one exception to the rule of culinary mediocrity. This was the Dickens Dinner, an eight-course meal based on Victorian recipes and with no expense spared. 'The restaurateur invited people connected with the Festival and members of the press. In those days of rationing, such a meal was a real treat and the tickets were really sought after,' recalled Prunella Guthrie, who gave up after the fourth course. 'Few people got further.'[37]

Another failure of the organisers was to anticipate the quantity of litter. This was a national shortcoming. A cartoon in *Punch* showed a directional sign in eight languages against which was another sign in English only — 'Drop no litter'. Britain was notorious for its untidy habits and it was naïve of Barry to blame manufacturers for using too much packaging:

After the first few days we were almost in despair, wading ankle-deep through litter and seeing a bright new exhibition in danger of becoming a slum. Something had to be done, quickly. We had placed 1,150 litter-bins about the site but these proved to be not nearly enough, and it is no good expecting people to be clean if one does not provide them with the means to do so. Several hundred more litter-bins were promptly ordered, and with the aid of these, of a revised and greatly intensified scavenging drill and of an occasional, not, I hope, too avuncular, appeal to good manners on the public address system, at the end of a month the problem had been mastered. Thereafter the place was kept remarkably clean. One could inspect the site of an evening after eighty or a hundred thousand people had been in and out of the turnstiles, and find it, certainly not spotless, but far from obtrusively dirty. As many as twelve tons of litter would be cleared away in the course of a day.[38]

Further into May, as the weather improved, the Festival was as popular at night as by day. With the wartime blackout a recent memory, the Festival illuminations were a powerful draw. A special treat for children born just before or during the war was to be taken to see the flashing hoardings at Piccadilly Circus. At the grand post-war switching on in 1949 a crowd of 50,000 sang the popular Blitz refrain, 'I'm gonna get lit up when the lights go on in London'. This writer, a country boy, recalls standing in awe before a simple neon sign above a sweet shop in Bury St Edmunds, sensing that somehow it promised an excitement way beyond the purchase of a threepenny bag of gobstoppers.

The Festival lights were something else again, surpassing anything London had ever seen. From the South Bank, a floodlit panorama stretched from Big Ben to St Paul's. A forest of luminous flags fluttered high above the turrets of Whitehall Court. Between pavilions on the Festival site, pavement lights twinkled while fountains were transformed into a kaleidoscope of colour. And there to transfix the public gaze was the Skylon, 'a giant pencil of lacy light against the night sky'. Michael Frayn called it 'a floodlit dreamworld'. An even younger visitor said it was 'like walking into a film set'. The *Guardian* suggested that a trip to the South Bank was 'as invigorating as a trip across the Channel, for the scene is quite as unfamiliar as a foreign seaside resort'.

Twice a week from early August, the night was enlivened by military bands playing under sweeping searchlights.

There was dancing on the Fairway led by Geraldo's Embassy Orchestra, one of the most popular of the big bands. Stars of stage, screen and radio took turns at the microphone. Throughout the day, the competitive spirit was demonstrated at the Sports Area, close by the Shot Tower, with strenuous activities ranging from fencing to weight lifting. Once the Battersea Pleasure Gardens were opened, passenger boats ran an ever crowded shuttle service between the two Festival venues.

And yet more was demanded – or, rather, it was thought that more was needed – to keep up the momentum. The brief fell to Antony Hippisley Coxe, a former features editor of the *News Chronicle* and, according to Paul Wright, 'one of the outstanding eccentrics of his time'. He had proved his worth by livening up the seaside section with a touch of vulgar fun – Blackpool meets Bournemouth, as he put it. From What the Butler Saw – carefully checked for indecency before being sanctioned – it was a short jump of imagination to the election of a Pearly King and Queen, the national symbol of Cockney London: 'Twenty boroughs from Acton to Woolwich were represented. We breakfasted off whelks, cockles and a mixed grill, washed down with Guinness. After a tour of the South Bank, we boarded a steamer for the Pleasure Gardens, and it was "Knees Up Mother Brown" all the way.'[39]

What else could the redoubtable Hippisley Coxe come up with? Well, how about a balloon ascent from the South Bank? Barry liked the idea; indeed, he was one of the first to step into the basket:

We were in the hands of George Long, a balloon pilot of veteran experience. There are, I believe, only two balloons in existence in this country, both of them belonging to the R.A.F. and only one active holder of a balloon pilot's licence. This is Mr Long, who took time out of his leave – he was attached to Cardington – to make the ascents from the South Bank and who told me that to qualify for a pilot's licence a balloonist must make six flights and one solo.[40]

After drifting back and forth on the Fairway in search of a fair wind, the balloon was launched:

We rose with surprising speed so that very quickly the pale upturned faces of the crowd below us looked like a bunch of toffee-apples. 'You,' said the pilot now, 'will be navigator', and pointing to an altimeter fixed to one side of the basket, of whose accuracy I had instantly the gravest doubts, he handed me an inadequate road map of London and suburbs. These were my instruments.[41]

After ninety minutes in the air, Barry, Long and the only other passenger, the wife of an air commodore from Balloon Headquarters at Cardington, made it as far as north Kent. Having passed over what looked to be a large hospital they landed on a road crossing at Dartford Heath. Almost immediately the police arrived, demanding to see passports – 'on the lookout for spies or contraband', surmised Barry. The hospital turned out to be an asylum, which in the circumstances was thought by all to be appropriate.

Another crowd puller was the Miss World contest, the brainchild of Eric Morley, who was to start *Come Dancing*, the BBC's longest running television series, and who launched commercial bingo in the early sixties. Miss World was planned as a one-off event but is still going strong.

Hippisley Coxe's crowning point was the high-wire crossing of the Thames. Charles Elleano, the intrepid performer, belonged to a circus family which had been in the business for generations. Technically from Alsace, or maybe Hungary, he told reporters that he had relations in four countries, spoke three languages and regarded the whole of Europe as his family home. 'We are nomads,' he declared, and as if to prove the point, he and his wife and children set up residence in two long caravans which he parked in a builder's yard beside Waterloo Bridge.

Finding the man was one thing, obtaining the wire was more difficult; it was a time of national shortages. When that problem was solved, the mass band of doubters and spoilers moved in on the act. The river police were dubious; so too was the LCC. Even the Metropolitan Water Board had a view – unfavourable, naturally. Eventually, Hippisley Coxe secured a reluctant go-ahead. The date and time were fixed – between 1 p.m. and 2 p.m. on Saturday 22 September, when low tide kept river traffic to a minimum.

Come the day there were close on 80,000 spectators inside the Festival compound and around the same number lining the Embankment and Westminster Bridge. Elleano believed in milking the crowd. Already running an hour late, the star of the afternoon announced that he had forgotten his *balancois*. Since his start point was on the north side of the river, there followed a race across Waterloo Bridge to retrieve the pole from the top of his caravan. A slow handclap grew in volume. In a Festival office, Barry was on the end of a telephone demanding action. The tide was rising and tugs with barges attached were beginning to come up on the flood.

And so, at 4 p.m., Elleano, in a scarlet and gold costume, finally set out. For Paul Wright, who had to answer for the publicity, it was a nightmare: 'Half the river's emergency services were afloat beneath him. When there was no going back, he appeared to stumble. Knowing his fondness for the wine bottle, I thought, this is the end. I believe now that it was all part of the act but at the time I could only think of the headlines.'[42]

The strongest memory for Hippisley Coxe was of a tug lowering its funnel to pass under Hungerford Bridge. 'Elleano was hidden in a cloud of smoke. As it cleared he was seen sitting on the wire.'

Twenty-seven minutes after he took the first step on the wire, Elleano jumped on to the South Bank. The crowd cheered, Paul Wright breathed again and Barry was left wondering how many days had been cut off his life.

Indirectly, Hippisley Coxe was responsible for another incident in Barry's Festival career that filled him with horror every time he thought about it. In London on a state visit, the King and Queen of Denmark were naturally keen to visit the Festival, knowing that it was in part inspired by Copenhagen's Tivoli gardens. Barry was deputised to show them round. Touring the section where the British love of the seaside was on display, he took a stick of Festival rock (a Hippisley Coxe innovation) from one of the girl attendants and snapped it in half to show the Queen the words 'Festival Rock' running right through the stick.

Would she, I asked, like a couple of sticks as mementoes? Yes, she would, but she had three children – could she have three sticks? Handing me three the girl said, 'that will be 2/3d.' To avoid embarrassment I dived into my trouser pocket only to find I hadn't a penny of small change. 'I'll pay you later,' I hissed in what I hoped was an inaudible whisper: 'this is Her Majesty the Queen of Denmark.' She registered no interest but repeated 'that will be 2/3d.' Queen Ingrid had by now begun to look in her own purse (but how should the Queen of Denmark on a State visit to England be carrying florins and sixpences?). A crowd stood about staring while, tension rising unbearably, I made another abortive attempt to penetrate the girl's defences. Mercifully at that instant the Science Director, standing at the Queen's left, came superbly to the rescue with the exact amount. But the crowning humiliation was to come. Accepting the money the girl next said, 'Can I have the [ration] coupons?'

Barry asserted himself. 'It was time to go. We went.'[43]

# CHAPTER NINE

A recurring joke in *Round the Horne*, the popular radio comedy series of the 1960s, was the Brad Smallpiece guide to fantastical attractions across the country:

> Well, there's Massed Goat Pandering at the Royal Nobblers Institute. Knock a Rabbi out of bed at Battersea funfair in aid of the Stuffed Mouse for Thailand fund. Hip Throbbing at Whipsnade, Finger Bogling at the Spotted Dick Memorial Hall, Hammersmith, and an exhibition of Gnome Clenching in the corset department of Sparkslew and Towser, chiropodists by appointment to ex-queen Marie of Rumania – Clapham. But I myself will make a beeline for the Master Carpenters Knot Hole of the Year contest which will be held in the saloon bar of the Orang-Utan's Arms, Stoke Poges.[1]

Some years ago I asked Barry Took, the co-writer of the show, where the idea came from. He credited Kenneth Horne, who had seized on the chance of parodying the roundup of weird and wonderful Festival happenings beyond the South Bank. Events like a shin-kicking contest in the Cotswolds, a mass choral rendering of 'folk songs of the English worker' at St Pancras Town Hall or the replacement of the tin shed with a new brick-built public convenience at Sunninghill. An exhibition 'showing Newark's contribution to the welfare of Britain' included the Newark Blue Smock and clay pipe-making. Nottingham presented 'Women through the Ages', a pageant of twenty episodes by 600 performers, and Aireborough Council gave guided tours of 'three sets of bungalows for the aged'. In Coventry, Lady Godiva rode yet again.

According to *The Times*, Leeds promised to be 'a centre of fun'. On 23 June, the Yorkshire battalion of the Parachute Regiment was slated to 'jump into Waterloo Lake in Roundhay Park'.[2] Promising 'something big', the Mayor of Ipswich saw 'no reason why members of the County Club should not fix up a special cricket match'.[3] Our Dumb Friends League put on a children's dog show while the West Sussex Women's Institute held a Festival of Good Entertainment, doubtless all very proper. Local histories were raided for heroic events. In Cardiff, the story of the nation was re-enacted in the Pageant Play of Wales.

It is easy to poke fun at provincial wavings of the Festival flag. But the money was simply not there for more than a few ambitious projects, as Barry was the first to acknowledge. His guidelines for local initiatives were suitably modest:

The cleaning and rehabilitation of ancient buildings and monuments. The conversion of buildings of historical interest into museums, libraries and art galleries, providing it does not involve new buildings. The clearing of canals. Tree, shrub and hedge planting schemes also decoration with window boxes. The conversion of derelict areas, including bombed sites, into gardens. The removal of useless and derelict buildings, sheds, etc. and any other 'eyesores'. The endowment of bursaries or scholarships in the arts and sciences. The rehabilitation of local crafts. Gifts of furniture to youth centres. The establishment of a civic theatre scheme or the inauguration of a repertory company. The setting up of a music club, etc.

The foremost ambition was for Britain to clean its face, to remove or disguise the blemishes that made so many towns 'inefficient, dirty, inconvenient, shapeless, without character or colouring'. The temptation to make 1951 a historical landmark was to be resisted. 'We want no legacy of cast iron Jubilee clichés.' If anything new was to be built, argued Barry, let it be attractive and practical like 'a well designed bus shelter' or 'changing the street lights from gas to electricity'.

Some district councils went in for more ambitious public works, such as a new sewage system. 'Houses, cottages and clubs have been built for old age pensioners. Playing fields and sports grounds have been made or improved. There are places where 1951 will see laid the foundation stone of the new Town Hall or where a new park will be opened for the first time.'[4]

Cultural achievements were to be marked by twenty-three arts festivals, wholly or partly funded by the Festival budget and mounted by the Arts Council. These included festivals at Aberdeen, Bournemouth, Cambridge, Dumfries, Inverness, Liverpool, Norwich, Oxford, Perth, St Davids and York. The first to open was at Bath. York presented medieval mystery plays, Stratford-upon-Avon produced Shakespeare, Cheltenham focused on music. Bristol's Colston Hall was reconstructed. The Walker Art Gallery in Liverpool was reopened and so too was Manchester's Free Trade Hall (blitzed home of the Hallé Orchestra). Also in Manchester, the John Rylands Library unveiled its treasures, including papyrus fragments of St John's Gospel and Caxton's edition of the *Canterbury Tales*. Edinburgh's international festival was set to become an annual event. Meanwhile, a gathering of the clans was to take place in August with a march-past of 1,000 pipers along Princes Street. Museums and galleries across the country mounted festival exhibitions ranging from the Hamilton bequest at Glasgow's Kelvingrove (the first time the complete collection of pictures had been shown) to a display of Regency cuisine at Brighton's Royal Pavilion. A Festival chorus three hundred strong gave voice in Durham.

By the end of November 1950, over a thousand local authorities had announced plans for the Festival. There were a few party poopers. Taunton and Malden decided to remain aloof. But after initial doubts most other refuseniks fell into line. Hull's festival budget of £20,000 was withdrawn and then just as quickly restored. Having declared the council kitty to be empty, Rochester managed to stage a Dickens pageant in the grounds of Rochester Castle.

Local bureaucrats could be a pain:

A landlord who took over an unsightly public house in Victoria, close to some industrial dwellings built in 1875, spent his own money putting up gaily-coloured awnings and placing trees in tubs outside his door, thus brightening the neighbourhood and earning the thanks of many residents. But the Westminster City Council told him that as his tubs obstructed the footway they must stand on his doorstep and not outside the door. Meanwhile, overflowing dustbins were standing shoulder to shoulder on every pavement in sight, waiting for the council dustmen. Tenants who complained were told that the council could not send dustmen into doorways to collect the bins, which must be left out on the pavements. Dustbins could brighten London in 1951, but not trees in tubs.[5]

But despite all obstacles and financial restraints, the national response was magnificent. In the end, some 1,600 towns and villages did their bit for the general uplift. Providing a new playing field or public garden, or equipping old ones with seats and litter bins, restoring an ancient building, renewing the church bells, floodlighting the town hall, planting trees or even encouraging window boxes, it was all part of what Barry called 'a gigantic tidying up campaign'. Tree planting was particularly favoured. Bedfordshire County Council alone planted close on two thousand trees. In Dover shell holes were turned into flower gardens. 'Never before has any country, anywhere, attempted such a widely divergent display of every aspect of national life.'[6]

Barry was on the invitation list for just about every out-of-London Festival event. He agreed to a punishing schedule of visits which began well before the official opening of the South Bank. But it was the cities in celebration that remained etched on his memory, starting with Chichester's floodlit cathedral. From the Bath Assembly Rooms he took away the indelible sight of John Barbirolli,

> in the greenroom after a superb performance of the Vaughan Williams Fourth, changing in the interval with trembling hands out of a wringing-wet dress-shirt. People congregate about him, offering comment, congratulation. He bows, pulls at a sandwich, wriggles himself into dry linen. His wife brings him a drink. No one, I suppose, who has not himself done it can know what the conducting of a symphony concert means in terms of intellectual effort, emotion or physical strain.[7]

No city, said Barry, was more successful than York in building its festival round the traditions and resources of the place rather than importing stock attractions from outside:

> Recitals of chamber music were given in the restored Merchant Adventurers' Hall; in the Art Gallery there had been gathered together a collection of paintings from the great Yorkshire houses . . . The city's 'liquid history' was not neglected either: a regatta and a carnival were held on the Ouse. Of an evening, to the evident pleasure of the crowds, the 'Old York Street Criers' cried their wares through the streets; towards dusk Guards were mounted at Clifford's Tower and took their posts on the city walls; while for good popular measure there was dancing each night in a Big Top in Bootham Park.

Impressive enough, but for Barry these attractions were merely the adornments of the two main features of York's festival, starting with the cycle of Mystery Plays, performed for the first time since 1572:

> This revival was a triumphant success, one of the great imaginative achievements of the Festival year. May it not be another four hundred years – or another four – before these plays are seen again. [They were to become an annual event.] Played in the open air, with the Gothic ruins and greensward of St. Mary's Abbey for stage and scenery, this pageant of Creation from the fall of Lucifer to the Day of Judgement made an unforgettable impression in visual delight, realism and dramatic force.

One episode in York appealed to Barry's love of incongruities:

> At the performance of the 'Dream of Gerontius' in the Minster, attended by both Archbishops, I had occasion in the interval to be conducted – a circumambulatory exercise as it proved – to a cloakroom in some outpost of the Cathedral, a place of small intrinsic interest but convenient no doubt for clergy and choir. On the floor of this place lay a discarded newspaper, and what kind of a newspaper if any at all might you be unsurprised to find in such a precinct? The *Church of England Newspaper*, a Diocesan Magazine, perhaps even the *Yorkshire Post*? A thousand guesses would not probe the heart of this ecclesiastical mystery – to my delight the

journal turned out to be none other than the *Sporting Times*.

Barry's welcome in Manchester was, as he put it, subdued. 'Maybe the city had never quite forgiven us for having chosen Liverpool for an arts festival in preference to themselves.' After the opening of the Land Travelling Exhibition, the high point of the visit was Laurence Olivier's presentation on alternate nights, before they were brought to London for a triumphant season at St James's Theatre, of Shaw's *Caesar and Cleopatra* and Shakespeare's *Antony and Cleopatra*, with Vivien Leigh as Cleopatra in both plays and Olivier as Caesar and Antony:

I am not sure what I was expecting, beyond unquestioned quality from these two. . . . In all my play-going life I had hitherto seen but three productions, and never yet an actress with the technique and temperament fully to achieve the blend of queenliness and wanton that is Cleopatra. Vivien Leigh did it. The production was first-rate, lovely to look at, compact, swift. To achieve coherence Olivier took some liberties with the text which the result well justified. Here was a great evening in the theatre. When I saw them in Olivier's dressing room afterwards, exhausted but happy, they knew, I think, that they were already across the threshold of one of the glittering successes of a Festival season which, in the theatre, was also to have its disappointments.

Barry spent a full week in Liverpool. There was much to enjoy:

Something was provided for everybody, from the most cultivated to the old people and children in tenements who, prevented from attending any functions themselves, had concerts brought to them in their own courtyards, with tea brewed on the balconies. The whole city most noticeably felt the Festival to be its own affair not something laid on by decree. The street decorations were among the most lavish anywhere, some of them very striking but perhaps rather too profuse in motifs to be a complete artistic success. What was remarkable was that the poorer the district, the greater seemed to be the enthusiasm, and these communities vied with one another for the honour of having provided the best street tea, which were a working class feature of the Festival, organised of course quite spontaneously.

In a full and rich arts programme, Barry identified an exhibition called 'The Story of Liverpool' as one of the striking events:

It told in a remarkably clear and vivid way the historical, sociological and commercial development of the city from a 12th century village to the great seaport and industrial centre of today. Nothing was sidestepped, neither slave trade, slums nor the devastation of the blitz. What made it more remark-able was the fact that it was almost entirely the voluntary work of art students. Industry had its say in an exhibition half in the open air run up on a bombed site, which quickly showed how successfully the Merseyside has been developing new light industries as well as the old established ones which made its reputation.

But what made the Liverpool Festival particularly memorable for Barry was the way in which it brought ordinary citizens into a truly communal enterprise:

Huge processions progressed through the streets rather in the style of Venetian pageants and the crowds rolled out in their hundreds of thousands to applaud. The newspapers produced complete special Festival editions. One evening I stood with the Lord Mayor and others high up on a platform above St. George's . . . to watch the converging procession and address the waiting crowd. All the dresses and the devices carried in the procession were made by amateur enterprise and the most striking use was made of colour. When the procession ended and gathered under the portico of St. George's Hall, it was already dusk and Bengal Lights flared up behind the columns of the portico, first red then green. But the river itself became the scene of the most spectacular pageantry. What were probably the biggest fireworks displays in the world were held on the river with fire boats passing up and down stream and the spectacle culminating in the simultaneous firing of 2,000 rockets. Half a million people turned out each time to enjoy this tremendous show.

In Glasgow, Barry was transfixed by a royal performance:

Two flunkeys step forward to open a window [of City

Hall] overlooking the square. Through the room moves Princess Elizabeth, steps out on to the balcony in the last of the June evening, and happily waves to the roaring crowd below.

The next memory was of the drive from Glasgow to Newcastle, a journey that sent Barry into lyrical paroxysms:

In the oblique rays of early June sun each tussock spread its separate shadow across the golden meadows; the earth, the air breathed with an innocence as in the first morning of the world. The road winds exhilaratingly into the uplands of Peebleshire, into a landscape of miniature mountains and swift streams not unlike the Luxembourg Ardennes, follows faithfully for several miles the course of the river, wriggles through Jedburgh, strikes out for the frontier at Castlebar, then swoops in giant switchbacks over vast, magnificent moorland almost to the gates of Newcastle.

Then it was off to Belfast, where the Farm and Factory Exhibition revealed that 'the innumerable tiny farms of Ulster (80 per cent of them under 50 acres) export together a quarter of a million gallons of milk a year to England and prodigious numbers of eggs – Ulster has a poultry population of about 18 hens to every human being'.

But Barry's strongest impressions were of Norwich, 'my childhood capital . . . where in the Wensum as a boy I had learned to swim, fish and row a boat'. The opening ceremony was in the market square, [flanked] on the left by superb St. Peter Mancroft and on the right by the old Guildhall with its handsome chequered flintwork; both of them, even the lofty magnificence of St. Peter's, dwarfed by the long expanse of the modern City Hall that fills the whole end of the square and looks twice as imposing because of the steep rise on which it stands. Not long ago Norwich was racked with controversy about abolishing the market stalls that cram the square with their tented roofs like a village in its own right set down in the heart of the city. The stallholders, thank Heaven, won the day. For me Norwich would be Norwich no longer without the striped awnings and busy medieval huddle of the market, with its pungent whiff of other markets across the North Sea, a reminder of the city's ancient Flemish associations.

Two additions to the city's amenities were ready in time for the Festival, the Colman Art Gallery and the Assembly House, saved from dry rot and decay to be 'exquisitely restored'. But, as ever for Barry, it was the cathedral that really held his interest. 'Architectural and historic interest apart, it is almost everywhere, quite simply, the best public building in the community.' In the evening he went to hear Beecham conduct Tchaikovsky's Fourth, 'as fine a performance as one is ever likely to hear'.

Next morning I took time off to revisit St. Peter Mancroft. Paul Wright, who was with me, can never resist an organ, and obtaining the key from an obliging verger he regaled me with a short recital.
And so back to London.

*Above:* Breakthrough into Modernism: the 1930 Stockholm Exhibition was the model for the Festival of Britain. *Courtesy of Arkitekturmuseet, Stockholm*

*Centre left:* Hugh Casson, architectural mastermind of the Festival, with a model of the Shot Tower, one of the centrepieces of the exhibition. *Getty Images*

*Centre right:* Gerald Barry who promoted the idea of the Festival and became its Director General. *Rex Features*

*Bottom:* Misha Black, James Holland, Ralph Tubbs and Hugh Casson working on plans for the Dome of Discovery. *Getty Images*

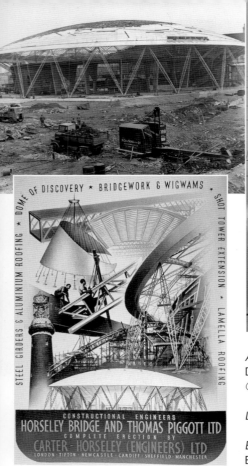

*Above left and above:* The Dome of Discovery and the Skylon under construction. *Getty Images*

*Left: TopFoto*

*Below:* The cartoonist Low gives Beaverbrook's critical view of the Festival.

Low, *Evening Standard*, 9.8.49

*Above: Alamy*

*Above right:* From right: Prime Minister Clement Attlee along with Winston Churchill and Lord Ismay (far left) at the Festival's opening. *TopFoto*

*Above:* The Royal Procession enters Trafalgar Square from the Strand, after the official opening ceremony by King George VI. *Getty Images*

*Above right: Getty Images*

*Right:* The official book of the Festival and a special edition London map for visitors. *Courtesy of A. S. Scott*

THE
FESTIVAL
OF
BRITAIN
1951

Welcome
to
LONDON

LONDON TRANSPORT
BRITISH RAILWAYS

The Dome of Discovery, *(top)* the Lion and Unicorn Pavilion *(above)* and the Skylon *(right)* attract the crowds. *Getty Images*

*Above:* The recently rediscovered *An Englishman's Home* by John Piper, commissioned for the Homes and Gardens Pavilion. Oil on 42 panels (477cm x 1547cm). Hugh Casson called it 'the one mural on the South Bank we can not afford to lose'.
*By kind permission of Liss Fine Art*
*© Piper Estate*

*Above:* At the Festival's Telecinema, visitors were able to experience pioneering three-dimensional pictures and stereophonic sound. *Topfoto*

*Left:* Tightrope walker Charles Elleano crosses the Thames for one of the most successful public relations stunts for the Festival. *Getty Images*

*Top:* The Battersea Pleasure Gardens, with a model of the 1851 Great Exhibition's Crystal Palace in the background. *Getty Images*

Two of the most popular attractions: Roland Emmett's The Far Tottering and Oyster Creek Railway *(above)* and the awe-inspiring Guinness Clock *(left)*. *Alamy*

*Above:* Children enjoying the boating lake in Battersea. *Alamy*

*Left:* A Festival carnival in Hucknall, Nottinghamshire. *TopFoto*

*Right:* The day before the festival closed, crowds take a last admiring look at Siegfried Charoux's *The Islanders* and Richard Huws' *Water Sculpture.* *TopFoto*

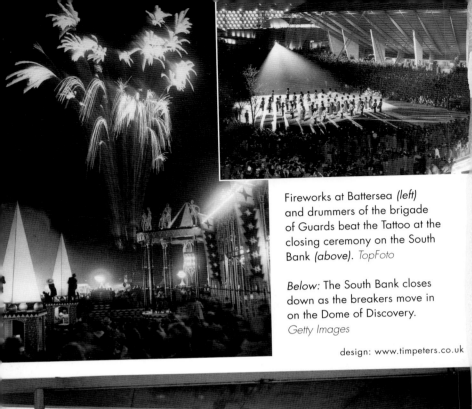

Fireworks at Battersea *(left)* and drummers of the brigade of Guards beat the Tattoo at the closing ceremony on the South Bank *(above)*. *TopFoto*

*Below:* The South Bank closes down as the breakers move in on the Dome of Discovery. *Getty Images*

design: www.timpeters.co.uk

If the organisers of minor events were disappointed not
to attract a personal visit from the Director General, they
could at least rely on a quotable message of support. The
Midlands village of Knowle, near Solihull, which presented
a week of the 'Revels of Arden', was told by Barry that it was
'setting a fine example' in helping to realise the hope he
shared with 'His Majesty the King and the Archbishop of
Canterbury that every family in the land will share in the
Festival'. This may have been pitching it a bit strong but by
now Barry's enthusiasm was stratospheric.

He even managed to find encouraging words for Trowell,
the official Festival village, which, late in the day, Barry had
decided was 'an unfortunate, indeed a rather thoughtless
choice'.[8] The problem with Trowell was that it started with
next to nothing to commend its depiction on a picture
postcard. As an adjunct to the Stanton ironworks on the
Nottinghamshire–Derbyshire border, it had found favour
as 'an example of what a small community has done to . . .
make itself a better place to live'.[9] But there was only so
much that could be achieved in a few weeks. By early May
there was a new children's playground and in prospect, a
cricket match 'played in the dress of a century ago'. There
was also an exhibition in the parish hall tracing the history
of the village. Barry had been expecting more originality, a
transformation, which would have been something of a
miracle since there was no money on offer. Brought up
against reality, he saw no alternative but to 'stick to our guns
. . . and see it through'. Trowell did not figure large in
Festival publicity.

The Festival's outreach beyond London to the rest of the
country did not depend entirely on local initiative. The two
major exhibitions outside the capital – Industrial Power at

Kelvin Hall in Glasgow and Ulster Farm and Factory in
Belfast – were financed by the central budget. Both cities
might justifiably have regretted drawing short straws in the
Festival lottery. Everybody talked of having fun, but where
was the fun in heavy engineering or in 'a narrative display
of Ulster's linen industries'? The designers did their best,
however, and excelled themselves.

The site for the Ulster exhibition was the new but
depressingly functional Castlereagh industrial estate on the
outskirts of Belfast. This was but the first of a succession of
unpromising circumstances faced by Yugoslavian-born
chief designer Willy de Majo, who had already overcome an
initial prejudice against the appointment to the post of a
man who was not British to the core. 'I got stuck with an
existing factory building with terribly low ceilings. The
solution I arrived at was to stretch an airy looking false cloth
ceiling across the whole 35,000 square feet which gave an
impression of height and was quite a technical feat.'[10]

Cheerful landscaping with a bandstand and an open-air
restaurant helped to lighten the instructional load of the
exhibition. Barry, who was at the official opening, declared
it a great success:

Here, as in London, fantastic weather had delayed
preparations. Only the night before an ornamental
canal in the front of the grounds had burst its banks
in a downpour, flooding flowerbeds and turning newly
laid lawns into a quagmire. But the Exhibition wore all
the same a cheerful and astonishingly finished air and
a fresh breeze from the sea set all flags fluttering.

What particularly impressed Barry was a 'model farm with

telephones from the living room by which the farmer could ring all the outbuildings'. Others were more taken with the quality of the restaurant meals, which far excelled those on offer on the South Bank. In fairness, the region having suffered fewer wartime shortages, the Northern Irish diet was more substantial if not more imaginative than that suffered on the mainland, but de Majo enhanced the taste with the style of presentation: 'I organised a special caterer, I insisted on that kind of detail right round. If I had to be in charge I wanted to choose the cutlery, I wanted to select the dresses of the waitresses and all that, and, in fact, the menus too.'[11]

Trying to outdo the South Bank was a de Majo speciality. To liven up the exterior of his exhibition he went for the Skylon effect, with a tapering metal structure that looked like an advanced communications aerial. It fell short of the magic of the Skylon, but as de Majo commented, 'we needed it so that people could see it from far away', a signal that there was excitement and pleasure to be had at the end of a bus route.

The Ulster Farm and Factory exhibition attracted 157,000 visitors over three months, twice as many as forecast. By contrast, Glasgow's exhibition of Industrial Power fell well short of expectations. The idea was to tell the story of Britain's contribution to heavy engineering, but Glaswegians were not inclined to devote their precious leisure to a subject many of them knew all about from their daily existence. This was a pity, since the exhibition was a masterwork of creative imagination by a group of designers led by Basil Spence, designer of the Sea and Ships Pavilion on the South Bank and soon to be the architect of the reborn Coventry Cathedral. Dramatic displays of the economic and social power generated by coal, steel, railways and shipbuilding climaxed with a Hall of the Future dedicated to atomic energy and predicting 'an age of plenty and comfort' or a regression to 'complete extinction'. Such sombre reflections were not calculated to inspire popular appeal, though the organisers surely deserved credit for not indulging in the propaganda of unrestrained enthusiasm. And despite poor attendances – 280,000 over three months, a third of the estimated figure – there was praise for the startling originality of the towering, crescent-shaped sculptured mural for the Hall of Coal illustrating coal as the god of nature pointing to a blazing sun. Hulme Chadwick was its designer. For the Hall of Hydro Electricity, Arthur C. Braven contrived to have visitors walk under twenty thousand gallons of water a minute crashing down on to a glass roof.

The accompanying storyline was less impressive. Late in the day it was realised that few who claimed to be scriptwriters knew anything about heavy engineering. The search went out for innocents who might be willing to learn on the job. One of the recruits was Michael Wharton, later for 28 years Peter Simple on the *Daily Telegraph*:

> I was given a ticket for the Library of the Institute of Electrical Engineers. There I asked the librarian to recommend a few elementary works. He produced a few and I took them away to a remote desk. All were completely unintelligible. But I had noticed a shelf containing such books as *Every Boy's Book of Electricity* and furtively taking these, I began my research. Every time the librarian came near I had to cover up the boys' books with the books he had given me. It was like

being back at school again. But I soon found I was getting interested in the history of electrical generation. It started with amber, the loadstone and the terrible iron mountain in the *Arabian Nights*, which sank ships by drawing out all their rivets if they came near it, and progressed by easy stages to Faraday, that saintly man who, if he could have foreseen the evils his electro-magnetic discoveries would make possible, from pornographic films to nuclear weapons, would surely have destroyed his laboratory and hanged himself. Soon I had mastered the basic principles. I worked on the project, on and off, for more than a year. Not being able to afford the rail fare to Glasgow, where this section of the Exhibition was located, I never saw the humming, clanking, booming end-product of my work. But even now I retain enough of what I learned then to be able to pose, if only for a few minutes, as an electrical engineer.[12]

Of the two travelling exhibitions, the converted aircraft carrier *Campania* had the edge as regards publicity. Tarted up with white paint and flags, the *Campania* was a miniature of the South Bank with, as one visitor noted, displays of 'everything from miners' singlets to plastic sink tidies'. Stopping off on its coastal voyage – the first port of call was Southampton – was the signal for a small army of reporters and photographers to gather at the docks. Such an unlikely proposition as a Festival showboat had news value. James Holland, who in addition to his responsibilities for the upstream section of the South Bank led the *Campania* design team, had problems in injecting a sense of fun into a severely confined space. But the ship itself was greeted with smiles of acknowledgement for an original and amusing idea.

Transforming the *Campania* for its peacetime role was not easy. The boat had been chosen primarily for its large hangar deck, but Holland soon found, as he put it, 'that it had all the stability of a biscuit tin'. For the internal structures the usual margins and tolerances had to be multiplied many times. After Southampton, with an official opening on 5 May, the *Campania* called at Dundee, Newcastle, Hull, Plymouth, Bristol, Cardiff, Belfast, Birkenhead and Glasgow, a round trip lasting until 6 October.

Also opening on 5 May, this time in Manchester, was the Land Travelling Exhibition, said by designer Richard Levin to be one of his least favourite assignments. Here was another version of the South Bank, but because it was visiting cities of the Industrial Revolution there was a stronger emphasis on industrial design. The challenge was to create an exhibition that could be adapted to four different sites. Manchester and Birmingham were able to provide covered premises but for Leeds and Nottingham, an acre of purpose-built tents made its appearance.

A fleet of trucks carried a bewildering array of items for show, including the latest designs of domestic objects like the clothes peg, hot water bottle, lady's hairbrush, clothes iron and − an ultra-modern touch − the corner television set, 'which provides good protection from glare'. There were scale models including a rail lounge car with all-round vision and a glass-fronted garden room. If attendance at the Land Travelling Exhibition (5,000 visitors daily, as against 8,000 for the *Campania*) fell below forecast it was not for the want of imaginative design. In the Corridor of

Time, a series of power-driven pendulums, suspended above the visitors' walkway, were seen in large facing mirrors, giving the illusion of infinity. By night the exhibition was brought alive by searchlight beams that pierced a red translucent roof.

Although the local Festival events were designed primarily for local people to enjoy, collectively they were touted as a tourist attraction with particular appeal to overseas visitors. But in 1951 travel was not easy. There was a shortage of passenger trains (freight came first on the railways), cars and buses were mostly of pre-war vintage and roads were narrow and winding. While Germany had its autobahns and France was well ahead in developing its autoroutes, Britain had to wait until the late fifties for its first stretch of motorway. At journey's end the hotels were a disgrace.

Official publications made light of the inadequacies while urging tourists, in the nicest possible way, to exercise patience and understanding. As editor of the Blue Guides, L. Russell Muirhead was brought on board to advise strangers to Britain who were bold enough to explore the highways and byways. His opening words of encouragement ('There are few English hotels without some honest merit') were immediately followed by a warning:

Visitors from overseas should remember that the hotel industry and its management are very strictly controlled in England, and, while this may perhaps too often be used as an excuse for deficiencies, it is frequently the genuine reason for the apparent difficulty of providing full comfort at all hours of the day and night.[13]

His top tip for obtaining half-decent service was 'not to expect too much nor to appear to know too much'. The breathtaking assumption that it was the customer who had to make the running was strongly endorsed:

> Good humour goes a long way, and a genuinely pleasant smile is worth many a sixpence. If you take the opportunity (as everybody should) of visiting a country pub, order your drink and consume it quietly; the habitués of the place will in due time engage you in conversation if you wish; they are as ready as anyone to enjoy the entertainment of conversing with a stranger when they are ready for it.

With the general shortage of hotel rooms, Muirhead judged it essential to book well in advance, otherwise 'It is quite possible, for example, to arrive in mid-week in a town like Northampton, Norwich or Shrewsbury, and have the greatest difficulty in finding a bed for the night.' As for the quality of accommodation:

> London is the only town that possesses great hotels of international first-class standard. The principal hotels in the other great cities of England – many of the largest managed by British Railways – go in rather for solid comfort than for luxury. More characteristic of English life are the principal inns in the smaller provincial towns which have not been totally rebuilt during the last hundred years; these have served travellers by road for many centuries, and, in a surprising number of instances actually retain a great part of their ancient fabric.

As a seasoned traveller, Muirhead had a few surprise recommendations for getting about:

> There is one form of public transport which, to my mind, is not sufficiently made use of by visitors from abroad who are not well enough off to use their own cars or to hire a car at will, and that is the ordinary service bus. These can be used, of course, for extended cross-country tours, provided that luggage is kept down to a small suitcase; but probably the most agreeable and profitable way of employing these cheap, comfortable and punctual vehicles is to choose one or two centres and radiate thence in all directions – taking half-day trips, day trips, or even longer journeys. Cheap return fares are the rule. By travelling on these local buses the stranger has a more intimate sight of the English countryside and its people, their houses, their inns, their crops, their cattle, and their industries, than he can gain from any other sort of mechanically propelled vehicle.

If buses were out of favour, the wandering tourist was urged to try cycling ('which demands a certain amount of muscular energy but the reward is out of all proportion') or go by foot:

> Even in these materialistic days, the walker – provided he (or she) is not too eccentrically clad – receives readier hospitality than any other traveller. I have personally been given food and drink, because I was hot and tired after a long walk, at an inn that was turning away motorists because of short supplies.

All that said, 'those who travel England on horseback are better received than anyone else'.

On this evidence the gulf between reality and the Festival promise of modern efficiency was still deep and wide.

# CHAPTER TEN

The mixed fortunes of London's Festival scene beyond the South Bank were a reflection of its extraordinary diversity. Two major exhibitions, that at the Science Museum in South Kensington and the creation of the Lansbury Estate at Poplar in East London, were supported by the central budget. For the rest, running the gamut from Hospitality at Home, staged by the Tea Centre in Regent Street, to a display of rare books at the Victoria and Albert Museum, financial backing came from a miscellany of private and public sources, with an occasional Arts Council subsidy compensating for any shortfall.

The Science Exhibition was really an overflow from the South Bank, a depository for items that were either too large to be accommodated on the main site or thought to be too complex to be appreciated by the general public. As such, it might well have fallen into the category of noble failures had not inspiration come from a young mathematician and biologist, Director of Research at the National Coal Board, who was destined to achieve television fame as a populariser of science and all-round egghead.

As the composer of the exhibition narrative, Dr Jacob Bronowski set about his task with all the infectious enthusiasm of a natural teacher. Starting with the physical and chemical nature of matter, he went on to give a lucid exposition of the structure of living things, plants and animals, climaxing with an introduction to the most recent areas of scientific research – including, under the heading Stop Press, 'what goes on in space'.

'There are no trick miracles here,' visitors were told, though, parading the aisles, many must have marvelled at a world made of atoms which could then be broken down into ever more minuscule elements. 'Here is the modern world,' declared Bronowski, 'standing straight and handsome on its base of science. The wonders of this exhibition are not larger than life; they are the fabric of modern life and they have grown of themselves from science.' The Archbishop of Canterbury, who, though to the fore elsewhere in the Festival, was not at the opening, might have demurred, especially when Bronowski came to his ringing declaration of humanist faith:

> This is an exhibition which looks inside nature. It shows the processes, living and dead, by which nature works. Here is the world for all to see, built transparently from the clear ideas of science. This exhibition is meant to make you feel at home with the knowledge of science, and to make you take pride in it, because it shows science as it is – fascinating, yes, but real and downright.

Bronowski made a triumphal return to this theme with his thirteen-part BBC television series *The Ascent of Man*, voted by industry professionals one of the one hundred greatest ever British TV programmes.

For the director, Ian Cox, and chief designer, Brian Peake, there was none of the pressure they were under at the South Bank to dilute the message of the Science Exhibition. The displays at South Kensington were for inquiring minds, not for day trippers in pursuit of amusing irrelevances. Even so, they attracted a higher than expected attendance at around 1,500 a day, confounding those who saw no appeal in an event of such 'advanced and technical character'.

You come into the exhibition through five rooms which take you, step by step, into the heart of the matter. Going through these rooms you seem to shrink like Alice in Wonderland, and the things round you seem to grow larger and larger. There are pencil and paper in the first room. Now you find yourself apparently shrinking, first to the size of the pencil, and then to the thickness of the paper; you see that the pencil lead slides off in layers as it writes. Another step, another thousand times smaller, and you see the structure of the graphite crystals which make up the pencil lead. And then a last step, you are ten thousand million times smaller than you began, and now you see into the atoms themselves. Each atom has a heavy centre like a small sun, and the electrons move round it in clouds. You have plunged headlong through these five rooms into the structure of matter, and are now ready to see, in a more leisurely way, how we come to know about it.[1]

Barry backtracked slightly on warnings that the Science Exhibition would be too heavyweight for popular taste: 'For a layman prepared to take his brains with him and give them a little exercise on fresh territory, this show was one of the best half-crown's worth in town.' Though he added, 'some of the new understanding one believed one had acquired would not stand the test of self examination next day'.[2] There was no need to read between the lines to conclude that this non-scientist was suffering a severe case of information overload.

The playful spirit was not entirely absent. In the section devoted to living structures, children warmed to the mechanical tortoises. Homing in on their generator when they needed a rejuvenating boost, and fitted with infra-red cells to stop them bumping into each other, they were almost indistinguishable from the genuine articles, except that the live tortoises had no access to artificial respiration. But they were not infallible. Brian Peake's most vivid memory of the whole exhibition 'was the appearance in my office on certain mornings of an assistant with a glum look, reporting further mortalities'.[3]

Having given somewhat grudging credit to the Exhibition's imaginative leaps, Barry awarded his accolade to the show's chief craftsman:

Many of the models were the invention of a young man of near, if not total, genius, Max Moffat, who lives in a small house on the edge of Dublin and does all his tricks in a hut at the bottom of his garden. Here he employs a staff of men and women who make everything themselves. The problems posed by the scientists and display-designers each had to be solved empirically on bench or drawing board; he would think out possible ways of illustrating this or that scientific fact which had to be 'exhibited', build a model, try it, and go on altering or improving or starting again until both the scientists and he were satisfied. When I paid a visit to his hut he was busy experimenting with a model that was to demonstrate the birth, growth and death of a star. Half a dozen other devices were standing about in varying stages of completion, each of which helped to illustrate a chapter in the story of matter.[4]

When the Exhibition closed, the models were handed on to schools, colleges and museums as permanent exhibits.

If Barry's semi-detached attitude to the Science Exhibition comes as no surprise, his holding back on the Live Architecture Exhibition is harder to explain. The social structure created by innovative architects for the forthcoming scientific and technological revolution was Barry's greatest concern. Yet the little miracle that happened in Poplar, in the least fashionable part of London, took place outside the orbit of the great and good. There was no formal opening, just a conducted tour for the Mayor of Poplar, a cursory inspection by members of the London County Council and a small ceremony to mark the handing over of keys to Alice and Albert Snoddy, Lansbury's first residents, on 14 February 1951.

The originator of the scheme was Frederick Gibberd, who in July 1948 wrote to the Festival's Council for Architecture to suggest that there was only one sure method of explaining architecture and town planning and that was to show on the ground what could be achieved. His idea was to take a bomb-damaged area and rebuild it as an exhibition. Not least of the attractions was the prospect of shifting most of the cost on to the LCC's housing programme.

Official sanction was forthcoming in August with Gibberd as one of the four contributing architects. He was commissioned to design the shopping centre and market square. Nominated for development was a thirty-acre riverside bombsite off the East India Dock Road, otherwise known to the LCC planners as Poplar neighbourhood No. 9. Jack Godfrey-Gilbert was the Festival's coordinating officer for the project. His first visit to the site was not encouraging:

> It consisted mainly of open derelict landscape, formerly occupied by terraced houses which had been completely devastated by the bombing and cleared away. There were the remains of a church on the corner of East India Dock Road and Upper North Street with some of the gothic arches still intact. There were derelict remains of houses here and there but the remainder of the site was completely flat except for one large square house occupied by a firm of chartered surveyors with the name William Clarkson written across the front. The whole area had an atmosphere of foreboding, gloom and despondency.[5]

The two immediate priorities were to deconsecrate the remains of the church (Hugh Casson quickly rustled up a bishop to perform the ceremony) and, more of a problem, to persuade the partners of William Clarkson to surrender their building. A deal was done over lunch, at which Godfrey-Gilbert promised the senior partner to secure for him a licence for a brand new office, which in those straitened times was a bit like telling his guest that he had won the Lottery. The alternative, a compulsory purchase order on a business that had long experience of delaying compulsory purchase orders into infinity, was too horrific to contemplate.

The biggest challenge was the clearing of a trail through local government bureaucracy. In the LCC labyrinth no less than ten committees had a say in the future of neighbourhood No. 9 and while they were deliberating on how many planners it took to make a simple decision, a battle was being fought between the LCC's Chief Architect and Chief Valuer for control over new housing construction, the former official representing socially conscious design and the latter efficiency and productivity. Victory went to the Chief Architect in 1950, after an exhibition promoting housing built to the specification of the Valuer's department was given a resounding raspberry by the critics. But the Valuer still had a major say in the choice of architects.

Meanwhile, neighbourhood No. 9 and its two adjoining sites, it was decided, merited a designation more resonant than simple numerals. Names of illustrious seafarers suggested themselves. Martin Frobisher, determined in 1577, at his second attempt, to find the North West Passage, led the nominations. In the end, however, the honour went to a recent local hero. One-time mayor of and MP for Poplar, George Lansbury was briefly a pre-war leader of the Labour Party. But he was chiefly remembered for his efforts to raise living standards in one of the most deprived areas of the capital. To associate his name with a new housing project, one, moreover, that was intended as a model for slum clearance, seemed an eminently suitable tribute.

Gibberd felt that the overall design, a compromise of LCC interests, was 'conventional and a bit tame'. J.M. Richards, one of the editors of *Architectural Review*, agreed. He criticised Lansbury's 'dull, less characterful external appearance', which followed too slavishly the nineteenth-century tradition.[6] All this was true, but with the desperate urgency of rehousing thousands of families, startling innovations too costly to be reproduced elsewhere were deemed inappropriate. And the outcome was a distinct improvement on what had gone before under the aegis of the LCC Valuer, who until recently had been giving the go-ahead on housing plans approved in 1934.

Some 400 new homes were built, a mix of two- and three-bedroom houses, flats and maisonettes, between them providing accommodation for 1,500 people. In outer appearance the buildings were a reminder of suburban dwellings that had sprung up in the inter-war years, though their very newness placed them in sharp contrast to the neighbouring terraced houses, grimy and cheerless after years of exposure to London's soot-laden air. Fitted bathrooms and relatively spacious kitchens also set them apart from older buildings.

Mrs Snoddy told the assembled press that her family was delighted with their new ground-floor flat. 'There are fitted cupboards and one to air clothes in, a stainless steel sink, hot water tanks. It's the sort of home to be proud of.'

Nine-year-old David Garred went with his parents to see the dawn of a new age. His mother could scarcely believe the all mod con kitchen: 'Compared with the scullery back home and the kitchen coal range this really was like the Hollywood films. A bathroom to yourself? No queuing on Saturday morning at the public baths for these lucky tenants. Oh, and just look at that, a toilet inside! My, that's what I call posh!'[7]

More than anything, however, what gave Lansbury its special character was the conscious effort to create an infrastructure for community living, starting with the first pedestrian shopping district to be built in Europe, a blue-tiled precinct of market stalls surrounded by small shops. There was sadness at the disappearance of the old Chrisp Street market, 'with its gas-lit stalls thronging with shoppers till late at night'.[8] But the electric lighting and the arcade to protect against the rain were welcomed. At each end of Market Square was a pub – the Festive Briton and the Festival Inn, the latter identified by an eccentric signpost with an elevated platform where figures representing typical Londoners danced round a maypole. There were also two churches, an old people's home and two schools, the latter praised for their imaginative use of space and light to produce an environment in which education could be fun. Plans for a health centre were abandoned when the NHS ran short of money.

Gibberd regretted that Lansbury made no exciting 'architectural statements' to inspire the younger generation, like the Dome of Discovery. But his budget did not allow for South Bank spectacles. The only opportunity for artistic license was provided by the Borough of Poplar. A symbol of civic pride was called for, such as a clock tower in the marketplace. We can imagine the conventional image that inspired the idea. Gibberd turned it into something exceptional:

I suggested we should not stop at a clock but also make it an 'Outlook Tower' from which to survey the surrounding panorama of dockland. And so it was that I designed a tower with two intersecting staircases (one for going up and the other for coming down), which start together but do not meet until the viewing platform – the prototype is the famous double staircase at the Château de Chambord. The building was given architectural expression by exposing the concrete framework of the landings and staircases, which cross each other like scissors, the diamond shapes formed by their intersections being left open for the view. It was a practical folly that gave pleasure.[9]

It was also a landmark that attracted queues of visitors waiting to climb the open-sided steps to the viewing platform: 'Those who dared to risk the top were amazed at their locality spread before them. The view on a clear day westward was towards the City and Tower Bridge. To the south was the Docks and the Thames, the north Crystal Palace and to the east Southend, or so the more imaginative said.'[10]

The excitement did not last. Unsupervised climbing was deemed to be unsafe and the staircases were closed.

The chief trouble with Lansbury was that little of it was finished in time for the opening of the Festival. Even the clock tower remained on the drawing board. It was not built until the following year. Linked specifically to the Festival, there was an exhibition of New Towns for Old in a tent on a corner of East India Dock Road, a Gremlin Grange mock Tudor house illustrating the structural defects of jerry-built housing, a Rosie Ice tea bar and, courtesy of McAlpines, a decorated crane to signal Lansbury from afar.

It was not enough. There were those who enjoyed

contemplating a building site, but it was a minority interest.
The official tally was of 87,000 visitors, but in the absence
of turnstiles it is hard to think of this as anything but a wild
guess. What is known is that the river bus service from the
South Bank was soon cut back and that six of the attendants
on hand to show people around were made redundant. Not
keen on being associated with a half-baked project, Gerald
Barry stayed away.

As one who listed his interests in *Who's Who* as people
and buildings, Barry was disappointed that the Festival
failed to make more of an architectural impact. Reyner
Banham, the harshest critic of Festival style, blamed Barry
and his cohorts for a failure of nerve. A devotee of Le
Corbusier, whose concept of the home was 'a machine for
living in', Banham promoted what he deemed to be 'sane
and rational design' against 'empiricism and compromise'.[11] If this meant the destruction of traditional
buildings to make way for high-rise apartment living with
traffic flyovers and elevated walkways, that was all a
necessary part of dragging the country into the twentieth
century.

But though Barry was proud to call himself a modernist,
he was sufficiently sensitive to social trends to realise that
the heritage culture was too strong to accept the thorough-
going modernism touted by Banham. Though many old
buildings were still to be swept away in the rush to replan
town centres and to meet the demand for decent housing,
the popular mood favoured a toned-down form of
modernism, with front and back gardens to detached or
semi-detached houses designed in recognisable styles that
paid homage to a gentler age. Many of those who lived in
towns and could not imagine being far away from shops,

cinemas and pubs were nevertheless devoted to the picturesque brick and gables more associated with rural life. As one critic detected, 'There is a corner of the English mind that is for ever Ambridge'[12] (it was on 1 January 1951 that the 'everyday story of country folk' started its record-breaking run on the airwaves).

Tower blocks were never popular. One of the first of London's post-war housing estates, at Roehampton, was heavily criticised for its 'barrack like' high-rise accommodation. Taking note of public demand, the new towns, eight of which were planned around London with six more to the west and north, subscribed to the conventions and restrictions of low cost, low density, low rise housing. The modernists were to have their day, but not yet. If Lansbury was a let-down for Barry and, even more, for modernists such as Reyner Banham, there were many who delighted in this updated but reassuringly familiar neighbourhood 'rising from the ruins of the blitz, a modern oasis set in a vast area of overcrowded streets'.[13]

Barry's itinerary may have omitted Lansbury but the Director General was certainly busy elsewhere in London. One of his first visits was to the Public House of Tomorrow, on show at the Victoria and Albert Museum. First prize in a related competition sponsored by *Architectural Review* went to Messrs Pollack, Prus, Hasler, Sharland and Negus, who as Barry proudly noted were also working on Festival projects. Their entry, said the judges, showed 'a genuine appreciation of pub character and at the same time a spirited and imaginatively modern quality'. The illustrations are of an interior that would not be unfamiliar to patrons of the modern wine bar or gastropub. Sadly, in the intervening half century, imbibers in search of convivial company had to put up with all that the judges railed against — 'copying the antique, equipping the interior with imitation old oak beams and ingle-nooks' or the 'chromium steel and plastics approach', both producing 'merely ersatz effects which have neither the advantage of modern convenience nor the charm of genuine age'.[14]

Barry weighed in with some unflattering observations on typical pub customers:

No improvement is possible unless we teach people to use their eyes. Nowadays the average user of a pub is not conscious of his surroundings, which is perhaps just as well, but the sad thing is that he has lost even the desire to look at what is on the walls: he simply does not know or care. If we want to encourage the man-in-the-street to appreciate the street, what better place to start than the house which is called the public house.[15]

This was Barry in one of his darker moods. But who is to say he was wrong?

Hospitality in the Home, an exhibition of contemporary furniture, was the joint effort of the Council of Industrial Design and the Tea Bureau. A distinctly middle-class affair, it put the emphasis on 'adaptability and the imaginative use of space and of furniture to create the right conditions for friendly entertaining'. The tour started with breakfast in the kitchen:

A colour scheme of lime yellow and bright green, with splashes of scarlet on the chair seats, and the hanging of pictures on the walls make this kitchen a pleasant place in which to start the day and very different from those modern kitchens which often resemble an operating theatre. Visitors, however, will soon see that 'fitness for purpose' has been the controlling factor in the choice of its furnishing and equipment: for example, the height of the table can be adjusted as required, the storing cupboards of aluminium have rubber sealed and dust-impervious drawers, and the laminated plastic tops of the low cupboards provide working surfaces which cannot be burned, scratched or stained.[16]

There followed lunch in the living room, a tea party in the nursery and high tea in the parlour ('Here, as elsewhere in the exhibition, potplants are used as an effective part of the decorative scheme'). Pride of place for the cocktail party was given to 'the sideboard, with a shallow wall unit, small table and a trolley with a lift-off tray for a selection of decanters, shakers and glasses'. The tour ended up in the bedroom, though there was no mention of the hospitality or entertaining that might take place there.

As unfashionable now as the suburban cocktail party are some of the suggested colour combinations. A living room with a 'bright blue carpet, a rich red wallpaper and printed fabrics of apricot and dark green' might be calculated to put diners off their food. But this was the fifties, when 'any colour as long as it's black or white' was a cardinal rule for most manufacturers and their paramount need was to brighten up their products.

Among Barry's favourite spinoffs from the South Bank were the 'book events', many organised by the National Book League with support from the Festival budget. Barry had great faith in the English language. He saw it as a powerful unifying force in his own country, and beyond its shores as a vehicle for moral improvement and for the transmission of peaceful democratic ideas.

Of the three major book exhibitions, two were north of the border in Glasgow and Edinburgh. The third was at the V&A, where 63,000 visitors turned up to view what Barry described as 'one of the most comprehensive collections of a nation's literature and learning ever gathered together in one room'. Over 800 books, themed chronologically, were on display:

The greatest single treasure was no doubt the tenth century 'Benedictional of St. Athelwold', an Anglo-Saxon masterpiece and one of the most exquisite (and best preserved) illuminated manuscripts in the world. (It was insured, they told me, for £50,000, but this was nominal.) But what out of these other priceless exhibits would be your fancy? Here was the first book ever to be printed in the English language ('The Recuyell of the Historyes of Troye': done by Caxton at Bruges before he set up his press in Westminster); here were a First Folio and a first edition of the Sonnets, a 'Gulliver' with corrections in Swift's own hand and the first draft of Gray's Elegy. Science, history, travel, poetry, sport, books for children: a manuscript version of 'The Three Bears', 1831 (a new discovery this, six years ahead of Southey and ending with the three bears tossing the old woman brusquely from the top of St. Paul's), the manuscript of 'The Wind in the Willows' — or the first issue (1874) of *Wisden*.[17]

Barry was particularly taken with the peepshow scenes from children's classics, which attracted a queue of adults in pursuit of lost innocence — 'grave old gentlemen creaking down on all fours to gaze through the peepholes made at a child's eye-height'.

But perhaps what drew me back most often were the numerous authors' manuscripts, with their sly hints of character: Dickens, fluent but crammed with second and third thoughts; trim, ornate Tennyson; Byron as untidy as you would expect; the over-neatness of Arnold Bennett; Eliot, flowing and scholarly; Siegfried Sassoon's curiously juvenile hand. Posterity, it would seem, has few more riches of this kind in store for it, authors nowadays composing direct on to the anonymous, or almost anonymous, typewriter. [What would Barry have made of the computer?][18]

Smaller exhibitions sponsored by professional bodies or local authorities risked being overshadowed by the South Bank. One of the most successful, starting as a joke, inspired a lengthy exchange of correspondence in *The Times* and after pulling in the crowds for four months embarked on a world tour.

The suggestion to stage an exhibition devoted entirely to Sherlock Holmes did not immediately appeal to the people's representatives of St Marylebone. They had in mind a more serious demonstration of the achievements of London's 'premier borough'; progress in slum clearance, for example. But when it became known that Marylebone's most famous, albeit fictional, son had been rejected as being unsuitable for a Festival icon, the press was quick to pick up on the story. Then a letter of outrage appeared in *The Times* above the signature of a certain Dr John H. Watson, 'late of the Indian Army'. A response was quickly forthcoming from a Mycroft Holmes, pointing out that Watson's military antecedents were questionable. In India he may have been, but only in his capacity as an officer in the British Army Medical Department, attached to the Northumberland Fusiliers, temporarily seconded to the Berkshires. There was also a letter from a Mrs Hudson, describing herself as a ratepayer, suggesting Madame Tussauds as the ideal venue for the exhibition. Stung into retaliation, a Professor Moriarty threatened to start throwing bombs if the Holmes exhibition took place.

The Council knew when to give in. The Abbey National Building Society, which occupied the premises closest to what might have been 221B Baker Street, gave over space for a reconstruction of Sherlock Holmes' sitting room as it would have been in 1898. Photographs, manuscripts and mementoes were loaned by devotees of the super-sleuth.

Sherlock Holmes proved to be a great crowd puller. The 50,000th visitor, the Very Reverend C.A. Rutherford, was presented with an inscribed copy of the Sherlock Holmes stories. When the exhibition closed in September it went on tour, along with a packet of Baker Street dust, starting in New York.

By contrast, the Exhibition of Exhibitions mounted by the Royal Society of Arts was a near disaster. Given the RSA's antecedents, the subject chose itself. It was here, in John Adam Street in 1760, that Britain's first art exhibition had been held. Among the participants, Joshua Reynolds showed his portrait of General Kingsley. But the star turn

was a Miss Moser, who carried off a first prize, along with
the Society's silver medal for flower paintings by candidates
under fifteen, 'as a further reward for her extraordinary
merit'. Needless to say, she was never heard of again. The
RSA struck gold as the initiator of the 1851 Exhibition
(originally planned for 1850 but, it should be noted, held
up by building delays). When Prince Albert caught on to the
idea, a triumph of nationalistic fervour was guaranteed.
Thereafter, the RSA did good work but had a tendency to
trade on past glories. Now, 1951 was a chance to restore the
sparkle with a reminder to the public of its central role in
putting the best of British on display.

Unfortunately, the Exhibition of Exhibitions was short
on anything visitors might want to look at. Many items
linked to past exhibitions had been lost in the Blitz. For
those that had survived, the Arts Council and others had
prior claim for Festival-linked events in the provinces. To
add to the RSA's woes, those who had exhibits to offer were
inclined to impose conditions. Thus the sales manager of
Thermos was prepared to loan 'brand vacuum jug model No
231Q', but made clear his irritation at the treatment
accorded his product at the earlier Britain Can Make It
exhibition, 'where the beauty and identity of this jug were
entirely lost'. It seemed that this innovative vessel was
'wired to the window pane of a hardware display in the
Street of Shop Windows and having no label of any kind
there was no indication that it was a vacuum vessel, still less
that it was of Thermos brand'. To prevent a recurrence of
such an egregious error, the RSA was required to give
prominent position to an 'ivorine stand label'.[19]

There was a more enthusiastic response from the Society
for Improving the Condition of the Labouring Classes (yes,

it was still operating in the 1950s!), which was only too happy to show a layout of the 'model dwellings' designed by Prince Albert a century before. It was not enough. The official opening by Princess Elizabeth attracted only mild interest, tinged with cynicism when she announced that the Albert Medal for 1951 had been awarded to her father. Paying visitors, of whom there were fewer than 4,000 against a projected 40,000 over five months, made unfavourable comparisons with the attractions of the South Bank, which was after all only a short walk from John Adam Street.

This was a view heard by many exhibition organisers who over-estimated the novelty value of what they had to offer. A history of the South Bank, cobbled together by the LCC for display in the foyer of the Royal Festival Hall, achieved an average daily attendance of just forty-six.[20]

Let Barry have the last word. He was in lyrical mood when he attended the opening of St Paul's Garden, rescued from the ruins of war surrounding the cathedral. Eleven years earlier he had stood on a City roof 'watching the flames circle the Cathedral and listening to their roar'. With him was his young stepson, Richard, who was to become the modernist architect Barry would have liked to have been. 'Remember this,' Barry had said. 'You will never see anything like it ever again.'[21] Richard took him to mean that they would never see St Paul's again.

It had been a struggle to get the garden ready in time. Persistent rain had held up planting and bulbs had rotted in the ground. 'But no matter how it looked today it would glow through many summers to come, the grass would be green, the fountains would cool the languors of clerk and typist during those parched interludes which in our paradoxical climate are never far separated from flood.'[22]

Listening to the brief speeches (it was raining on the morning of the opening), Barry thought how wonderful it would be if there was a pedestrian bridge from the south side of the Thames leading directly to St Paul's. Might not the Festival help to realise the vision? It would have been small comfort for him to know that it would take another half century and another celebration with another dome for his hopes to be realised.

# CHAPTER ELEVEN

What is art? In any other European country, the question would have sounded faintly ridiculous. But in Britain of the 1950s, even a broad definition was elusive. The popular reaction against anything new was shared by many of the cultural elite (one reason why European artists of the inter-war years are so poorly represented in British collections) and extended from the fine arts to music, literature, drama and film, though some even disputed that film deserved consideration as an art at all.

The Festival was committed to promoting British culture and the fledgling Arts Council was on hand to keep the dominant group of architects and designers up to the mark. But with notable exceptions, inspiration was lacking. When Hugh Casson asked for ideas for reconciling art and architecture to make a satisfying whole, his design team was unable to think beyond the obvious names – Henry Moore, Jacob Epstein, Graham Sutherland, Barbara Hepworth, John Piper. These and other leading British exhibitors on the international circuit were duly invited to make their mark on the Festival, but in a manner that kept them at arm's length from the decisions that were crucial to a coherent display:

The commissioning procedure was simple. Once the artist was agreed the papers would drop into the gearbox of the Contracts Department and the artist would emerge with his brief — always in two parts: first the production of sketch or maquette (at which point, if necessary, relations could be broken off on payment of an appropriate fee), and then the completion and delivery of the work.[1]

Lacking firm guidance, artists felt free to give their own interpretation of what the Festival was all about and then were surprised when the reception of their work was less than wholehearted. Epstein was particularly incensed:

I conceived the idea of making a figure that should embody youthful courage and resolution, and the result was the over life-sized bronze entitled 'Youth Advancing'. The figure was gilded and placed looking over a sheet of water. I worked very strenuously and earnestly on this work giving up several portrait commissions to execute it on time. Imagine my surprise, to put it mildly, to receive with the compliments of the organizers of the exhibition a review referring to it as a mere 'pot boiler'.[2]

Sadly, the critics were right. Epstein's *Youth Advancing* was a cliché in bronze made more conspicuous by the absence of any relationship with its surroundings. It has to be said that Epstein was not easy to manage. Nor, indeed, was Moore:

Barry called a special meeting at Savoy Court, so that

Epstein and Moore could select sites for their sculptures. Both grand chaps, but agree sites together? They were as compatible as oil and water. After the purpose of the meeting was explained there was rather an uncomfortable pause until Moore, in his down-to-earth way, suggested we have separate sessions. Moore and I went down to the Savoy Brasserie, where he bent over a plan held flat by pepper pots on the marble-topped table, and cogitated over direction of light, the viewer's eye level, type of background, and height of the plinth, while I sipped coffee. One of my dreams, working while relaxing at a café table, French style, and here I was at last. Returning to the conference room, we discovered that Epstein had been less fussy. He did not care where his piece was placed, so long as it was 'here', pressing his thumb on the centre of the concourse, the site reserved for the Skylon.[3]

Contributions by other well-known sculptors, notably Lynn Chadwick's hanging mobile in metal and canvas, Reg Butler's abstract in wrought iron, Hepworth's *Contrapuntal Forms* and Frank Dobson's *London Pride*, the latter now back on the Festival site as an eye-catching feature of the Thames walkway, were well received but failed to make the impact they deserved. Misha Black put it down to an '*embarras de richesse*': 'When there was so much to see and experience, when the Skylon soared to the sky and the Dome of Discovery spanned the days of the year, it is not surprising that a carved block of stone only eight feet high [fashioned by Henry Moore] should seem, to most, of little importance.'[4]

But this was to hit the point without noticing it. The Skylon and the Dome were themselves works of art which commanded attention for their innovative force. They, above all other Festival creations, measured up to Barry's highest aspiration, to make art, engineering and architecture as one.[5] When visitors saw the Skylon and the Dome they had a glimpse of the future. When they chanced upon Moore, Hepworth or Epstein, they were more likely to recall long-past battles for attention and recognition.

A reminder of the controversy once engendered by the now famous sculptors was provided by the *Sunday Pictorial*, which alleged that Mitzi Cunliffe's group of statuary, representing the Origins of the Land and the People, was obscene. Taking fright at the prospect of an erotic infusion into his family show, Herbert Morrison sent Barry post haste to Manchester to inspect the work in progress. Asked what he was supposed to be looking for, Morrison solemnly voiced his conviction that the Festival had inadvertently commissioned a study in sodomy. Barry recalled:

I examined it *very* carefully, from every angle, and with the dirtiest mind I could summon. I don't *like* it enormously, but it has some strength and a quiet grace (especially the two heads and necks from the back view). But by no stretch of the vilest imagination could it be called salacious. (Incidentally the axes of the two bodies are so divergent that any malpractice would be anatomically impossible.) I should think he [Morrison] would hate it as a work of art (and a lot else on the S. Bank!) but anyhow we shall see. I've told her to go right ahead and get the piece to London as soon as a place is ready for it. Then I'll invite Morrison to see it – and if he still thinks it objectionable his blood must be on his own head.[6]

Morrison's aversion to anything too far out of the ordinary undoubtedly had an inhibiting effect. 'Better safe than sorry' was the guiding principle for art arrangers. Of the eleven exhibitions mounted by the Arts Council, pole position was given to Henry Moore's retrospective at the Tate Gallery. In the publicity stakes, the Open Air Exhibition of International Sculpture in Battersea Park, though containing little that was startling, except perhaps to the untutored who thought it was part of the fun fair, took second place to Hogarth (also at the Tate), Victorian Photography at the V&A, Traditional Colonial Art at the Imperial Institute and Historic Plate of the City of London at the Goldsmiths' Hall.

If sculptors, particularly young sculptors, felt sidelined, painters had even greater cause for complaint. Their chief showcase, British Contemporary Painting 1925–50, highlighted the earlier years specified in its title, which were hardly contemporary. Moreover, the Arts Council's New Burlington Galleries proved to be too small to take all the pictures, with the result that the exhibition was split with the Whitechapel Gallery. There, the architectural watercolourist Barbara Jones, examples of whose work ranged across the South Bank from the seaside section to the Lion and Unicorn, produced a mixed bag of tricks called *Black Eyes and Lemonade*, a quote from the Irish poet Thomas Moore:

> A Persian's heaven is easily made:
> 'Tis but black eyes and lemonade.

Though doubtless some of the iconoclastic painters felt more at home at the Whitechapel than in the New Burlington Galleries, which favoured the more traditional artists, they were at risk of sinking in a mishmash of popular culture:

Things currently on sale in the shops and posters on the hoardings, plaster and plastic ornaments and a fine 1951 fireplace in the shape of an Airedale dog were all displayed as works of art. People began to realize that indeed they were. Visitors were eased into the idea by a row of ships' figure-heads and cases of other acceptable art-objects, and were brought gradually to accept comic postcards and beer labels. All through the exhibition the new and commonplace were seen near the old and safe, and by the end most people felt able to accept a talking lemon extolling Idris lemon squash and Bassetts Liquorice Allsorts isolated under a spot light. A few adjustments had to be made; we had borrowed two waxworks from Madame Tussauds – Queen Anne for general appeal and the beloved late Chief Rabbi for Whitechapel. The first local visitors were delighted to see him, but later the Synagogue felt that he was too near the talking lemon for dignity. So we swapped the waxworks round, though the visual balance was destroyed, and Queen Anne stood nearer to the lemon.[7]

Directors of the central London galleries were invited but none showed up. Whitechapel was too far off the beaten track, while the paintings were too far off the mainstream. The best chance for newcomers to be noticed was provided by the Arts Council exhibition of *Sixty Paintings*. The idea was to encourage artists to undertake larger-scale works, which, given the post-war shortage of materials and of wealthy patrons, had gone out of fashion. The minimum size for a picture was set at 45 inches by 60. This brief had the added advantage for the Arts Council of relieving it of the responsibility of picking names out of a hat. The few artists who were comfortable with the grand scale chose themselves.

In the event, fewer than sixty were prepared to take up the challenge, almost certainly because it came with the smallest possible financial incentive. If some of the sculptors felt hard done by (their fees were in the £350 to £400 bracket[8]), the painters had to make do with a free canvas and the promise that they would be part of a selling exhibition visiting twelve cities. The Arts Council was committed to buying five of the pictures.

Some outstanding work was produced, notably Lucien Freud's *Interior Near Paddington*, a disturbing image of a bespectacled man in a raincoat (a child molester?) beside an ominously large potted plant. Others tried hard to capture what they assumed to be the Festival spirit with depictions of old favourites such as the Cornish landscape and hop picking in Kent. The award of £500 to William Gear, one of the few abstract painters exhibited, caused such an uproar as to provoke questions in Parliament.

The murals on the South Bank, art at its most visible, also tended towards the familiar. Big hitters like Ben Nicholson and Graham Sutherland were seen in juxtaposition with beginners such as Geoffrey Clark, who was still a student at the Royal College of Art when he designed a screen in coloured glass and cast iron for the Transport Pavilion.

Sutherland gathered plaudits for his huge mural for the Land of Britain Pavilion, but most praised was Victor Pasmore's ceramic abstract on the east wall of the Regatta Restaurant, otherwise more noted for the spectacular views across the Thames than for the quality of food served within. Pasmore was determined to try something different:

> Of the various ways of extending architecture by the addition of painting and sculpture two stand out: one is to reinforce it harmonically by repeating its forms; the other is to transform it optically by means of contrast. I decided on the latter course . . . a complementary image sufficiently dynamic to change the architecture. So, with the idea of 'exploding' the Regatta Restaurant, I painted a full-size maquette on the floor of the gymnasium at the Central School of Art.
>
> The architects gave me full support in this venture even to the extent of granting my request not to have the tiles 'pointed', a decision which greatly distressed the tile craftsmen. But I had to explain that we were not tiling a swimming pool, but constructing a jazz painting, so the more uneven the tile grid the more movement we would get in the painting. Nevertheless the process of having the design copied on to tiles for firing in ceramic also proved inhibiting as it had to be done only in small sections in a tiny workroom. As a result neither I nor my assistants could ever see what we were doing. When finally they did arrange the complete work on the ground I wanted to rearrange the painted tiles in new and

independent positions; but this proved to be too costly an operation.[9]

The up-market Regatta Restaurant, designed by Misha Black, had another artistic distinction in that it launched the Festival Pattern Group. This was the creation of the Council of Industrial Design, or rather of its chief industrial officer, Mark Hartland Thomas, who was persuaded that crystal structure diagrams, the epitome of modern science, could inspire original and exciting motifs for textiles, cutlery, pottery and other household items. He was to be disappointed. While twenty-eight manufacturers joined the project, contributing furnishings and tableware and a dash of colour to the restaurant, the designs proved to be too fussy and intricate for popular consumption.

With so much to catch the eye on the South Bank, a work of art needed to be itself a spectacle to command attention. Richard Huws got it right with his *Water Sculpture*, which was kept in perpetual motion by a succession of buckets filling, tipping and emptying into each other. Mesmerised onlookers would not be moved on until they had seen the full cycle.

A spectacle of another sort was provided by a small boy who caught his head under one of the legs of Moore's *Reclining Figure*. Pushing and pulling were to no avail until someone applied liberal quantities of soap. According to Barry, the boy 'was finally liberated by his whole body being lifted into horizontal position and slid out like a missile from the breach of a gun'.[10] His mother reported that her son's neck had never been so clean.

If, in Festival terms, the visual arts came in on the coattails of architecture and design, there was at least a suggestion of change, of the new nudging up against the traditional. This was one up on literature or drama, which seemed caught in a time warp, the favoured practitioners totally innocent of the impending revolution that would turn icons into has-beens.

Literary fiction was least well served by the Festival. Despite Barry's advocacy of the English language as a force for good, there was no programme for writers. Perhaps this was just as well given the myopia of the grand old men of letters who sneered at Festival pretensions. Leading the pack was Evelyn Waugh, who used his epilogue to *Unconditional Surrender* to take an undeserved and unprovoked swipe at modern times:

> In 1951, to celebrate the opening of a happier decade, the Government decreed a festival. Monstrous constructions appeared on the south bank of the Thames, the foundation stone was solemnly laid for a National Theatre, but there was little popular exuberance among the straitened people, and dollar bearing tourists curtailed their visits and sped to countries of the continent, where, however precarious their position, they ordered things better.

Even further from the right came a blast from the artist, author and one-time fascist sympathiser Wyndham Lewis, whose advanced sense of his own social and intellectual superiority put him in the front line of festiphobics. In the foreword to his novel *Rotting Hill*, he raged against the Festival as a product of socialist machinations:

In 1945 we ended a second, a six-year spell of war. We came out of this a ruined society, our economy destroyed, our riches vanished, our empire reduced to a shadow of itself, but our island-population (optimistically built-up to the absurd total of fifty millions) undiminished and requiring just as much food as when we had the money to pay for it. Naturally everybody was dazed. But into this situation burst a handful of jubilant socialists, voted into power, with an overwhelming majority, on the Labour ticket. They were in no way dismayed by the national situation; they proceeded to extract by huge taxation, direct and indirect, the colossal capital needed to stage a honeymoon for the liberated manual-working mass. This of course gave no one any time to despair at the disappearance of national prosperity. The majority of the nation was highly stimulated: and if the landed society was taxed out of existence, the middle class in rapid dissolution, on the whole England became a brighter rather than a darker place. To symbolize this extraordinary paradox the capital city burst into festivities all along the south bank of the Thames; there was whoopee at Battersea, there was the thunder of orchestras in a new national concert-hall, a thousand peep-shows, culminating in a Dome of Discovery lower down the river. This was staged in the ward sanctified by Shakespeare. In the Parliament the lamb lay down with the lion; the Tory bleated softly and snoozed beside the rampant socialist lion: all England seemed to have decided to forget that it had lost everything, and to live philosophically from day to day upon the Dole provided by the United States.

A kinder reception could be expected from J.B. Priestley, whose wartime broadcasts had made him a man of the people, a kindly pipe-puffing uncle who knew what was best for us. For Priestley, the Festival did not go far enough: at the inaugural concert at the Festival Hall he had complained of 'the homely and rather melancholy smell of moth balls'.[11] Yet his own contribution, *Festival at Farbridge*, described by him as a comic novel, was rooted in a familiar north country urban setting with a cast of stock characters.

Heading the campaign to persuade an introverted provincial town to stage its own festival are three outsiders (shades of *An Inspector Calls*) who expose the prejudices and hypocrisies of mean-spirited citizens. There is Commodore Tribe, a cheerful conman with a heart of gold, Laura Lacy, a sturdy young independent who organises everyone and Theodore Jenks, the man she loves, who happens to be passing through Farbridge and stays because he likes the place, a mystery that is never adequately explained.

Priestley's scatter-gun satire takes in a visit to Farbridge of the BBC *Any Questions* team with its resident rustic who talks gibberish with a Dorset accent, and a session of the local communist cell, represented by a railway clerk given to Marxist clichés, an angry teacher and a prim, intellectual typist. What Priestley was attempting was to show that Britain needed to wake up and gather its energy. The Festival message comes over in a conversation led by Mr Jordan, a retired wealthy businessman:

'One reason why I want a Festival. Give people a jerk — start them enjoying life. Too worried, most of them. Or half asleep. Most of the girls in shops now are half asleep.'

'Yes, they are,' said Laura. 'I've noticed that. They haven't any interest in serving you, so they're making it drearier and drearier for themselves. Is that politics? Some people seem to think it is.'

'I don't think it is,' said Theodore.

'Of course it isn't,' cried Mr Jordan. 'Nothing to do with government. Psychological. Drift of the times. Bad influence of the press too. Hate the press. Wrong values all the time. Glorifying rubbish.'

The only other novel that connected to the Festival was John Moore's *Dance and Skylark*, which in style and theme, with its gentle ribbing of small-town committees, was Priestley all over again.

In similarly indulgent vein, the humorist Stephen Potter (book critic of the *News Chronicle* under Barry) drew on the Festival to apply his science of One-Upmanship ('How to make the other man feel that something has gone wrong, however slightly') to exhibitions in general. 'Exhibitionship,' he declared, 'is the name for various ploys and gambits connected with the art of being, or seeming to be, a visitor to an exhibition.' This had to be distinguished from the art of exhibiting, which Potter called 'Barryship'. The basic rule of Exhibitionship was to stand out from the crowd:

For instance, if the notice says 'TURN LEFT' instantly turn right. Do not trudge round in a crocodile. If there

is an injunction to keep moving, stand stock still, eyes
fixed on the ceiling.

Again, to suggest that you have the artistically
awakened eye and can form your own opinion in
perfect independence of the kind of judgement which
the lay-out and emphasis of the exhibition seem to
demand, pause a long time before some object which
has nothing to do with the exhibits — say a fire
extinguisher or a grating in the floor through which
warmed-up museum air rises — and say, 'The
influence of William Morris, even here', or just, 'Now
*that*, to me, is a beautiful object.'

The best way to praise the exhibition is to say, 'It's
a great jaunt, a delightful affair and a huge success.
Exhibitions always are a huge success.'

You can then criticize.

After showing that you yourself are a jolly and
exhibition-minded person, and have enjoyed, in
the old days at the White City, the model of the
Astronomer Royal in margarine, you can then be
generally nasty by complaining that this particular
show lacks the indefinable something, the gaiety
perhaps, of the Petit Palais Exhibition at Varence in
1931 (designed by Pompipier), or the feeling for
Internationalism which one got frightfully from that
wonderful Füldenbliegen Collection in the Rond Tor
at Uppsala.[12]

If the Festival left authors to their own devices, there was
more direct encouragement to poets with £1,100 in prize
money offered for the best of what turned out to be a
disappointing crop. In his introduction to a collection of

the prize-winning efforts, published as *Poems 1951*, John
Hayward declared the vast majority of entries to be
extremely bad. 'It was disturbing to find such widespread
ignorance of the nature of poetry and such technical
incompetence.'[13]

Though drama qualified for a relatively generous
handout, most of it went on popular revivals. The pride was
in great acting, preferably with a touch of novelty, as at St
James's Theatre where Laurence Olivier and Vivien Leigh
performed in the London run of Shaw's *Caesar and
Cleopatra* and Shakespeare's *Antony and Cleopatra*. Alec
Guinness played and lost as Hamlet in modern dress, John
Gielgud brought *The Winter's Tale* to the Phoenix, and if that
was not enough Shakespeare, *A Midsummer Night's Dream*
was on at the open-air theatre in Regent's Park. The Old Vic
had seven classics in repertory, three of which were
Shakespeare's.

Young directors were in evidence – Michael Benthall,
Peter Brook and Frank Hauser among them. But of young
dramatists there was scarcely a sign. In retrospect the most
promising was John Whiting, who won the Arts Council
competition 'for a new play of contemporary significance'
with *Saint's Day*. Along with two other entries, *Poor Judas* by
Enid Bagnold and *Right Side Up* by C.E. Webber, *Saint's Day*
was presented for three weeks at the Arts Theatre.

The critics hated it. Iain Hamilton in *The Spectator*
dismissed the production as 'beyond description, far less
analysis', while *The Times* found it 'of a badness that must be
called indescribable . . . fantasy plunging portentously in a
sea so dark and wide and stormy that the shores of reality
are rarely glimpsed'. And so it went. The kindest reviews
were from those like Alan Dent of the *News Chronicle*, who

found this 'strange, mad, baffling little play . . . too startling to be tedious, too scatterbrained to be a bore'.[14]

The play was indeed unusual and complex, a thousand miles away from the drawing-room drama so beloved by West End producers and, it must be said, by their audiences. *Saint's Day* is set in the dilapidated house of Paul Southman, an equally dilapidated poet-pamphleteer who is surrounded by oddballs including Stella, his pregnant granddaughter, her husband Charles, twelve years her junior, and a mysterious servant, John Winter. They are expecting a guest, Robert Procathren, a representative of the literary elite. News from the village is of three soldiers who have escaped from a detention camp and are now marauding and looting. A pistol is produced. The nervous and reserved Procathren is persuaded to aid in the defence of the house. The gun goes off accidentally and Stella is killed. Thereafter chaos reigns until the village is burned. Procathren returns to the house with the soldiers, who are ordered to take out Charles and Paul and hang them. Charles has spent his last hours completing a mural using the dead Stella as a model.

Audiences were not sure whether to laugh or scream. The all-pervading menace, the violence, though off-stage, and the passive acceptance of death was disturbing to a public used to plays with a beginning, a middle and a happy ending (unless, of course, it was Shakespeare).

There were those who recognised in Whiting a dramatist who would change the very nature of theatre. George Devine, who within five years was to lead a stage revolution at the Royal Court, was strong in his defence, while for the twenty-year-old Peter Hall, *Saint's Day* was 'the first truly *modern* play I had seen in my life'. Hall went on, 'Looking back now [this was in 1979] Whiting was a passionate and ironic evangelist, preparing the way for Beckett, for Pinter, for Arden and for Bond.'[15]

Depressed by the reception to *Saint's Day*, Whiting came to rely on the movies for a regular income, accepting commissions as they came along and turning out a succession of competent scripts, most of which never made it to the screen. One of his best efforts, still worth viewing, was *The Ship that Died of Shame*, where he was so far down the production pecking order that they misspelt his name as Whitting on the publicity posters. He produced at least three more plays of durable quality – *The Devils*, *A Penny For a Song* and *Marching Song* – before dying of cancer at forty-five.

Among the commercial plays loosely associated with the Festival were a dull Priestley (*The Golden Door*) and a lightweight Peter Ustinov (*The Love of Four Colonels*). Apart from *Saint's Day*, the only new play to aim for the intellect was a verse drama by Christopher Fry called *A Sleep of Prisoners*. Commissioned by the Religious Drama Society, the storyline was suitably biblical. Four captives of war are locked in a church. Each has a dream which he plays out as a modern variation on an Old Testament story: David and Goliath, Cain's murder of Abel, Adam hearing the voice of God, and Abraham and Isaac. The underlying message is that Everyman is responsible to himself for the way the world goes, and it is only through the assumption of responsibility that mankind will find peace.

Said by Fry to be 'the production with which I have been most completely happy',[16] *A Sleep of Prisoners* has not endured, being too worthy and platitudinous for modern audiences. But at the time verse drama was in fashion and

Fry, along with T.S. Eliot, was seen as a leading exponent. The play had an added distinction. Not only set in a church, it was actually played in churches, starting in St Thomas's just off Regent Street. As a theatrical venue it was difficult to think of anywhere less likely to attract an audience. Tucked away behind the shops, it was not the easiest venue to find. But thanks to the originality of the idea, at a time when churches were rarely used for commercial performances, and the interest in seeing how Fry met the challenge, the pews were filled. Ronald Searle drew haunting skeletal figures for the programme cover. No drinks or ice-cream were served: such frivolities would have disturbed the mood of the play. Applause was not invited. At the end, the audience sat in silent approval. The cast was led by Denholm Elliott, who was to become one of Britain's finest character actors on stage and screen but was then billed even more grandly as the natural heir to Gielgud.

Opposition to the Festival surfaced in *The Lyric Review*, for which Noël Coward, who thought the South Bank and Battersea both in frightfully bad taste, had four members of the cast under umbrellas singing a number called 'Don't Make Fun of the Fair':

> Take a nip from your brandy flask,
> Scream and caper and shout,
> Don't give anyone time to ask
> What the Hell it's all about.

One theatrical event prompted by the Festival was welcomed with great ceremony and then laid to rest for 25 years. The campaign to build a national theatre had its origin in the mid-nineteenth century, when melodrama and burlesque threatened to overwhelm serious drama. Over the next century, like a slow-burning fire, the arguments in favour flared up occasionally, only to be smothered by a fresh load of objections. Then, in 1948, the London County Council proposed a national theatre on the South Bank. Three years later, midway through the Festival, Queen Elizabeth (soon to be the Queen Mother) unveiled a foundation stone close to the Festival Hall. Dame Sybil Thorndike, one of the grand dames of the theatre, spoke an ode composed by the Poet Laureate, John Masefield. It began:

> Here we lay stone, that, at a future time,
> May bear a House, wherein, in days to be,
> Tier above tier, delighted crowds may see
> Men's passions made a play thing, and sublime.

Bouquets of flowers and herbs mentioned in Shakespeare's plays were exchanged and the Queen declared her belief 'that the stage can express with its truth, enrich with its laughter and adorn with its poetry, and pageantry, the life of the nation'.

Doubtless inspired by the royal tribute, theatrical managers and producers were quick to offer their services in helping to create this living monument to the performing arts. Among those who wrote to the Clerk of the LCC was C.A. Crathorn, who, describing himself as a pioneer of the Odeon theatres and one-time manager of Erdington Amusements, invited particular attention to his experience, along with that of his wife, in leading Olde Tyme dancing demonstrations. His letter ended with a flourish.

'With modesty, I claim to possess an UNRIVALLED record in the entertainment world.'

In the margin is a scribbled addendum from the Clerk. 'Whatever would he claim if he weren't modest.'[17]

Mr Crathorn was premature with his application. Ten years after the foundation stone was laid there was still not enough money to start building a theatre. While negotiations with the government and the LCC continued fitfully, a National Theatre Company was based at the Old Vic. It was to remain there until 1976 when the Olivier, the first of the three auditoria at what is now the National, opened with a production of *Hamlet*.

Like literature and drama, Festival music was predominantly conservative; the classics taking pride of place in concerts across the country. Benjamin Britten was one of six composers commissioned by the Arts Council to write or complete opera scores, but *Billy Budd* was a long time coming and was not given its first public airing until the Festival was over. This left the field clear to Ralph Vaughan Williams, whose *Pilgrim's Progress* preceded the Festival by a week. New choral and orchestral works, also sponsored by the Arts Council, failed to make their mark, or perhaps they were simply overshadowed by the single biggest, most newsworthy musical event of the year – the opening of the Festival Hall.

The first major public building to be completed in London since the end of the war, and a welcome successor to the Queen's Hall which had been destroyed in the Blitz, the Festival Hall was a notorious bone of contention between the kings of the podium. Sir Malcolm Sargent, Chief Conductor of the BBC Symphony Orchestra and already the star turn of the Last Night of the Proms, was all in favour of it, creating in his mind's eye a people's palace for music on the South Bank. As early as October 1948 he was lobbying the LCC for a leading role in attracting audiences. 'I am deeply interested in music for the people and spend most of my time thinking about it.' He went on to say that he was eager to get the organising committee 'cut and dried' before 'the vultures assemble to devour it'.[18]

One of the spoilers he may well have had in mind was Sir Thomas Beecham, who was already miffed at being sidelined over the reopening of Covent Garden. Having called on the government to build a new concert hall he was then, as he saw it, studiously ignored as the plans evolved. His temper boiled over. The façade of the Festival Hall was 'repellent', a 'Zeppelin on stilts' which would not look out of place among 'the gas holders of Beckton or the factories that line the Great West Road'.[19]

Beecham was further incensed when he was passed over as principal conductor for the Festival Hall's inaugural concert. The prize went to Arturo Toscanini. 'I am not, nor ever have been opposed to the appearance of eminent foreigners in this country,' he told the *Daily Telegraph*, 'but I do hold the unshakeable opinion that an event such as the opening week of this new hall should be dominated by native art and artists.'[20]

Which is what happened, but not in a way that pacified Beecham. When Toscanini withdrew after suffering a minor stroke, insult was added to Beecham's injury when Malcolm Sargent stepped forward.

Those outside the circle of musical prima donnas found it hard to understand what the fuss was about. For Barry, the Festival Hall was all that he desired in a cultural flagship. Completed well on time, it was of distinctively modern design, there were clear sightlines to the stage from every part of the 3,000-capacity auditorium and though the acoustics were not as good as first claimed, they were a lot better than at the Albert Hall – the only venue, as Beecham observed, where a conductor could hear his performance twice in the same evening. Best of all, the auditorium, suspended within an outer shell of dressing rooms, offices and restaurant, was totally soundproof, a vital consideration with a busy commuter railway passing close by.

The Festival Hall's opening concert was Sargent's triumph. The high points were 'Land of Hope and Glory', 'Jerusalem' and Sargent's own boisterous version of Thomas Arne's 'Rule Britannia' for soloist, chorus, state trumpeters and full orchestra. 'It was a rendering more notable for its athleticism than its musicianship,' wrote Barry, 'though no doubt the latter was irreproachable. Altering the normal rhythm of the familiar music to give it a more compelling swing, orchestra and choir brought the audience to a fine pitch of patriotic emotion which demanded and received a full encore.'[21] King George VI led the audience in a standing ovation.[22] When it was Sir Adrian Boult's turn to wave the baton he had to wait with increasing impatience while the ovation for his colleague rolled on. At the reception afterwards, the King told Sargent that 'Rule Britannia' should be played at every concert. Sargent pointed out that it might not always be appropriate. 'In that case,' declared the King, 'I won't be there.'[23] Beecham was eventually converted to the Festival Hall. He went on to conduct there on no fewer than ninety-three occasions.[24]

And then there was film. In the time it took to complete the groundwork for the Festival the British movie industry had peaked at its best year ever before tipping over into a long decline. The war had brought out the best in film-makers who had responded to the public demand for stories that were at once stimulating, inspiring and entertaining. The momentum was kept up after 1945, with Carol Reed, David Lean, Michael Powell, Robert Hamer and Alexander Mackendrick exercising their world-class talents to create what are now accepted as screen classics – *The Third Man*, *Brief Encounter*, *Kind Hearts and Coronets*, *Fallen Idol* and *Great Expectations* among many other box-office successes. And, for once, with that unlikely movie magnate J. Arthur Rank devoting his fortune from corn milling to build a production base the equal of any American rival, money was no object. Weekly cinema attendances were close to or even exceeded 35 million.

But a reaction set in. Instead of supporting Rank in his efforts to break into the American market and thus become a dollar earner, the government, in the person of Harold Wilson, eager to exercise his propensity for interfering in matters of which he knew nothing ('a bit pompous for a man in his thirties,' noted Barry[25]), decided to save precious dollars from leaving the country by imposing a 75 per cent levy on foreign movies shown in British cinemas. Rank, who by now was financing half of Britain's film output, was not consulted. Much to his fury, he had to give up on his hopes for a favourable distribution deal in the USA.

An even more inept government attempt to control the industry started with a quota system for movie imports. Set at 45 per cent in October 1948, this arbitrary figure produced a rash of complaints from cinema owners who were short on new features to fill their programmes. The quota was dropped to 40 per cent and then, in 1950, to 30 per cent.

The impact was traumatic. Pressure to turn out 'quota quickies', all best forgotten, weighed down on quality and innovation. The Ealing comedies have rightly secured a place in cinema history but the plots were soft and undemanding, projecting a society addicted to cosy incompetence, certainly not an image the government favoured. The problems of holding on to standards and to audience loyalty were made all the greater by a wobbly financial structure (Rank was understandably having second thoughts on how to spend his money) and by an increasingly sophisticated output from Hollywood with movies that had universal appeal. By 1949, cinema attendance was in freefall, seventeen British studios were idle or had been sold off and a third of the membership of the film technicians' union was unemployed. British film-making, declared the *New Statesman*, was 'facing disaster'.

This, then, was the sorry state of the industry when the recently created British Film Institute (BFI), led by Denis Forman, the future head of Granada Television, was charged with putting together a mini-festival of screen entertainments including a contribution from the new, up-and-coming medium of television. To add to Forman's difficulties, after two years at the BFI helm he was still trying to match the authority and prestige of the Arts Council:

I found the Film Institute to be not only dim but sleazy. The outgoing Director, Oliver Bell, was also the Chairman of the Magistrates Association, and although reputed to be the scourge of petty criminals he was certainly pretty lenient with himself. He and other senior staff, including the Secretary (who was said to have appeared in jackboots and a Nazi armband until the outbreak of war made this unwise), spent a great deal of the day in Soho drinking clubs and seemed to regard bogus expense claims as a simple and perfectly acceptable way of augmenting their incomes. The rest of the staff were rarely to be seen at their desks but were 'viewing films' or 'visiting schools'.[26]

Forman had recruited young and talented staff to revitalise the Institute's journal, *Sight and Sound*, and to counter 'the smug suburban self-satisfaction of the British cinema',[27] but while the BFI manifesto won applause, producers were slow to catch on.

Jack Ralph, late of the National Film Board of Canada, famed for animation, was brought in to give substance to the vague aspirations of the Festival organisers. A committee of movie luminaries, including producer Michael Balcon and directors Anthony Asquith and John Grierson, was set up to support his efforts. The task of creating a Telecinema, or Telekinema (there was some confusion as to what to call it), went to W. Wells Coates, architect of the Lawn Road Flats in Hampstead. It was to be the first theatre in the world 'in which big screen television, three dimensional pictures and stereophonic sound can take place on an equal footing'.[28]

Though recognised as a major talent and strongly supportive of Festival ideals, Wells Coates was a troubled soul who could be difficult to work with. This is maybe why he was sidelined to one of the less prestigious buildings, tucked away as it was next to the railway arches between the Festival Hall and Waterloo Station. The finished product was a grey, oblong concrete structure, far removed in style from the traditional flamboyant high street cinemas but, in consequence, lacking warmth or any expectation of excitement within.

For those who persevered there was a surprise in store, for the interior of the Telekinema was highly innovative. The foyer doubled as a projection room and television studio with the cameras and other equipment behind glass. For most visitors this alone was worth the price of admission, since it was the first time they had seen, as it were, behind the screen. Few, indeed, had ever seen a television set. For the auditorium Wells Coates did away with the proscenium arch familiar to cinema- and theatre-goers in favour of a perforated frame, much like the frame of a painting, which splayed out from the screen. To give all-round comfortable viewing, instead of a continuous downward rake from rear to front, the seats closest to the screen were on a rising slope.

What to show proved more of a challenge than how to show it. As the Festival buildings began to take shape there were press reports of frenetic studio activity. Carol Reed, consistently the best director then working in Britain, was said to be busily reading scripts, Frank Launder was slated for a movie centred on the 1851 Exhibition and at Elstree Studios there was talk of an adaptation of Thomas Hardy's *The Mayor of Casterbridge*. Doubtless the latter was in itself a worthy project, but a few eyebrows must have been raised when it was announced that Richard Todd, a popular actor of limited range who was always more comfortable playing military roles and who was soon to achieve renown for his leading role in *The Dam Busters*, was to star as the mayor.

None of these projects materialised. Instead, audiences

were rewarded with *The Magic Box*, a joint effort by various members of the British film industry to prove that it was still in the major league. As a movie of all the talents it only went to prove the old adage about too many cooks.

The problems started with a weak story, a hagiography of William Friese-Greene, an early dabbler in cinematography who failed to realise his ambition to project colour on to the screen. To suggest that he should rank with other pioneers of moving pictures was a nonsense that even such talents as Eric Ambler, who wrote the screenplay, and John Boulting as director, could not disguise. After 'Britain Can Take It' (the wartime slogan) and Britain Can Make It, this movie was more like *Britain Can Fake It*.

The challenge of producing a dramatic structure for a story that was essentially one of failure (Friese-Greene died unacknowledged and in poverty) was made all the greater by the decision, seen as a good promotional idea at the time, to provide walk-on parts for every British working actor whose name had ever appeared above the credits, and for a good few more besides. In its early screenings, the plot of *The Magic Box* was sacrificed to audience participation in often voluble competition to identify the stars under their makeup. Seen today, the movie is more a demonstration of fleeting fame. Apart from Laurence Olivier as a policeman and Richard Attenborough as Friese-Greene's assistant it is hard for anyone but a devoted movie buff to put a name to the players, who have mostly descended into the movie graveyard of daytime TV. Robert Donat, one of the few British film names known in Hollywood, fought debilitating illness to portray Friese-Greene in a reprise of his soft-centred performance in the title role of *Goodbye Mr Chips*.

*The Magic Box* was late in arrival; its premiere was held as the Festival was closing. The critics damned with faint praise and the movie duly bombed. With commendable restraint, Richard Attenborough has classified the movie as 'not one of John Boulting's finer directorial achievements'.[29]

The documentary, soon to switch from cinema to television, fared better than drama, at least in terms of productivity. With modest financial support from the BFI, commercially sponsored production units offered their largely elegiac interpretation of what it meant to be British with movies such as *Air Parade*, a patriotic depiction of aviation history, and *Waters of Time*, a conducted tour of the Port of London.

*Waters of Time* was judged to be the best of the documentaries. As related by the film critic C.A. Lejeune,

It describes the progress up-stream from the Nore of the cargo steamer *Highland Princess*, shows how she noses her blunt way into the narrows at Gallions Reach; how the little river tugs take charge, and push and pull and nudge her into dock; how the wide river becomes a busy, land-locked water-way; how the ship is unloaded and re-loaded and turned round; what sort of men swarm about her decks and what sort of goods go swinging down into her hold; how the harbour-master signs off another job, and *Highland Princess* sets out on a new voyage; what London looks like as the buildings are left behind, and the dock becomes a river, the river becomes an estuary, and the estuary becomes the sea. . . .

Lejeune added:

> Nothing could be more exact than the detail displayed
> in this account of a single, routine shipping operation,
> but nothing would be more inexact than to give the
> impression that *Waters of Time* simply describes a
> shipping operation and stops there. The *facts* about
> the steamer *Highland Princess* are merely the begin-
> ning. From these facts the producer goes on to set his
> fancy free on the theme of London River.[30]

The director was Basil Wright, a veteran documentary
maker who doubled as the chairman of the BBC's *Sunday
Critics* programme. The commentary was by Paul Dehn, the
critic and poet who had lately and successfully turned to
movies as co-writer of *Seven Days to Noon*.

What is striking now about the documentary output is the
avoidance of any topic that could be seen as even mildly
controversial. This was not entirely the fault of those
behind the cameras. A top level fear of politics tarnishing
the Festival spirit was so great as to lead to the withdrawal
(censorship by another name) of a documentary on the
troubled region of Kashmir. What is surprising is that
directors who were noted for their sturdy independence
went along with the official line.

But the prize for cloying sentimentality must go to
Humphrey Jennings, a doyen of the documentary movement. Beyond the hallowed confines of the British Film
Institute it is hard now to take Jennings seriously. Yes, he
was a pioneer of the documentary and, yes, he made a
notable contribution to the war effort by capturing the
stoicism and courage of ordinary people in films like *Fires*

*Were Started*. But in a limited canon there are some real clinkers. Even his fondest admirers concede that his inept use of non-professional actors produced dull, monotone performances, while his biographer designates *The Cumberland Story* as 'quite the most boring long film Jennings ever made',[31] which given some of his other efforts is really saying something.

Jennings' distinction was in portraying on screen an idealistic social harmony – all working to a common purpose – which, however misleading in reality, fitted neatly into the Festival's propaganda remit. The result was *Family Portrait*, a 23-minute attempt to explain the success of a 'small, varied and restrained' nation in its ability to combine curiosity, inventiveness and practical application, with a love of pageantry and 'simple pleasures' as the binding force.

Rather than a call for renewal, this was a comfort blanket for the middle-class and middle-aged. Apart from a brief shot of a football match, young people were notable by their absence. There were, however, lots of old men in ceremonial dress engaging in traditional rites. As revealed by Jennings, life in Britain looked to be excessively boring.

The success of the Telekinema (close on half a million visitors were eager to pay a separate admission charge of two shillings) was not so much artistic as technological. Abiding memories are of watching, through Polaroid eyeglasses, the 3D image of an actor batting a ball into the audience, who either tried to catch it or ducked behind their seats. Those caught on camera as they entered the Telekinema saw themselves projected on the big screen, a brief moment of notoriety that was soon to be repeated across the country as television took hold of the living room.

Young visitors held fast to the memory of their first programmes on television. Pete Pennington, who was eight in 1951, was mesmerised by an on-screen cricket match. 'Being short I had difficulty in seeing over the crowd but I don't think I have watched a match with so much interest ever since.'[32]

The Telekinema, or National Film Theatre (NFT) as it was known after 1952, proved to be a lifeline for the BFI. 'We introduced a new class of membership at five shillings per head,' recalled Denis Forman, 'and put on the screen the classics of the cinema (many of which had never been seen in London before) and a ravishing series of contemporary films arranged and presented by the *Sight and Sound* team.' BFI membership shot up from 2,000 to 26,000:

The newly joined members flocked to the theatre which was often booked out, and this gave rise to another problem. The news got around in the film trade, whose leading figures had been persuaded in the cause of art to allow us to show the films free, that the Telekinema now under the name of the National Film Theatre was making money. There were cries of 'unfair competition', 'exploitation' and 'we've been conned'. Walter Fuller, the general secretary of the Cinematograph Exhibitors Association, took the matter up with me personally. His office was in the same building, several storeys above the BFI. Frequently he would pop down to deliver vague threats and make intimidatory noises. He had green teeth and whilst he talked he kept flashing sinister underworld smiles at me. His whole manner was unnerving and he would usually make his exit, still flashing, and tapping his nose on one side, saying, 'I'm sure you know what's good for you, old boy.'[33]

In 1956, the Wells Coates building was demolished to make way for a new NFT under Waterloo Bridge.

# CHAPTER TWELVE

The last Saturday in September was party night. Everybody was invited and as the crowds rolled over Waterloo Bridge it seemed that everybody had accepted. It was a fair measure of the success of the Festival that so many were eager to take this final opportunity to enjoy the South Bank. One pleasure was denied them. The regular evening open-air dance on the Fairway had to be abandoned. There were just too many people milling around. As a *Times* reporter coyly put it, 'So large were the crowds that never for a moment was there any dancing other than that which can only rank as rhythmic movement within the narrowest possible limits of space.'[1]

This unintended restraint on natural exuberance was welcomed by society's more puritanical elements. On earlier visits to the South Bank, Barry had frequently encountered the self-appointed guardians of decency. 'You never know what dancing will lead to,' he was told by one busybody. 'There could be an outbreak of jiving.' Heaven forfend.

One night, Barry was standing at the Fairway alongside a policeman:

The dancing seemed quite orderly to me but the constable was not so easily satisfied and pointed out a male member of the crowd whose conduct clearly displeased him. So I asked him what he was doing wrong. 'Didn't you see him, Sir,' said the constable, *'he was bent double!'* I remarked that so far as I knew it was not an offence against English law to bend double and so far as I know he remained unapprehended.[2]

Dancing on the Fairway was one of the big successes of the season:

It was fascinating even to watch moving spotlights playing on the swirling crowds, the small lights twinkling underfoot and the illuminated fountains and buildings framing the dark pool of dancers in a rectangle of brightness. Young couples would start streaming across the Bailey Bridge for the dancing the moment the two-shilling entry fee came into operation at half-past-eight. Star worship was rampant. Film and radio stars would come to the microphone on the Dome podium half-way through the evening, 'say a few words', autograph a bouquet which would then be presented to the winner of the spot dance. Sometimes there were unexpected visitors to the platform, once an elderly man who had walked to the South Bank all the way from Chelmsford.[3]

The morning of Saturday 29 September was warm and dry, 'clean, misty, pale in colour, sharp and thin to the nose', wrote Hugh Casson. The first turnstiles clicked open at 9 a.m. They clicked at an accelerating rate throughout the day until, after dark, the mass of bodies seemed to move as one, 'carved horizontally by the violet slices of the arc lamps'.[4] Up in the control tower the general manager, 'a tense silhouette', was seen with a telephone at each ear.

A crowd-pulling programme of entertainments was led by Geraldo and his Orchestra. The stars of radio, rarely seen in the flesh in this pre-television age, took their turns at the microphone. After their appearances Casson noticed Richard Murdoch and Kenneth Horne, who often worked together as a comedy duo, walking off arm-in-arm until they parted, each to his own Rolls-Royce.

Top of the bill was Gracie Fields. Her lure, said the starstruck Barry, proved irresistible:

> She sang and sang and the crowds adored her and clamoured for more. I was struck that night by her strictly professional modesty about her own work: in the Royal Pavilion afterwards, congratulating her, I said tritely enough that she had been wonderful. 'No,' she answered, 'I wasn't wonderful, I was just all right.' Miss Fields must permit me to keep my opinion that in her own incomparable style she was on this night, as always, magnificent.[5]

An encore of 'Wish Me Luck', Gracie Fields' signature song, ended the cabaret. As the crowd thinned, Casson noted the 'sleepy tots, couples hand-in-hand, a few determined drunks – teeth sucking little men in large check caps clasping glasses of light ale'.

The South Bank stayed open until midnight. But when, spot on time, the official farewell – 'The exhibition management wishes you good night' – was heard over the loudspeakers there were only a few stragglers left to respond.

There were many enduring memories. James Gardner was sitting next to Herbert Morrison at a farewell dinner in the Riverside Restaurant:

He steered me out into the crowd to see the great firework finale. The whole of London seemed to be there, and we soon lost contact in the press of bodies which ebbed and flowed wherever there was standing ground. It was amazing so few had to be pulled out of the lake. Near me, a party had made space to do a 'Knees Up Mother Brown' as waves of singing swept the crowd. Then, as the last star slowly fell tracing a sparkling trail to be met by its mirror image on the lake, there was such cheering as had not been heard in Britain since Mafeking night.[6]

The closing ceremonies were held the following day. After the speeches, community singing was led by the massed bands of the Brigade of Guards and the BBC Choral Society. All the old favourites were given a Thames airing – 'A Long Way to Tipperary', 'All Through the Night', 'Jerusalem', 'Rule Britannia', 'Abide with Me' and 'Land of Hope and Glory'.

The last act, with the crowds on the Fairway as its principal throng of witnesses, was the striking of the flags – the Union flag and the Festival flag. The crowds lingered yet awhile singing again, but unaccompanied, songs of farewell. The sounds began to grow scattered and distant, until at last the Fairway was deserted and the South Bank had known its last festival visitor.[7]

In all, eight and a half million people visited the South Bank, half a million short of target. Barry was inclined to skirt this unwelcome intelligence by pointing out that another eight and a half million paid to enjoy the Battersea Pleasure Gardens. Lumping together the two figures he was able to claim credit for the Festival attracting more than one in three of the entire population, a sleight of hand that ignored the fact that many went both to the South Bank and Battersea. But there was really no need to dissemble. By any statistical criteria, the Festival had scored some palpable hits.

The record day for the South Bank was 22 September, when 158,365 people visited the exhibition and 75,923 were on site at the same time. Nothing was heard from the 'experts' on crowd control who, earlier, had warned that 20,000 was the upper limit. Nationwide, three and a half million guides were sold. Schools had responded enthusiastically to concessionary charges for group bookings. Over half a million schoolchildren saw the Exhibition in organised parties, the present writer among them.

There was also a record number of overseas visitors, up from 610,000 in 1950 to 700,000. They were reckoned to have boosted the national economy by £18 million, twice the cost of the entire Festival. Almost a third of the tourist traffic was from North America, a welcome source of dollar earnings. These figures were all the more impressive given the obstacles to international tourism. The Australian reader of a lyrical guide to Britain ('the glory of the superlative cathedrals and beautiful old churches; the quaint charm of picturesque inns and little villages; the pomp and pageantry, customs and ceremonials') was warned that he had to go through a series of bureaucratic hoops before even boarding the ship:

Australian residents wishing to travel overseas must first obtain a release from the Taxation Department, given only when one is completely out of their debt. Shipping companies are forbidden by law to issue steamer tickets until this certificate has been produced. A British passport costing about 3o/- entitles the holder to travel anywhere in the Empire within a period of five years.

Each person is permitted to take up to £500 sterling, which, with the 25% exchange added, will cost you another £125. Only about £10 is allowed in actual cash, the rest being made up of travellers' cheques for use on board, at ports of call en route, and on arrival. These cheques are issued by Cook's Travel Agency and by the Bank of New South Wales, are of various denominations and will be cashed by almost anyone anywhere. However, it is advisable not to take too many of these, but to have the main bulk of your funds transferred to your bank in London by letter of credit. This opens a temporary working account for you in England during your stay.

Each traveller is permitted to take 50lbs. of groceries, which is carried free by the ship along with the passenger's other personal baggage. Certain firms specialise in this work and will pack for you and deliver on board. Cameras, binoculars and other such personal possessions are duty free if being carried and used.[8]

The prize for the most impressive statistic must go to the Thames bus service, which recorded more than five million passengers. Incredibly, no one at the Ministry of Transport thought it worthwhile to incorporate the scheme in the London traffic plan, though the Festival did bequeath five new river piers, at the South Bank, Hammersmith, Blackfriars, Old Swan and Battersea Park.

Among the unsung heroes were the staff of the South Bank Advance Ticket Office in Whitehall Place. They dealt with 88,000 letters in the twelve months the office was open. The daily post included a good many collector's items, including this application for a refund:

Flight Lt. A.D.J. was one of the navigators on the Lincoln Aries III which in mid-July flew over the North Pole non-stop from Iceland to Alaska. The Aircraft was stranded in Alaska waiting for a new engine to be flown out and he was therefore unable to use the South Bank Exhibition tickets which he had bought, due to the unserviceability of his plane.

Every day throughout the Festival fifty-one balloons were released from the South Bank, each carrying a voucher for free entry to the Exhibition. The finders were invited to write in for their tickets. Among the correspondents was Mr Ratcliff from Wandsworth, whose letter is reproduced as written:

Dear Sir, I wish to apply for tickets, as regards the time the balloon comes down. Well its a funny thing where they drop. Im a railway linesman, and today I was walking as per routine from Hayes to West Drayton, and believe me its some walk. Perhaps you would not understand, but I would like to take some of your people one day, for the same self walk (I guess you would go home hungry) anyway thats beside the point but today I noticed this voucher with a busted red balloon, and of coarse its our Job to notice everything, and believe me its not every day we pick up something worth picking up, so in my holidays which starts in a few weeks, I shall be very pleased to have a tour round the south bank, and as a man who likes a bob each way, I think it's a very sporting gesture, where these balloons will drop, so heres wishing you all the best and really I don't know whom I am writing to.[9]

For the many who were strangers to London, finding their way about could be a problem. A traveller from Bolton sought practical help:

Dear Sir/Madam, As I have never been to London before, I am intending to go during the Festival and it will mean having time off work, which will not have to be to long.

I wonder (Nay) I hope you can Furnish me with a Map or small diagram of the Roads street etc or any details that will help a stranger to locate anything of interest around or near the Festival as I shall have 2 boys of mine with me which will be enough, apart from after effects of Bereavement (it is the change mostly that I am coming for) If you can help in this respect or put me on to the proper place I would be most grateful and indeted to you, we may come on our own or we may come by organised party, I don't know what station we shall arrive at, but I shall be leaving here Sunday Midnight and arrive Monday Morning.

Please say where the Festival is being held and I would like (time permitted) to visit Buckingham Palace and see the changing of the guard (if Possible).

If there is any charge for the Map (or the trouble I have caused) please let me know (in first instance) then I can return same.

If you cannot do any of these things for me Please let me know the Name, No ect of the Map and I'll try and get it near home.

Thanking you _very_ _very_ Much.[10]

There were the inevitable complaints of expectations sorely disappointed. From Chingford came a cry of anger from parents who had nowhere to leave their infants:

We are furious – FURIOUS – to think that we and our two elder children cannot visit the South Bank Exhibition BECAUSE we also have a year old baby.

If the 'Daily Mail' Ideal Home Exhibition can provide a crèche _why can't you_?

My neighbours don't like minding babies – I've tried it before.

Before any trouble starts at the gates please remedy this glaring omission.

I am writing to all the principal newspapers.

Yours truly . . .[11]

And from a refused refund:

Received your reply. I am disgusted. You can stuff your
F of B up your Jumper. I had a poisoned ankle at time
of our visit. I think you could have stretched a point.
Hope your conscience pricks you.
 Now I will take myself to the Battersea Fun Fair and
have 2/- worth of your lights later.[12]

In the weeks after the closure, such was the buoyant
mood among the Festival's progenitors that hopes were
kept alive of somehow perpetuating, if not the Festival
itself, at least the spirit of the event. It was not to be. The
incoming Conservative government, led by a visibly ageing
Winston Churchill, wanted no part of this socialist-
inspired experiment in social engineering. With the King
near life's end (in September he had a lung removed after
the discovery of a malignant tumour), Tory eyes were set
firmly on the coronation of Princess Elizabeth, an occasion
that was calculated to restore national pride and self-
confidence with the promise of a second Elizabethan age. It
was to be another party, but one with a difference that was
little noticed at the time. While the Festival looked to the
future, the Coronation was an exercise in mass nostalgia,
less a celebration of what could be than of what was: Britain
as a heritage site.
 The politician charged with managing the transition was
David Eccles, Churchill's choice for Minister of Works. An
MP since 1943, Eccles had come to the notice of the Prime
Minister for his wartime service coordinating the Anglo-
American munitions programme. As a devotee of the arts
and an enthusiast for the expansion of higher education, he

had much in common with Barry. But though he might have shared Barry's objectives and was noted for outspoken views that were not always in accord with government policy, Eccles was not about to sully his first weeks in office by taking on a fight he knew he could not win. The Festival was a lost cause while the Coronation, which also came within his remit, was his opportunity to make his mark as a political high-flier.

By the time the Tories returned to power, in late October 1951, the job of dismantling the South Bank exhibition and of dispensing with staff was already under way. Hugh Casson's dismissal had coincided with the Festival's official opening. Popping into his office before rushing off to the ceremony, he had found a roneoed letter on his desk telling him that his services were no longer required. Other members of the planning and design team were similarly discarded.[13] By the time Eccles became involved, the Festival payroll was down to around one hundred. Never one to exercise tact in breaking bad news, the minister lost no time in writing formally to Barry:

> I am most anxious that the Government should show its determination to reach decisions about the South Bank site as quickly as possible and generally to clear up the affairs of the Festival of Britain. I see no reason why within the next month we should not reach decisions of principle regarding the clearance of the South Bank site and its interim use . . .
>
> In these circumstances I have to consider your own position. There would I think be criticism in the House of Commons if we were to continue the appointment of a Director General for any long period

after the end of the Festival and I should like to be able to say that your services ceased at the end of the year. I should, however, propose that the appointment was formally terminated on 31st January, 1952. I understand that in fact you contemplated taking some well earned leave as from the end of December so I hope the arrangements I propose will be acceptable to you.[14]

This came as a shock to Barry, who had anticipated clearing his desk at a more leisurely pace. Responding to the peremptory directive he stressed that he had 'no desire to linger'. But 'There is necessarily a good deal still to be done in winding up a project that took three full years to plan and I do not see how I can be in a position to hand over my responsibilities for the satisfactory discharge of the financial and physical affairs of the Department, the preparation of our Report as directed and so on, before the end of January at the earliest.'[15]

Eccles agreed, reluctantly. Writing to Barry on 18 December he also came to terms over a holiday allowance:

I understand that the Treasury have already laid it down that no member of the Festival Office staff could take after 31st January, 1952 more than 36 days cumulative leave in all. This arrangement was no doubt intended for the ordinary staff, but I think you will agree that it would be appropriate to adopt the same principle to the senior posts including your own. On the assumption that you will carry on your work until 31st January and take your leave after that date this would mean that your appointment would be formally terminated on 15th March.[16]

In recognition of Barry's persistence as a negotiator, there is in the margin of Eccles' letter a scribbled addendum: 'This is the result of long argument and is the best I can do.'

Barry served out his notice in the role of Festival apostle. Now Sir Gerald (the dubbing of Hugh Casson had to wait until the New Year's Honours, when Paul Wright and James Gardner also collected OBEs), the soon to be retired Director General was in hot demand for articles, lectures and after-dinner speeches. His invariable starting point was a favoured anecdote of Festival life. One such was the following request from the secretary of a darts club: 'Is it possible to send me also a Blank Notepaper with Festival of Britain Heading to place the Notice on our Notice Board, as it will also bring the Festival to other Patrons of the House attention. I believe in advertising anything British.' Another was a much quoted letter from Glasgow:

> I am writing to you, to find out, if, you have any of the persons aftermentioned, on your books, and if you have, you could furnish me with their addresses, all from Glasgow,
> Jean Arthur, Comptomotor Operator
> Andrew Harris, Draughtsman
> Andrew Reid, Sketch Artist
> At home here, we are very worried about their whereabouts, one is my sister, the other two are brother in laws.
> I will be very indebted to you, for your help in locating them.[17]

Having put his audience in receptive mood, Barry launched into a passionate plea to the government and the London County Council not to allow the South Bank to regress to its former dereliction. Many and varied were the suggestions. Though Barry was reconciled to losing most of the Festival buildings (except for the Festival Hall they were, after all, temporary structures), he had hopes that the Arts Council would take on the Lion and the Unicorn Pavilion as an art gallery 'such as Paris has in the Orangerie, the Jeu de Paumes and the Chaillot Palace'. Along with the Telekinema and the administrative block running parallel with Waterloo Road, a boundary could be formed to mark out a public garden consisting of land and waterscapes left over from the Exhibition: 'With such comparatively simple adjustments the South Bank could keep the reputation it has won and continue to attract a public until its more permanent development can begin.'[18]

Casson was also on the campaign trail. Ever the committee man, he suggested to the LCC that he, the Council's chief architect and the chief officer of parks should get together to plan for the future of the South Bank:

We drew attention to the newly disclosed panorama of the North Bank – 'marching', as James Bone put it, 'as majestically as a policeman to its proper climax at Scotland Yard', to the newly appreciated use of the river, to the pedestrian, informally scaled exhibition layout which had proved so popular and so workable, to the importance of attention to detail, to the legacy of good will for the area left by the exhibition. We recommended the temporary retention of certain buildings and facilities (including the Shot

Tower and Boat Pier), the maintenance of public access.[19]

The *Sunday Times* ran a competition on what should be done. The prize of £100 went to D. Mason Jones of Linton near Wetherby in Yorkshire, who suggested for the upstream section a Theatre Square flanked by a hotel and an airway terminal while downstream could accommodate an exhibition and recreation centre.[20] A letter from the administrator at the Old Vic reminded readers that the foundation stone for the National Theatre was in place; surely a good omen. In that he was very much mistaken.

The 1851 Exhibition had set an instructive precedent in relocating the Crystal Palace to Sydenham in South London. Now that Paxton's wondrous icon had been destroyed by fire, could it not be replaced by the Dome and the Skylon? Too expensive, said the Treasury, who then spent too long quibbling over possible deals to attract private investment for the Festival icons.

All the ideas lobbed at the Ministry of Works bounced back. The unstated message, clear to anyone who could read between official lines, was that there was no money for a socialist memorial. It took nearly a year for Casson to fix a meeting with Eccles to discuss the South Bank. He emerged thoroughly discouraged: 'It seems probable that there will be a mixture of LCC gardens, a fireworks display ground and a helicopter landing ground for the new BEA air terminus in the old Waterloo entrance building.'

Meanwhile, demolition continued apace. The Skylon and the Dome went to scrap. What was left of the Festival was sold off at public auction in December, 'a cold and melancholy farewell', wrote Barry.

The fans turned up in strength. 'South Bank aficionados struggled to the underground clutching plaster doves, race chairs, light fittings and butterflies immortalized in plastic cubes.'[21] The inner circle of planners and designers fought for mementos.[22] Casson's daughter, Nicky Hessenberg, recalls 'a number of curious items which arrived at home — two lobster creels, plaster white doves, wooden and cane models of different types of fish and a 6ft 6ins leather box from the Sports Pavilion'.[23]

Radio reporter Audrey Russell acquired two doves for a guinea each:

I gave one to Richard Dimbleby as a souvenir of the many broadcasts we had shared. I also bought an elegant white wrought iron garden chair. When I received my purchases I realized how fragile were the plaster doves and how heavy the chair. There were no taxis to be seen and half way across the now deserted concourse the chair had to be left behind. The dove is still my souvenir of the Festival. I wonder what became of the chair.[24]

Over one hundred job lots went under the hammer. They ranged from a sculpture of an Iron Age chariot to a mural on the history of television. Barry's favourite entry in the auction catalogue was item 849, 'A Large Leather Figure of a Man and Wooden Ditto of a Woman, and a Quantity of Wooden Fish'. But he searched in vain for the apocryphal offering, 'One Boot Jack, one Stuffed Polecat, one Enema, and Farrar's Life of Christ'.[25]

Four years after the sale, the Town Clerk of the Borough of Willesden wrote to his LCC opposite number to complain that three ticket and paybox kiosks bought by his council had never been delivered. The sum of £53 was outstanding. What did the LCC propose to do about it? Nothing was the answer. The Ministry of Works replied likewise. After another round of letters, the Treasury settled the debt.[26]

Scientific and technological displays were reassembled in schools, colleges and museums. The Barbara Hepworth group went to Harlow New Town and the Henry Moore reclining figure to Leeds Art Gallery. Reading University adopted the 'Farming Year' murals from the Dome and the two murals, 'Plankton' and 'The Marmalade Cat', were displayed at Langbourne School in West Dulwich. The great bell of the Lion and the Unicorn, cast specially for the South Bank at the Whitechapel foundry, found a new home at Kelvedon Church in Essex. The components of the bailey bridge across the Thames to Northumberland Avenue were demanded back by the army.

Battersea was reprieved. The Pleasure Gardens were to remain open, subject to regular profitability checks. Starved of investment, they staggered on for twenty-five years, growing ever more tatty until they succumbed to the competition of Disney-style theme parks. As for the South Bank, 'Nothing remained but the embankment wall, the boat pier, the trees, the circle of turf marking the Dome of Discovery and the Festival Hall, marooned on its empty, windswept site.'[27]

# CHAPTER THIRTEEN

Gerald Barry wanted everyone to have a good time but he also intended the Festival to be an agent for change. The melding of modernist design with breakthroughs in science and technology offered a tantalising glimpse of the future, an objective worth working for. Or so Barry hoped.

Imaginative teenagers who felt smothered by the dreary uniformity that was post-war Britain were quick to get the message. For Arnold Wesker it started with a ticket to see Christopher Fry's *A Sleep of Prisoners*: 'A play in a church! That was a new horizon — as was the entire Festival of Britain.'[1]

Mary Quant and Terence Conran were among those who experienced a Road to Damascus impetus to their careers, as did a whole generation of art students who went on to revolutionise advertising, stage design, topography and photography. Barry headed his list of achievements with the 'great experiment' of cooperation between art and commerce to 'work closely together on a united creative project', so that when the Festival opened it 'did represent most of what was best at that time'.[2]

From 1951 notice was served on 'the days of varnish, brown paint and porridge wallpaper'.[3] Items intended for everyday use – pots and pans, curtains and chair covers, work surfaces and carpets – added colour to their utility.

Landscaping came into its own with the Festival, demonstrating that a balance between humans and their environment could not be achieved without planning. It was surely no coincidence that soon after the Festival closed the Women's Institute launched a nationwide Keep Britain Tidy campaign.

After an initial period of letdown ('We thought our lives were made only to find there was no work,' says Terence Conran[4]), modern styles found their market. Habitat and Heals were pure Festival, as too were Ercol and G-Plan furniture. It was the Festival that prompted enlightened manufacturers to the value of research in design and 'to the advantage of bringing in the industrial artist to cooperate in the design of goods', even if the 'South Bank quickly deteriorated into a cliché for every coffee bar or renovated pub'.[5]

Design education came into its own with courses set up across the country, albeit they were often an adjunct to technical education rather than part of the university network. Academic recognition did not come easily. Even so, many of the most enduring images of the next decade, from Alec Issigonis' Mini to Robin Day's lightweight polypropylene chair, owed much to the Festival. David Mellor, destined to be Britain's leading designer of cutlery, who was at the Royal College of Art in 1950, was so imbued with the Festival spirit that he took up a travelling scholarship to Sweden and Denmark where he acquired the essence of 'timeless minimalism'.

With justification, Barry claimed credit for a 'quickened sense of community' and for 'new fields of creative initiative'[6] which left towns and villages better off at the end of 1951 than they had been when the year began. On the simplest level he was thinking of tree-lined urban streets, playing fields and bus shelters (over one hundred of which were built). He noted too the town hall steps that carried tubs of flowers and observed that the view from park benches was taking on a richer and more varied floral aspect. More substantial achievements were the historic landmarks reconstructed or restored. In addition to Bristol's Colston Hall, Manchester's Free Trade Hall and the refurbished Walker Gallery in Liverpool, these included the Assembly Rooms at York and Norwich, the Guildhall at King's Lynn and Buckland Abbey (reopened as the Drake Museum) in Plymouth.

As a direct result of the Festival, the Arts Council and the Council for Industrial Design, rechristened the Design Council, came into their own as cultural lobbies with access to government funds. In the following decade, grants to museums, galleries and the performing arts increased fourfold. Arts administration adopted an educative role which showed up most obviously in the retreat of intellectual snobbism from public exhibitions. In the pre-Festival years, curators had been obsessively over-protective of their most treasured items, hiding them away behind wire grilles for fear that they might be sullied by contact with the uninitiated. Here is Christopher Hobhouse reflecting on a typical pre-war museum display:

> on the one side, are all the trumpery flotsam of learning, stuffed mammals and fossils, stuck into glass cases and labelled in the hope of filling some vacant mind. And here, on the other side, are some of

the loveliest things on earth, whole rooms of English furniture, and the Raphael cartoons, and Pellé's bust of Charles the Second — here they are, snatched from the hands of private men, sterilized, caged together in tasteless surfeit, imprisoned without hope of release. Here too, perhaps saddest of all, is a great staff of experts — unhappy custodians, bound by hated necessity to the prisoners of their great seraglio, yet pleased with a gloating pleasure that other men cannot get near them to enjoy them. From beyond their glass cages a few German and Japanese students of all ages come and blink through their spectacles at them and go away again, having added one more piece of information to the silly pile. Domestic servants make assignations among the period panelled rooms. And on Bank Holiday, when it is wet outside, quite a lot of people go.[7]

The Festival, with its imaginative layout of exhibits, changed all that. One example can serve for many. The Victoria and Albert Museum was accustomed to arrange items by similarity of shape and form rather than by age. Thus, five hundred porcelain vases were lined up in no particular order. Scholars could be relied upon to sort them out. Post Festival, objects were arranged by period with helpful captions attached.

But as Barry was the first to concede, whatever credit attached to the Festival, the cultural breakthrough was on a narrow front. The excitement of the new felt by many younger visitors to the Festival was not always shared by their elders who were more receptive to the whimsical glorification of the British character, the pride in national achievement and the sheer exuberance of the Festival spirit, to the packaging more than the contents.

Critics blame Barry for losing an opportunity to advance truly radical ideas as, later, young designers were accused of too close an association with art as opposed to the raw commerce that reached out to the people. But this was to ignore the reality of a society in painful transition.

The aftermath of a world war found Britain tired and resentful, aware of its status as an international has-been but scared of losing what little influence it still had to the superpowers and their acolytes. The public demand was for reassurance, which is why the future was presented in a context that respected and even glorified tradition, albeit in a manner that stopped well short of blatant nationalism. As Barry put it, 'we tried to say our piece disarmingly, with wit and an occasional dig at ourselves'.[8] To have attempted more would have risked stoking the ire of those who wanted no change at all, a powerful lobby that could have stopped the Festival in its tracks.

Comparison with the Nordic countries, the envy of social and cultural radicals, is instructive. As small nations with a firm economic base and homogenous societies, Sweden, Denmark and Norway were in a far stronger position to demonstrate the liberating force of modern design. The distance Britain had to cover to catch up was plainly demonstrated by one of the big talking points of the Festival. Visitors welcomed the soft toilet paper, an unfamiliar luxury, in all the public lavatories. It was several years before it made its appearance in the average home. Moreover, four years after the Festival a mere 18 per cent of households boasted a washing machine while only eight per cent had refrigerators.[9]

Deprivation supported conservation, a reluctance to give up what was familiar for fear of being cast adrift. Hence the aversion to open-plan living, even when it could be shown to have advantages over the poky downstairs front and back rooms characteristic of the vast majority of houses in the UK. The middle class was more receptive to innovation, particularly when it came to labour-saving devices; even so there was a reluctance to move on from the standard reproduction furniture in bay-windowed houses, the mark of genteel respectability. So it was that while home interiors benefited from Festival design it was in a somewhat rarefied form, a contrast to the high quality, mass-produced design of Scandinavia.

The challenge of nudging forward the process of change was toughest for the young architects. It all began so well. Standing out sharply against its dull surroundings, the South Bank exhibition quickly became the routine starting point for any discussion on post-war building. 'For the first time for generations,' wrote Hugh Casson, 'architecture has been talked and written about by people who are not architects.' If the Festival was distinguished by one particular characteristic it has to be its lightness of touch. To wander the South Bank in its brief span of glory, not alone but in the company of thousands of other visitors, was to enjoy an exhilarating sense of freedom to move about without hindrance or simply to stand and stare at unfamiliar sights without being pushed on or told to keep in line. And the buildings themselves seemed lightweight, not in any trivial sense but in projecting clean, smooth shapes that might have inspired, or have been inspired by, a science fiction vision of a space city. The contrast with what had gone before, notably the Victorian monoliths so despised by Barry, but also the crowded tenements familiar to industrial towns and even the model working-class housing represented by the claustrophobic Peabody buildings, was only too apparent.

This toning down of European modernism has been dubbed 'picturesque' for its updating of traditional designs to match the practicalities of modern living and for its emphasis on recreating the spirit of an interdependent community thought to be characteristic of the village and small town. The surviving Festival interpretation of picturesque is the low-rise development of the Lansbury Estate, where a mix of maisonettes and flats linked by open spaces and a pedestrianised market eventually offered some 9,000 London East Enders modern comforts in a setting that allowed room to breathe. It was a development that set the pattern for the New Towns promoted by the Attlee government as a 'daring exercise in town planning'. Of the Lansbury pioneers, Frederick Gibberd was the chief planner for Harlow, while Geoffrey Jellicoe worked on the plan for Hemel Hempstead and Judith Ledeboer designed one of its neighbourhoods. But it is in Coventry, where Basil Spence, who had undertaken two major projects for the Festival, won the competition for the rebuilding of the war-damaged cathedral, that Festival architecture has its enduring memorial. The Godiva shopping centre with its fountains, flower tubs and raised walkways has been described as 'perpetual South Bank' while the cathedral 'marks the apotheosis of the Festival'.

Enter through the bomb-site leftovers of the old Cathedral, go down the steps and into the new. On the vast glass entrance screen John Hutton engraved a host of ascending Mintons. On a side wall, Epstein's St Michael strikes down the Devil: both have the same ravaged bronze eyes as the 'Advancing Youth' beside the Homes and Gardens pavilion. John Piper's stained glass flushes into incandescence behind the rough-hewn boulder font. The jutting choir stalls, the hi-fi ceiling, the pillars made to appear barely to touch the floor, the inscriptions round the walls, the wrought iron thorns in the Gethsemane Chapel where a gingerbread angel kneels with crystallographic motifs on its tunic and fern wings, the Recommended Circulation: the building, its furnishings and fittings amount to a total recall.[10]

But it was not long before the Festival style was challenged. A tougher breed of social engineers moved in on the scene, their arrogance matched by blunted sensibilities. The damage they caused to people and places scarred the country in ways that can be seen to this day.

# CHAPTER FOURTEEN

After the Festival was cleared away, one of the prime sites in central London was without any sort of development plan. When hopes of creating an arts complex around the Festival Hall foundered on government parsimony, the South Bank presented a 'dismal picture of neglect and decay'.[1] Writing to the *Daily Mail*, a concert-goer reported on the depressing experience of a riverside stroll where she encountered 'large masts with broken cords, woodwork shabby and lacking paint, large cement bowls containing half-dead weeds, two flowerbeds with nothing growing, dirty sidewalks and sordid dinginess abounding'.[2]

By day, what had been the Dome but now looked like a bombsite was used for parking by County Hall employees, an easy accommodation which gave the lie to the retort from London County Council leader Sir Isaac Hayward, 'We are doing as much as we can.' The follow-up was a weakly defensive feature in *Cooperative News* promising that the 'new embankment will be a democratic place with a popular mix of entertainments'.[3] In fact, negotiations were already well advanced to hand the site over to commercial developers.

Initially, the favoured scheme was for an air terminal,

along with a helicopter pad and a hotel, both of which would appeal to wealthy American tourists.[4] Though itself unwilling to get into the hotel business, the LCC invited bids for a 99-year lease on 'this commanding position . . . between County Hall and Waterloo Bridge with its uninterrupted view of the north bank of the river'.[5] There was a poor response. The only serious offer, from Hilton, came with the condition that the LCC should share the investment, a commitment deemed by that bureaucratically cautious body to be a risk too far.

Gerald Barry pushed hard for a start to be made on the National Theatre, as the most suitable partner for the Festival Hall. But having lost his power base, Barry no longer commanded attention in high places. David Eccles, the minister responsible for the arts, kept him at arm's length, hinting at one point that Barry's Festival connections were not helpful in promoting the Design Centre, the Design Council's permanent exhibition space in Regent Street,[6] an enterprise that Barry had tried to make his own. Rebuffed by the government and in need of an income, Barry pursued other interests. He became the LCC consultant for the development of the Crystal Palace site and an adviser on public relations to the National Farmers' Union. Disappointed not to be made Director General of the BBC, he found some consolation in his appointment as head of education programmes at Granada Television. But however rewarding, there was no question that Barry had been sidelined.

For the rest of his career, Barry never came close to that high point of the Festival when all things were possible. Instead, he could only look back on what might have been. His saddest moment was in 1960 with the closure of his beloved *News Chronicle*. Though he had long ceased to be involved in the running of the paper, the liberal principles which governed its editorial were still dear to Barry's heart. That the *News Chronicle*, with a circulation of 1.4 million (higher than that of most of today's newspapers), was unable to match the appeal to advertisers of the populist *News of the World* (8 million copies weekly) or the *Mirror* and *Express* (each around 4 million) laid bare a society that fell a long way short of Festival ideals. The manner in which the *News Chronicle* ended its run was even more disquieting. Looking to an easy gain in circulation, the Beaverbrook and Rothermere papers ganged up to encourage the print unions to demand wage increases they knew the *News Chronicle* could not afford. Faced with labour militancy backed by capitalist greed, the *Chronicle*'s proprietor, Lawrence Cadbury, a weak vessel at the best of times, was relieved to strike a deal that merged his paper with the *Daily Mail*, a misalliance that gave scant regard to readers' interests.

The turn of events in Fleet Street was a financial blow for Barry. His first preference shares in Daily News Ltd, worth £10,000 when he received them as part of his compensation package for vacating the editorial chair, slumped to under half their nominal value. His hopes for gaining the sympathy of the Cadbury family and, maybe, a cheque to make up the difference were, predictably, disappointed.

As the other Festival knight, Hugh Casson was in a stronger position to make his voice heard. Mixing easily with prestigious clients who helped him build a thriving architectural practice and ever ready to join committees promoting worthy causes, Casson made frequent pleas for a culture-led revival of the South Bank. But always he came up against the conservative establishment, for whom the arts were a costly extravagance with no hope of a political return. For these little Englanders, a more attractive public morale booster, one that suited the tenor of the now ruling party, was the coronation of Elizabeth II.

Renowned for his sentimental devotion to royalty, Churchill saw the coronation as an opportunity to revive the patriotic spirit and love of empire that he believed had been undermined by his Labour predecessors. Like Herbert Morrison, Churchill wanted the people to be in celebratory mood, but more for what had been than for what might be. Though there was much talk of a second Elizabethan age, the coronation was essentially backward looking. The appeal of nostalgia was enhanced by the advent of mass television. Whereas the Festival had only the radio for its BBC coverage, 56 per cent of the adult population (around 20 million) watched the coronation service on screen. The coronation also did better in attracting overseas visitors, a million in total with 200,000 from the US alone.

Here, if anywhere, was the boost to Britain's exaggerated respect for tradition which critics later blamed for the slow pace of modernisation. The coronation, with its parade of imperial dignitaries, gilded coaches and heavy state ritual, was an invitation to the public to sit back in smug satisfaction at the country's effortless superiority. The chief beneficiary was the heritage industry.

That the Festival has also been attacked for giving too much attention to the past is partly in consequence of the two big public events of the 1950s being locked together in the collective memory. Then again, the chief aspiration of the Festival, to build a better future on a strong national foundation, was all but forgotten in the increasingly ferocious debate on reconstruction and planning, a debate in which the apostles of Le Corbusier, an architect with an outsized imagination whose visions for modern living were on the grandest possible scale, held the high ground.

The generation for whom Gerald Barry and Hugh Casson had been such adroit impresarios in 1951 had had nothing much to do once the South Bank show was over. Apart from the handful of pioneering public offices, the only private work available was minimal housing and an occasional factory or office block, the latter commonly entrusted to the sort of older firm that knew its way through the controls and did not waste time or money on 'architecture'. The result was one of the dimmest decades in our architectural history.[7]

With the rush to modernisation, propelled in the early 1960s by Harold Wilson's 'white heat of technology' government, the Festival style gave way to brutalism, a bilingual pun on the French *béton brut* (new concrete) and *art brut*, coined by the art and architecture critic and one-time Festival consultant Reyner Banham. Much of what the brutalists set out to achieve in terms of higher living standards could only be applauded. Their failure, and that of Le Corbusier, was to treat people like units to be slotted into a box-like configuration. When the people failed to appreciate what was being done for them it was always they, not the architect, who was judged to be at fault.

The concept of building ever higher to compress the greatest possible number of people into the smallest possible circumference and thus to make the best economic use of limited space was anathema to Festival planners. They would be shocked and pained to see the Canary Wharf skyscrapers that now hem in the Lansbury neighbourhood. But at least these buildings, or many of them, have a shape and style that enlivens the view. The trouble with so much post-Festival development, 'a flood of the worst kind of bastardised architecture the country has ever seen'[8] for which the Festival is unfairly held responsible, is the conformity of a dull imagination.

The favour bestowed on concrete as a wonderfully adaptable building material is a case in point. Seen with the Festival eye, it opened up vistas for architects as artists. But concrete also lent itself to prefabrication, factory-produced slabs and columns that could be thrown together to make cheap accommodation, a far cry from the Festival ideal — or, for that matter, from the Le Corbusier ideal, which demanded 'sun, space and greenery'. Significantly, Le Corbusier's early buildings were whitewashed, while the concrete of Britain's urban spawn deteriorated to sludge grey, if it did not first succumb to shoddy workmanship.

The Festival had no part in this. Rather, the finger should be pointed at avaricious developers, dim-witted councillors, the ethics of the brown envelope and the national imperative to do everything on the cheap. Inevitably, brutalism, a loaded word for any creative concept, came to represent wholesale destruction to make way for a heavyweight urban sprawl bisected by expressways, parking lots and windswept pedestrian piazzas. Even technology failed to deliver on its promises:

Post-war buildings began to come to pieces: they blew up, collapsed, leaked, burnt out, had their roofs blown off. The spacious new houses and flats that people could not afford to heat suffered appallingly from condensation. In the high flats, the lifts failed and there was no one on hand to repair them: in the sealed office blocks, the air-conditioning failed or the external cladding fell off. Those who had the courage to employ expensive *avant-garde* designers found themselves at worst ruined or at best embarrassed by experimental technology that went wrong. Those who were forced to employ the cheapest found 'cutting corners' could end in even more spectacular disasters. People began to look back with regret not only at the styles of the old architecture but at its comparatively safe technology.[9]

The collapse of Ronan Point, a south London tower block, its concrete slabs tumbling like decked dominoes, ended the love affair with high-rise living. That was in 1968, but the malign effect of brutalism lingered on as developers pursued the lowest common denominator at the highest possible profit.

For the Festival trailblazers, who 'made people want things to be better and to believe that they could be',[10] there was a terrible irony in the fate of the South Bank. There, brutalism was allowed to reveal its ugliest face.

Having decided to let the site go to the highest bidder, the first post-Festival project approved by the LCC was the construction of Shell Oil's UK headquarters. Few kind words are ever said of the Shell Centre, the first building in London to rise above the Palace of Westminster's Victoria Tower. Originally incorporating a downstream block, now converted to apartments, the only virtue of the Shell Centre is that its cladding of Portland stone has weathered better than the raw concrete of neighbouring buildings. But to look across the water to the old Shell headquarters or, indeed, to Somerset House, is to realise how the new construction materials and techniques touted by the Festival as the essence of modernist creativity were degraded to serve the trite and the tawdry. If the Shell Centre is eye-catching, it is for its unrelenting and intrusive banality. Any hope of softening its impact with an attractive surround was lost thanks to a restrictive covenant that prevented building between the Shell Tower and the Thames.

But what of the cultural enterprises long promised by city politicians? Pressure on the government to help finance the National Theatre culminated in July 1958 with a firm rejection from the then Chancellor, Derick Amory, for a grant of £2 million.[11] If London wanted an arts centre on the South Bank it would have to pay for it. The challenge was taken up with plans for two new concert venues, the Queen Elizabeth Hall and the smaller Purcell Room, and an art gallery now known as the Hayward after LCC leader Sir Isaac Hayward.

With the vogue for brutalism at its height, it was perhaps inevitable that modern architecture should be represented by grey concrete slabs. Led by Hubert Bennett, the LCC's chief architect, the design team reserved their imagination for the interiors while the façades were cold and uninviting. It is almost as if they saw culture as the equivalent of foul-tasting medicine: you had to suffer before it did any good.

But whatever disagreement there was over the outward appearance of the three newcomers to the London arts scene, there was soon a united chorus of disapproval for the warren of subterranean walkways that became the haunt of winos and a refuge for the homeless. The underground car park with its inadequate lighting was equally depressing and, at night, downright threatening.

But a focus for the arts, however ill-presented, revived the lobby for a National Theatre. Its foundation stone, proudly unveiled at the Festival, had, noted Casson, spent several years being wheeled around London on castors looking for an alternative home. The various other options having been considered and rejected, the South Bank came back into favour. Though the original site had been taken by the Hayward, land could be cleared just the other side of Waterloo Bridge. The budget allowed for three auditoria, the Lyttelton, the Olivier and the Cottesloe, the latter designated for experimental theatre. The architect was Sir Denys Lasdun, a leading exponent of brutalism, who had already made his mark on the South Bank with the new National Film Theatre tucked away under Waterloo Bridge.

As the National Theatre's artistic director, Peter Hall shared many of the frustrations experienced by Gerald Barry as the Festival took shape. Labour and management appeared to operate in different worlds, the work was often substandard and, inevitably, target dates were missed. By 1975, while the completion of the Lyttelton was on track, the Olivier and Cottesloe were way behind schedule.

The overall concept won Hall's approval: 'Lasdun's work is triumphant. He has divested concrete of its brutality. It's slender, delicate and in beautiful geometric patterns. I think the theatre is a masterpiece.'[12] But as the date for the opening productions approached, Hall took a less rosy view of the operational features:

Very little worked at the National during that first improbable year. The doors stuck, the hinges screamed hideously when latecomers were admitted, and the stage-lighting switchboards regularly plunged us into darkness. The address system calling the actors bled through from the dressing rooms into the auditoriums and startled the public. The ventilation system overheated the air in the hot summer and froze it as the autumn chill arrived. Everybody – actors, staff and audience – lost their way: Denys Lasdun's direction signs were so tasteful as to be invisible. An actor in *Plunder* who, true to Ben Travers, spent an entire act in pyjamas, found himself in the foyer rather than in the wings and couldn't navigate his way back to the stage. 'Teething troubles,' said the builders philosophically, as yet another set of snags presented themselves.[13]

Or, as Gerald Barry might have said, déjà vu.

When the problems were eventually sorted out, the general relief was such as to temper any doubts about the quality of the building as a whole. There was praise for the acoustics and visibility, the quality of light and air and the standards of comfort for audiences in the auditoria and bars (though no one thought fit to mention the defect common to all London theatres – the shortage of lavatories). For his exteriors, Lasdun was treated respectfully, at least by the critics who were grateful for a change from the 'standard expectations of stucco, mirrors and red velvet'. But while the informed view fell well short of the verdict of the guide on a Thames pleasure boat ('And on the right, ladies and gents, we have the ugliest bloody building in London'), there were those who were worried by the 'dark and sombre' look of the National, particularly when it rained, and by the 'large areas of greyness'[14] that stood in contrast to the more cheerful façades lining the north side of the river.

Give it time, said Lasdun's admirers. Highly visible change is never welcomed unreservedly. If experience teaches us anything it is that yesterday's blot on the landscape is frequently tomorrow's beloved icon. If this is true, one can only say that for the National, the gap between yesterday and tomorrow seems interminable. While praise is high for the standards of production and performance, anecdotal evidence suggests that the theatre itself has still to find its niche in public affection. Everything about it, from its blackish, pitted surfaces to the bleak entrances in the shadow of Waterloo Bridge, challenges the performers to transcend their environment. That they invariably do so speaks volumes for the quality of British acting. The same might be said of the artists who grace the walls of the Hayward and the musicians who perform in the Queen Elizabeth Hall and the Purcell Room.

The abolition of the Greater London Council (GLC) in 1985 brought good and bad news for the South Bank. The bad news was the sale of County Hall, a traditional municipal building of the 1920s, to a Japanese consortium, a deal that passed up the chance to make space for a major arts centre. Instead, most of County Hall was converted into a hotel, with the new owners retaining the right to build a giant underground car park to the east towards the Festival Hall. Not surprisingly, this has inhibited the development of the Jubilee Gardens.

The good news was the transfer of GLC responsibility for

the South Bank to a South Bank Board, an offshoot of the Arts Council, charged with managing the concert halls and the Hayward alongside the National Theatre and the National Film Theatre. For the first time there was a semblance of coordinated planning. It was not a moment too soon. While the South Bank boasted premier cultural institutions, the overall site was judged to be a disaster area. In 1991, on the fortieth anniversary of the Festival, Hugh Casson asked rhetorically 'what other city would stomach the squalid approaches to the South Bank', while Simon Jenkins, now chairman of the National Trust, then editor of *The Times*, declared the site to be 'derelict in thought and fact . . . a monument to indecision'.[15] Though a lot of money was needed to correct the errors of four decades, there was a serious hope that this familiar obstacle might at last be removed with a little help from the National Lottery.

A competition to select an architect to transform the 1960s buildings was won by the Richard Rogers Partnership. Appointed masterplanners for the South Bank Centre in September 1994, the project was managed by Ivan Harbour. Well aware that public affection for brutalism was muted but that demolition was not an option, he came up with the idea of building a canopy – a Crystal Palace – over the Hayward and Queen Elizabeth Hall to soften the concrete effect and create a friendlier, more intimate environment. This would also free up otherwise unused space for all the year-round cultural events.

It was a brave and imaginative concept that had much of the Festival about it, encouraging visitors to 'arrive early and stay late' to enjoy a mixed programme of concerts, exhibitions and informal events – 'dance at lunch, jazz in the evening, club at night'.[16] It was not to be. With the economy in poor shape, the mid-1990s was not a good time for grand schemes. When New Labour came to power after the 1997 election, its claim to be able to handle the national finances 'prudently' counted against public undertakings with high visibility. Even with a generous allocation from Lottery profits, the Crystal Palace was an expense too far. Instead, it was decided to focus on immediate priorities, starting with the restoration and refurbishment of the Festival Hall, said to be in a 'deplorable state'.[17]

There was backing too for the transformation of the NFT into a National Film Centre, though the budget, pitched at £160 million, was cut by two-thirds. Meanwhile, with the build-up to the Millennium, the South Bank beyond Waterloo, made easily accessible by its riverside walk, was sprouting first-rank visitor attractions ranging from the reconstruction of Shakespeare's Globe Theatre to Tate Modern, the latter opened in 2000 in the brilliantly converted Bankside Power Station. The Millennium Wheel, soon to be as familiar to the London scene as the Eiffel Tower is to Paris, was, like the Eiffel, originally intended to be temporary. Common sense prevailed. Would that the Skylon had been similarly favoured.

Also part of the Millennium celebrations was the reincarnation of the Dome of Discovery. Too large for the South Bank – at 365 metres in diameter, it was to be the world's largest building of its type – the site for the new dome was the reclaimed Greenwich Peninsula, a wasteland of toxic sludge. Commendable as a policy of regeneration, the project broke the first rule of the 1951 Festival planners, to operate only where there was easy access by public transport. The new Jubilee Line took London's Underground to North Greenwich, but this still left too much foot-slogging for a day's outing. The building itself, designed by Richard Rogers, was an impressive landmark but the exhibits, sponsored by major companies (a second Festival rule carelessly ignored), had little in the way of a unifying theme and were generally thought to be substandard Disney. As Minister for the Millennium for eighteen months, Peter Mandelson fell short of his ambition to emulate his grandfather, Herbert Morrison, who loved to be known as Lord Festival.

The cost of the Millennium Dome was £789 million, well ahead of a budget that had anticipated greater popular support. In the event, instead of the 12 million visitors forecast, only 6.5 million turned up over the entire year, a figure lower than the attendance for the South Bank Festival, which only ran from May to September. The Dome is now a sports and entertainment centre.

The new century inspired another try at a masterplan for the South Bank site. This one is the brainchild of Rick Mather Architects. Rejecting the grand slam solution, Peter Cully has produced a blueprint for a 25-year staged development incorporating three new public spaces – Festival Riverside, Southbank Centre Square and Festival Terrace. With work completed on the Festival Hall and its adjoining line-up of shops (the first new buildings on the site in forty years), the Queen Elizabeth Hall, Purcell Room and Hayward are next in line for a radical updating.[18]

Early improvements for the public areas include raised walkways so that the Thames is always in view, better signing so that visitors will know how to get into buildings without a route map, the redirection of delivery vans underground, the widening of terraces to appeal to strollers, the cleaning of the concrete façades and clever lighting to make constructive use of otherwise forbidding space, such as the new restaurant opened under Hungerford Bridge. Before long we may see a reconstruction of the Skylon. Jack Pringle, who worked with Sir Philip Powell at Powell and Moya, is leading a fundraising campaign to restore this celebrated icon, though it is less likely to make its reappearance on the South Bank than at one of the Olympic sites where commercial sponsors are showing interest in a unique opportunity to promote their wares.[19]

Sixty years on, the South Bank is beginning to rediscover the Festival spirit. With no less than twenty-one cultural landmarks spread out over as many acres along the Thames walk, visitors have the choice of over one thousand paid performances a year. It has taken long enough, but Gerald Barry might concede that the wait has been worthwhile.

# EPILOGUE

Reminders of 1951 are still to be found on the South Bank. There are regular ferry services from what was the Rodney Pier and is now known as the Festival Pier. Close by is the country's tallest unstayed flagpole, a gift to the Festival from British Columbia, re-erected on site for the Queen's Silver Jubilee. Best of all is Frank Dobson's magnificent *London Pride*, a bronze sculpture of two female figures commissioned for the Festival and now back where it belongs courtesy of Dobson's widow, Mary.

The Festival Church of St John the Evangelist, close by the Waterloo roundabout, had its latest restoration in 1998. Built in the 1820s as part of a government-sponsored programme to keep a restless populace in order, St John's had its roof taken off by a bomb in 1940, remaining open to the skies until its 1951 reconstruction. The simple barn-like design, characteristic of the early nineteenth-century Greek revival, now has a Grade II listing as a place of historical interest.

Harder to find is the elm tree planted in September 1971 in memory of Gerald Barry, who had died three years earlier aged seventy. And, of course, there is the Festival Hall, splendidly restored but still awaiting new entrance steps.

It is little enough to show for one of the great cultural events of the last century. But if the visible heritage of the Festival is hard to find, this is not to dismiss its impact on the popular imagination. For the first time since the war, ordinary citizens were given a vision of the future which took them beyond the everyday concerns of keeping body and soul together.

They might not have liked everything they saw but they were made aware that design was for living, that the arts need not be elitist and that technology was stronger in promise than in threat. The Festival was a beacon for change. The light may have flickered over the years, but for those five glorious months in 1951 it was bright and strong.

# BIBLIOGRAPHY

Colin Amery (ed.), *The National Theatre*. Architectural
  Press, 1977
Mary Banham and Bevis Hillier (eds), *A Tonic to the Nation.*
  *The Festival of Britain 1951*. Thames & Hudson, 1976
Ernest Barker, *The Character of England*. Clarendon Press,
  1947
Michael Bird, *The St Ives Artists. A Biography of Place and*
  *Time*. Lund Humphries, 2008
Christopher Booker, *The Neophiliacs*. Collins, 1969
*Britain's Town & Country Pattern*. Faber & Faber, 1943
Cheryl Buckley, *Designing Modern Britain*. Reaktion Books,
  2007
Ruth Butler, *The Festival of Britain and the Buildings of the*
  *1950s*. Brighton Polytechnic School of Architecture, 1992
David Cannadine, *Making History Now and Then*. Palgrave
  Macmillan, 2008
E.J. Carter and Ernö Goldfinger, *The County of London Plan*.
  Penguin, 1945
Nigel Cawthorne, *The New Look*. Hamlyn, 1996
Laura Cohen, *The Door to a Secret Room*. Scolar Press, 1999
*Designing the Future of the South Bank*. Academy Editions,
  1994

Becky E. Conekin, *The Autobiography of a Nation. The 1951 Festival of Britain*. Manchester University Press, 2003

Charlotte and Peter Fiell, *Decorative Art 50s*. Taschen, 2000

Naomi Games, Catherine Moriarty, Jane Rose, *Abram Games. His Life and Work*. Princeton Architectural Press, 2003

James Gardner, *Elephants in the Attic*. Orbis, 1983

Janie Hampton, *The Austerity Olympics*. Aurum Press, 2008

Brian Harrison, *Seeking a Role. The United Kingdom 1951–1970*. Oxford University Press, 2009

Elaine Harwood and Alan Powers (eds), *Festival of Britain*. Twentieth Century Society, 2001

Robert Hewison, *In Anger. Culture in the Cold War 1945–60*. Weidenfeld & Nicolson, 1981

Harry Hopkins, *The New Look*. Secker & Warburg, 1963

Lesley Jackson, *The New Look. Design in the Fifties*. Thames & Hudson, 1991

James Knox (ed.), *Cartoons and Coronets. The Genius of Osbert Lancaster*. Frances Lincoln, 2008

Bernard Levin, *The Pendulum Years. Britain and the Sixties*. Pan Books, 1970

Patrick J. Maguire and Jonathan M. Woodham (eds), *Design and Cultural Politics in Postwar Britain*. Leicester University Press, 1997

José Manser, *Hugh Casson, A Biography*. Viking, 2000

Jeremy Melvin, *FRS Yorke and the Evolution of English Modernism*. Wiley, 2003

John Montgomery, *The Fifties*. Allen & Unwin, 1965

Harry Mount, *A Lust for Window Sills*. Little, Brown, 2008

Charlotte Mullins, *A Festival on the River*. Penguin, 2007

George Orwell, *Orwell's England*. Penguin, 2001

Paul Overy, *Light, Air and Openness*. Thames & Hudson, 2007

Richard Overy, *The Morbid Age. Britain Between the Wars.* Allen Lane, 2009

Kenneth Powell, *Powell & Moya. Twentieth Century Architects.* RIBA Publishing, 2009

Eva Rudberg, *The Stockholm Exhibition 1930.* Stockholmia Förlag, 1999

Eric Salmon, *The Dark Journey. John Whiting as Dramatist.* Barrie & Jenkins, 1979

Michael Sissons and Philip French (eds), *Age of Austerity 1945–1951.* Penguin, 1964

D.J. Taylor, *After the War. The Novel and England Since 1945.* Chatto & Windus, 1993

Ralph Tubbs, *The Englishman Builds.* Penguin, 1945

Nigel Whiteley, *Reyner Banham.* MIT Press, 2002

Paul Wright, *A Brittle Glory.* Weidenfeld & Nicolson, 1986

# NOTES

## Chapter One

1. Harry Hopkins, *The New Look*, Secker & Warburg, 1964, p. 91.
2. Gerald Barry, Cantor Lecture, published in the *Journal of the Royal Society of Arts*, 12 May 1952, p. 676.
3. Paul Greenhalgh, *Ephemeral Vistas*, Manchester University Press, 1998.
4. London Metropolitan Archives, LCC/CL/GP/2/64.
5. RSA Archive, Festival of Britain.
6. Ibid.
7. The widow of a prominent banker, Lady Swaythling was best known as the mother of Ivor Montagu, film-maker and critic, table tennis champion, card-carrying communist and alleged Soviet spy, and of Ewen Montagu, judge, writer and wartime intelligence officer who conceived Operation Mincemeat or, to use the title of his own book and that of the movie, *The Man Who Never Was*. The full story has now been told by Ben Macintyre in *Operation Mincemeat* (Bloomsbury, 2010).
8. Bernard Donoughue and G.W. Jones, *Herbert Morrison, Portrait of a Politician*. Weidenfeld & Nicolson, 1973, p. 19.
9. RSA Archive, Festival of Britain.
10. *The Memoirs of Lord Ismay*, Heinemann, 1960, p. 448.
11. Gerald Barry, Oxford Extramural Lecture, 13 August 1940. The 'National Plan for Great Britain' was published as a supplement to *Weekend Review* on 14 February 1931.
12. Michael Frayn, 'Festival', in Michael Sissons and Philip French (eds), *Age of Austerity 1945–1951*, Penguin, 1964, p. 323.

13. Hugh Casson in Mary Banham and Bevis Hillier (eds), *A Tonic to the Nation. The Festival of Britain 1951*, Thames & Hudson, 1976, p. 76.
14. Paul Wright, *A Brittle Glory*, Weidenfeld & Nicolson, 1986, p. 35.
15. Kingsley Martin in the *New Statesman*, 21 March 1968.
16. Gerald Barry, letter to Herbert Morrison, 4 February 1948. Barry family archive.
17. Barry, Oxford Extramural Lecture.
18. Gerald Barry, 'The Place of the Architect in the Post-War World', *Journal of the Royal Institute of British Architects*, July 1946.
19. Gerald Barry, unpublished memoir.
20. Denis Forman, *Persona Granada*, Andre Deutsch, 1993.
21. Ibid.
22. Barry, Cantor Lecture, published in the *Journal of the Royal Society of Arts*, August 1952, p. 674.
23. Barry, unpublished memoir.

## Chapter Two

1. *Observer*, 9 September 1951.
2. *A Tonic to the Nation*, p. 76.
3. Ralph Tubbs, *Living in Cities*, Penguin, 1942, p. 18.
4. Ibid., p. 36.
5. Ralph Tubbs, *The Englishman Builds*, Penguin, 1945, p. 8.
6. Ibid.
7. Gerald Barry, unpublished diary, 26 February 1951.
8. Hugh Casson in *A Tonic to the Nation*, p. 72.
9. Ibid.
10. Michael Frayn, 'Festival', in Michael Sissons and Philip French (eds), *Age of Austerity 1945–1951*. Penguin, 1964, p. 320.
11. 'One Man's Week', *Leader Magazine*, 9 July 1949.
12. Eva Rudberg, *The Stockholm Exhibition, 1930*, Stockholmia Förlag, 1999, p. 192.
13. Ibid., p. 194.
14. J.M. Richards, quoted in Laura Cohen, *The Door to a Secret Room*, Scolar Press, 1999, p. 112.
15. Patrick J. Maguire and Jonathan M. Woodham (eds), *Design and*

*Cultural Politics in Post-war Britain*, Leicester University Press, 1997, p. 58.

16. Geoffrey Holme to Lord Samuel, 9 March 1947. RSA Archive.

17. *Marks of Distinction. The Memoirs of Elaine Blond*, Vallentine Mitchell, 1988, p. 129.

18. Ibid.

## Chapter Three

1. Director General's statement to the first Festival Council meeting, 31 May 1948.

2. Gerald Barry, unpublished memoir.

3. Barry, unpublished memoir.

4. House of Commons, 10 February 1949.

5. Paul Wright, *A Brittle Glory*, Weidenfeld & Nicolson, 1986, p. 33.

6. Jeremy Melvin, *F.R.S. Yorke and the Evolution of English Modernism*, Wiley Academy, 2003, p. 57.

7. Barry, unpublished memoir.

8. Ibid.

9. A.N. Wilson, *After the Victorians*, Hutchinson, 2005, p. 273.

10. Gerald Barry, Cantor Lecture, published in the *Journal of the Royal Society of Arts*, 19 May 1952.

11. Ibid.

12. Wright, *A Brittle Glory*, p. 35.

13. Ruth Butler, *The Festival of Britain and the Buildings of the 1950s*, Brighton Polytechnic School of Architecture, 1992, p. 126.

14. Quoted by Hugh Casson, *National Life Story Collection Newsletter*, Summer 2001.

15. *A Tonic to the Nation*, p. 77.

16. Ibid.

## Chapter Four

1. James Gardner, *Elephants in the Attic*, Orbis, 1983, p. 70.

2. Hugh Casson in *A Tonic to the Nation*, p. 78.

3. Ibid.

4. Ibid.

5. *The Sphere*, 2 June 1951.

6. Later achievements of Freeman Fox & Partners included the Forth

Road Bridge (1964), the first of two Severn road bridges in 1966 and the Humber Bridge in 1981.

7. Ralph Freeman in *A Tonic to the Nation*, p. 91.
8. Hugh Casson in *A Tonic to the Nation*, p. 78.
9. Misha Black papers. V&A AAD/2008/2/3/1/26.
10. Naomi Games, Catherine Moriarty, Jim Rose, *Abram Games: His Life and Work*, Lund Humphries, 2003, p. 25.
11. Gardner, *Elephants in the Attic*, p. 72.
12. Kenneth Powell, *Powell and Moya*, RIBA Publishing, 2009, p. 33.
13. Harry Mount, *A Lust for Window Sills*, Little, Brown, 2008, p. 107.
14. Gerald Barry, *Delphi*, Second Quarter, 1951.
15. Harriet Atkinson, 'Imaginative Reconstruction: Designing Place at the Festival of Britain 1951', thesis, Royal College of Art and Victoria and Albert Museum, 2006. To be published by I.B. Tauris in late 2011 as The Festival of Britain: A Land and its People.
16. Ian Cox in *A Tonic to the Nation*, p. 63.
17. *Hansard*, 7 July 1948.
18. Sonya Rose, *Which People's War?*, OUP, 2003, p. 200.
19. Ernest Barker (ed.), *The Character of England*, OUP, 1947, p. 27.
20. Gerald Barry papers, notes dated 21 July 1952.
21. Gerald Barry, address to the Council of Churches, undated.
22. Cheryl Buckley, *Designing Modern Britain*, Reaktion Books, 2007, p. 11.

## Chapter Five

1. Victoria and Albert Museum archive, AAD/2008/2/3/1/1.
2. *Daily Express*, 29 April 1949.
3. Hugh Casson in *A Tonic to the Nation*, p. 79.
4. London Metropolitan Archives, LCC/CL/GP/2/64, 31 May 1949.
5. Gerald Barry, Cantor Lecture, published in the *Journal of the Royal Society of Arts*, 22 August 1952.
6. London Metropolitan Archives, LCC/AR/TP/4/40.
7. *South London Press*, 1 June 1949.
8. London Metropolitan Archives, LCC/CL/GP/2/65.
9. Clerk of Council to Festival General Manager, 22 August 1950 (Est. c. (Ch) 19.8). London Metropolitan Archives.
10. London Metropolitan Archives, LCC/CL/GP/2/65.

11. Ibid.
12. Museum of London, Festival memory archive.
13. Gerald Barry, unpublished diary, 1 January 1951.
14. Ibid., 1 February 1951.
15. Ibid., 10 January 1951.
16. Festival Daily Press Summary, 20 March 1951. London Metropolitan Archives.
17. *South London Press*, 19 June 1949.
18. Gerald Barry, unpublished memoir.
19. Barry, Cantor Lecture, 22 August 1952.
20. Barry, unpublished diary, entry undated.
21. Council for Industrial Design, Annual Report 1950/51.
22. Quoted in Paul Greenhalgh, *Ephemeral Vistas*, Manchester University Press, 1998.
23. *A Tonic to the Nation*, p. 96.
24. Barry, unpublished memoir.
25. Barry, Cantor Lecture, 22 August 1952.
26. London Metropolitan Archives, LCC/CL/GP/2/65.
27. Valerie Grove, *Laurie Lee*, Viking, 1999, p. 259.
28. Ibid., p. 258.

## Chapter Six

1. Gerald Barry, *London Calling*, 15 December 1949.
2. Becky E. Conekin, *The Autobiography of a Nation. The 1951 Festival of Britain*, Manchester University Press, 2003.
3. Gerald Barry, unpublished memoir.
4. James Gardner, *Elephants in the Attic*, Orbis, 1983, p. 73.
5. Ibid., pp. 74–5.
6. Ibid., pp. 76–7.
7. Ibid., p. 78.
8. James Gardner in Mary Banham and Bevis Hillier (eds), *A Tonic to the Nation. The Festival of Britain 1951*, Thames & Hudson, 1976, p. 121.
9. Gardner, *Elephants in the Attic*, p. 84.
10. Gerald Barry, unpublished diary, 31 December 1950.
11. Ibid., 2 January 1951.
12. Judith Taylor, personal secretary to the Entertainments Manager,

in a letter to her parents. Museum of London, Festival memory archive.

13. Barry, unpublished diary, 7 January 1951.
14. Ibid., 12 March 1951.
15. Ibid.
16. Ibid.
17. Gardner, *Elephants in the Attic*, p. 79.
18. Barry, unpublished diary, 31 March 1951.
19. Gardner, *Elephants in the Attic*, p. 80.
20. Ibid., pp. 84–5.
21. Ibid., p. 85.
22. Ibid., p. 80.

## Chapter Seven

1. *Country Life*, 11 November 1976.
2. Janie Hampton, *The Austerity Olympics*, Aurum Press, 2008.
3. Paul Wright, *RSA Journal*, May 1995.
4. Michael Frayn, 'Festival', in Michael Sissons and Philip French (eds), *Age of Austerity 1945–1951*, Penguin, 1964, p. 326.
5. Gerald Barry, unpublished memoir.
6. Ibid.
7. Ibid.
8. Ibid.
9. Paul Wright, *A Brittle Glory*, Weidenfeld & Nicolson, 1986, p. 36.
10. *A Tonic To the Nation*, p. 171.
11. Barry, unpublished memoir.
12. Gerald Barry, unpublished diary, 19 February 1951.
13. Ibid.
14. *Hansard*, Vol. 481, no. 21, 28 November 1950.

## Chapter Eight

1. Gerald Barry, Cantor Lecture, *Journal of the Royal Society of Arts*, 22 August 1952.
2. Gerald Barry in Mary Banham and Bevis Hillier (eds), *A Tonic to the Nation. The Festival of Britain 1951*, Thames & Hudson, 1976, p. 22.
3. Ibid.
4. Ibid.

5. *A Tonic to the Nation*, p. 93.
6. *The Memoirs of Lord Ismay*, Heinemann, 1960, p. 451.
7. Ibid.
8. Ibid.
9. *A Tonic to the Nation*, p. 167.
10. Barry, unpublished memoir.
11. Ibid.
12. Ibid.
13. *The Memoirs of Lord Ismay*, p. 451.
14. Paul Wright, author interview.
15. Barry, unpublished memoir.
16. Ibid.
17. Ibid.
18. Arnold Wesker, *As Much as I Dare*. Century, 1994, p. 264.
19. Richard Morse. Museum of London, Festival memory archive.
20. Betty Phillips. Museum of London, Festival memory archive.
21. Hugh Marshall. Museum of London, Festival memory archive.
22. Audrey Russell in *A Tonic to the Nation*, p. 169.
23. *Illustrated London News*, 3 May 1951.
24. *Country Life*, 27 April 1951.
25. *La Nation Belge*, 4 May 1951.
26. *Nöel Coward Diaries*, ed. Graham Payne & Sheridan Morley, Weidenfeld & Nicolson, 1982, 12 and 21 June 1951.
27. *Harold Nicolson, Diaries and Letters 1945–1962*, ed. Nigel Nicolson, Collins, 1968, p. 206.
28. David Harris. Museum of London, Festival memory archive.
29. F.H.K. Henrican, designer, Agriculture and Country Pavilion, in *A Tonic to the Nation*, p. 107.
30. T.H. Hendrick, Production Manager of the designer consortium Cockade, in *A Tonic to the Nation*, p. 163.
31. Ibid.
32. Barry, unpublished memoir.
33. E.S. Turner, *The Listener* 21 August 1969.
34. *A Tonic to the Nation*.
35. Robert Hewson, *In Anger: Culture in the Cold War 1945–60*, Weidenfeld & Nicolson, 1981, p. 55.
36. *The Times*, 5 May 1951.

37. Prunella Guthrie. Museum of London, Festival memory archive.

38. Barry, Cantor Lecture, 22 August 1952.

39. Antony Hippisley Coxe in *A Tonic to the Nation*, p. 89.

40. Barry, unpublished memoir.

41. Ibid.

42. Paul Wright, author interview.

43. Barry, unpublished memoir.

## Chapter Nine

1. *Round the Horne*, 26 March 1967.

2. *The Times*, 6 April 1951.

3. *East Anglian Daily Times*, 12 December 1949.

4. Festival of Britain guide book.

5. John Montgomery, *The Fifties*, Allen & Unwin, 1965, p. 31.

6. Adrian Ball and David Knight, *Festival Diary*, Town & County Publications, 1951.

7. Gerald Barry, unpublished memoir.

8. Gerald Barry, unpublished diary, 15 February 1951.

9. Becky E. Conekin, *The Autobiography of a Nation. The 1951 Festival of Britain*, Manchester University Press, 2003.

10. Mary Banham and Bevis Hillier (eds), *A Tonic to the Nation. The Festival of Britain 1951*, Thames & Hudson, 1976, p. 156.

11. Ibid., p. 157.

12. Michael Wharton, *The Missing Will*, Chatto & Windus, 1984, pp. 237–8.

13. *Britain Today*, Festival Number, May 1951.

## Chapter Ten

1. Official guide, Science Exhibition.

2. Gerald Barry, unpublished memoir.

3. Mary Banham and Bevis Hillier (eds), *A Tonic to the Nation. The Festival of Britain 1951*, Thames & Hudson, 1976, p. 146.

4. Barry, unpublished memoir.

5. *A Tonic to the Nation*, p. 160.

6. *Architectural Review*, December 1951, p. 242 (quoted in Harriet Atkinson, 'Imaginative Reconstruction: Designing Place at the Festival of Britain 1951', thesis, Royal College of Art and Victoria

and Albert Museum, 2006).

7. David Garred. Museum of London, Festival memory archive.
8. Ibid.
9. *A Tonic to the Nation*, pp. 140, 141.
10. David Garred. Museum of London, Festival memory archive.
11. Nigel Whiteley, *Reyner Banham. Historian of the Immediate Future*, MIT Press, 2002, p. 11.
12. Christopher Frayling in Boris Ford (ed.), *The Cambridge Cultural History: Modern Britain*, CUP, 1988, p. 173.
13. *The Sphere*, 2 June 1951.
14. Official Festival programme.
15. Notes for a speech, Barry papers.
16. Official Festival programme.
17. Barry, unpublished memoir.
18. Ibid.
19. RSA Festival archive.
20. *The Times*, 15 August 1951.
21. Richard Burton, author interview.
22. Barry, unpublished memoir.

## Chapter Eleven

1. Hugh Casson in Mary Banham and Bevis Hillier (eds), *A Tonic to the Nation. The Festival of Britain 1951*, Thames & Hudson, 1976, p. 80.
2. John Montgomery, *The Fifties*, Allen & Unwin, 1965, p. 29.
3. James Gardner, *Elephants in the Attic*, Orbis, 1983, pp. 72–3.
4. Misha Black in *A Tonic to the Nation*, p. 83.
5. Christopher Barry, author interview, 2009.
6. Gerald Barry, unpublished diary, 9 March 1951.
7. *A Tonic to the Nation*, p. 131.
8. Misha Black, papers, V&A AAD/1980/3/35.
9. *A Tonic to the Nation*, p. 102.
10. Gerald Barry, private papers.
11. Quoted in Robert Hewison, *In Anger, Culture in the Cold War 1945–60*, Weidenfeld & Nicolson, 1981, p. 55.
12. Stephen Potter, *One-Upmanship*. Hart-Davis, 1952, pp. 66–7.
13. Ibid.

14. Eric Salmon, *The Dark Journey*, Barrie & Jenkins, 1979, pp. 128–9.
15. Ibid., p. 9.
16. Christopher Fry, author interview.
17. London Metropolitan Archives, LCC/CL/GP/2/65.
18. Ibid., LCC/CL/GP/2/64.
19. *Financial Times*, 9 May 1951.
20. John Lucas, *Thomas Beecham, An Obsession with Music*, Boydell Press, 2008, p. 326.
21. Gerald Barry, unpublished memoir.
22. Richard Aldous, *Tunes of Glory: The Life of Malcolm Sargent*, Hutchinson, 2001.
23. Ibid.
24. Lucas, *Thomas Beecham*, p. 327.
25. Barry, unpublished diary, 2 March 1951.
26. Denis Forman, *Persona Granada*, Andre Deutsch, 1997, p. 24.
27. Ibid., p. 25.
28. British Film Institute Press Release, 30 April 1951.
29. Richard Attenborough and Diana Hawkins, *Entirely Up to You, Darling. Scenes from a Life*, Hutchinson, 2008, p. 189.
30. *Britain Today*, Festival Number, May 1951.
31. Kevin Jackson, *Humphrey Jennings*, Picador, 2000, p. 189.
32. Museum of London, Festival Archives.
33. Forman, *Persona Granada*, p. 27.

## Chapter Twelve

1. *The Times*, 1 October 1951.
2. Gerald Barry, unpublished memoir.
3. Ibid.
4. Hugh Casson, diary of the final week of the Festival.
5. Barry, unpublished memoir.
6. James Gardner, *Elephants in the Attic*, Orbis, 1983, p. 85.
7. *The Times*, 1 October 1951.
8. Leonard Kendall, *A Visit to Britain*, Paterson, 1951, pp. 6–7.
9. Gerald Barry papers.
10. Ibid.
11. Ibid.
12. Ibid.

13. José Manser, *Hugh Casson, A Biography*, Viking, 2000, p. 147.
14. David Eccles to Gerald Barry, 5 December 1951. Gerald Barry papers.
15. Gerald Barry to David Eccles, 7 December 1951. Gerald Barry papers.
16. Eccles to Barry, 18 December 1951. Gerald Barry papers.
17. Gerald Barry papers.
18. *New Statesman*, 13 October 1951.
19. V&A, AAD/2008/2/3/1/17.
20. *Sunday Times*, 16 December 1951.
21. Misha Black in Mary Banham and Bevis Hillier (eds), *A Tonic to the Nation. The Festival of Britain 1951*, Thames & Hudson, 1976, p. 85.
22. Hugh Casson to A.F.C. Brown, 1 October 1952.
23. Museum of London. www.museumoflondon.org.uk/archive/exhibits/festival/tangible.htm
24. *A Tonic to the Nation*, p. 168.
25. Gerald Barry, unpublished diary, December 1951.
26. London Metropolitan Archives, LCC/CL/GP/2/68.
27. Hugh Casson in 1988. V&A, AAD/2008/2/3/2/17.

## Chapter Thirteen

1. Arnold Wesker, *As Much As I Dare*, Century, 1994.
2. Gerald Barry, RSA lecture, June 1961.
3. John Wright in Mary Banham and Bevis Hillier (eds), *A Tonic to the Nation. The Festival of Britain 1951*, Thames & Hudson, 1976, p. 170.
4. *Observer*, 15 April 2001.
5. Barry, RSA lecture, June 1961.
6. *New Statesman*, 13 October 1951.
7. Christopher Hobhouse, *1851 and the Crystal Palace*, John Murray, 1937, pp. 152–3.
8. Gerald Barry, 'After the Ball is Over', *New Statesman*, 13 October 1951.
9. David Kynaston, *Family Britain 1951–57*, Bloomsbury, 2009, p. 668.
10. William Feaver in *A Tonic to the Nation*, p. 54.

## Chapter 14.

1. Letter to the Chief Clerk, County Hall. London Metropolitan Archives, LCC/CL/GP/2/105/1-97.
2. *Daily Mail*, 31 May 1952.
3. *Cooperative News*, 30 August 1952.
4. London Metropolitan Archives, LCC/CL/LEA/1/18.
5. Ibid., LCC/CL/GP/2/108.
6. David Eccles to Gerald Barry, 24 June 1953. Gerald Barry papers.
7. Lionel Esher, *A Broken Wave*, Allen Lane, 1981, p. 59.
8. Christopher Neve, *Country Life*, 25 November 1976.
9. Esher, *A Broken Wave*, p. 80.
10. Hugh Casson in *A Tonic to the Nation*, p. 81.
11. London Metropolitan Archives, LCC/CL/LEA/1/19.
12. John Goodwin (ed.), *Peter Hall's Diaries*, Hamish Hamilton, 1983, p. 35.
13. Peter Hall, *Making an Exhibition of Myself*, Sinclair Stevenson, 1993, p. 275.
14. Colin Amery (ed.), *The National Theatre. An Architectural Review Guide*, Architectural Press, 1977, p. 22.
15. *The Times*, 3 May 1991.
16. Ivan Harbour, Rogers Stirk Harbour & Partners. Author interview.
17. Michael Lynch CBE, AM, Chief Executive of Southbank Centre. Author interview.
18. Peter Cully, Rick Mather Architects. Author interview.
19. Jack Pringle, Pringle Brandon Architects, Skylon campaign, www.voteforskylon.com

# ACKNOWLEDGEMENTS

The hero of the 1951 Festival of Britain was Gerald Barry. The Festival was essentially his creation, a heady mix of inspirational ideas and entertainment which to this day remains a controversial talking point among architects, designers, planners, sociologists and social historians. This former editor of a national newspaper was a visionary with an imagination that was both original and practical. Would that someone like him had been in charge of the Millennium celebrations.

Though my knowledge of Barry is inevitably second hand it has been made real by his family, who have been most generous in sharing their memories. My particular thanks go to his son, Christopher Barry, his stepson Richard Burton and his daughter-in-law, Jacqui Barry. I have also been fortunate in gaining free access to the wealth of information contained in Barry's unpublished collection of private papers, held in part by the family and in part by the London School of Economics Library. I am grateful to the staff of the LSE Library for their ever willing assistance and also to the staff of the London Metropolitan Archive, the Victoria and Albert Museum, the London Museum, the BFI National Archive, the Royal Society of Arts and the

London Library. For background to the 1930 Stockholm Exhibition I am indebted to Frida Melin and Torun Warne of Stockholm Arkitekturmuseet. Updates on the latest developments on the South Bank come courtesy of Michael Lynch, former chief executive of the Southbank Centre, Ivan Harbour of Rogers Stirk Harbour + Partners and Peter Cully of Rick Mather Architects. Constructive criticism and fruitful discussion were the happy result of meeting Harriet Atkinson, who chose the Festival as the subject for her Royal College of Art thesis to be published by I.B. Tauris (*The Festival of Britain: A Land and Its People*) in late 2011. My assistant Jill Fenner has made sense of my otherwise indecipherable scrawl and Fred Pesket and his friends at the Festival of Britain Society have given welcome encouragement along the way.

## A NOTE ON THE TYPEFACE

The font used for the title and chapter headers in this book is Festival, designed by Philip Boydell and cut by Monotype in 1950 as the official display face for the 1951 Festival of Britain. Used for all official Festival announcements, Festival Titling was made available for general use in 1952. It was designed to have a festive feel, a character that even today makes it a useful face for display and advertising use.

# INDEX